55

50¢

DATE DUE

GAYLORD			PRINTED IN U.S.A.

AGAINST THE TIDE

AGAINST THE TIDE

wilhelm röpke, 1899-

translated by Elizabeth Henderson

HENRY
REGNERY
COMPANY
CHICAGO

61,511

Foreword

The present volume contains studies that reflect the life's work of a great humanist and outstanding economist and sociologist who generally has been considered the intellectual father of the economic recovery of Europe. The title, *Against the Tide*, is well chosen. Wilhelm Röpke not only was a distinguished scholar; he also was a courageous man who steadfastly spoke out against the prevalent trends, irrespective of whether they favored fascism, the welfare state, or Marxism. His work is a good demonstration of Thomas Mann's assertion that great things are here in spite of opposition. Röpke sought the truth and stood up for his opinion in a way that was dreamed of only by philosophers.

Shortly after the French Revolution, Fichte, who considered true scholarship the highest form of divine grace bestowed on men, stated that the scholar must be the *morally best* human being of his age, a priest of truth, in the service of truth, committed to truth, willing to do and dare everything for it, to suffer persecution, hatred, and even death. This far-reaching, nearly superhuman, and perhaps truly humane devotion Nietzsche probably had in mind when, having studied Burckhardt's uncomforting prognoses, he hoped that in the new brave world of secularism scholars would humanize men after Christianity had failed to do so, even at the cost of martyrdom.

Unfortunately, this hope has not come true. In today's

student riots, we wonder whether we should be more ashamed of the insurgent students, of the teachers who support them, or of the professors and academic administrators who allow themselves to be intimidated, thus encouraging a behavior that must lead to the destruction of the very prerequisites of humanism: free instruction and learning. We also wonder about the professors who during the past decade went along with the tide, teaching a "value-free" science and promoting a devaluation of property rights, and thus laid the groundwork for today's destruction of humanistic values. The failure of today's academicians to stand up for the values of our civilization, to fight socialist gradualism and communist terrorism, reminds us of the failure of German scholars to fight positivism and the fascist gradualism and terrorism of Hitler's National Socialists.

Wilhelm Röpke was not one of them. Blue-eyed, tall, blond, rugged looking, born in a part of Germany that is known for its nordic types, not compromised by Marxism, Röpke could have made the most of the opportunities the Hitler movement would have afforded him. He refused the temptation. He was a humanist, not an opportunist. Having spent his formative years in places where Schiller had lived, and also having been influenced by Kant, Röpke became one of the great libertarian humanists of our century.

Röpke not only preached liberty and humanism against the tide; he also brought sacrifices for them. The youngest university professor in the German-speaking world at the age of twenty-four, he soon attained a reputation as a libertarian. It has been said that if during the depression the German government had followed his advice, it could have mastered the economic emergency and Hitler would never have come to power. He denounced the *Tat* circle, an "action" group of intellectuals opposing capitalism, men who paved the way for National Socialism. He urged farmers not to vote for their enemies, the National Socialists. After the latter had come to power, he kept on attacking them. A few hours before the

Reichstag burned, Röpke, comparing a colleague to a gardener in the sense of Voltaire's famous line in *Candide,* "mais il faut cultiver notre jardin," said at his burial that "he probably no longer fitted into our time which is about to destroy the garden of culture and to restore the original wilderness." In Frankfurt, the birthplace of Goethe, where Röpke gave his last lecture as a German professor, his speech was characterized as much by a defiance of the Hitler regime as by an accurate prognosis of what lay ahead. Shortly thereafter, he became the first professor to leave Germany in protest against that regime.

Following an invitation by Kemal Pascha, Röpke became a professor of economics at Istanbul, where he decisively contributed to the reform of the university. In 1937 he joined the distinguished graduate Institute of International Studies in Geneva, Switzerland. In the summer of 1940, when after the fall of France there was imminent danger of a German invasion of Switzerland, Röpke turned down attractive offers from American institutions in spite of the persecution that would have threatened him and his family in case of an invasion. He preferred fighting Hitler from close by.

But he fought not only the brown danger. Having denounced Marxism as early as he denounced National Socialism, Röpke never wavered in pointing out the red danger. Analyzing André Gide's report on the Soviet Union, Röpke emphasized the "terror, the culture-murdering uniformization of all life, the servility, the lies of propaganda, the misery" in Russia, a totalitarian state characterized by an absence of freedom and humanism where men lead the lives of insects. When National Socialism had been defeated, Röpke increased his efforts to warn of communism. Just as prior to the Third Reich he had fought not only the National Socialists but also intellectuals who paved the way for them, he now not only denounced Communists but also intellectuals, the "anti-anticommunists" who have aided the spread of communism since World War II, who were blind to the fact that Marxist socialism was as dangerous as National Socialism. He warned the naive and blind whom the Italian communist Togliatti once called "useful idiots," the professors whom the Bulgarian communist leader Dimitroff accounted to be worth red armies. Adamant in refusing to accept invitations to join professional societies that in his opinion did not sufficiently recognize the danger of communist totalitarianism, Röpke consistently cautioned against arrangements with the Communists, feeling that a true understanding with them and the elimination of mutual distrust would not be possible.

National Socialists and Communists honored Röpke in their own way. The former listed him as one of the professors to be dismissed and banned his book *The Social Crisis of Our Time*—fortunately only after a few hundred copies had been distributed in Germany. In Hungary *The Social Crisis of Our Time* rallied the antitotalitarian opposition to such an extent that when a National Socialist government came to power in 1944, it immediately announced that "the time of Röpkeism is now over." In an encyclopedia published in East Germany, Röpke is described as "liberalist, opponent of the USSR; his theories of 'planned capitalism' attempt to defend and perpetuate imperialism." Another verdict runs as follows: "By identifying monopolism and socialism, Röpke succeeds better than any other defender of monopoly capitalism in the design of bourgeois political economy to suppress class struggle and to defame the socialist camp. This makes Röpke's theory one of the most dangerous bourgeois economic theories. . . . Röpke thus must be considered an especially shrewd and therefore especially dangerous representative of the modern bourgeois point of view."

Röpke fought not only against the brown and red tides; he also fought prevalent trends toward less totalitarian planning of the economy. Having denounced the New Deal as early as 1934, he never ceased to take issue with economic planning as proposed by Lord Keynes and his orthodox disciples, who abounded and seemed to have their way in the free world. Through and after World War II, Röpke stood up firmly to the great majority of influential economists when he warned against the advocacy of a planned economy and expressed the fear that planning and collectivism would prevent the economic recovery that he felt was inevitable under a free economy.

The correctness of his opinion was first demonstrated in Germany. His friend Ludwig Erhard, Minister of Economics under Adenauer and later Chancellor, has told how during the war he illegally got hold of Röpke's books, the contents of which he "devoured like the desert the life-giving water." Erhard repeatedly emphasized his debt to Röpke when, against the opposition of the military government, he introduced the market economy in West Germany. Röpke's arguments were decisive in persuading the West German government to reject Keynesian solutions, which were suggested by leading Anglo-Saxon economists. Röpke's study of the early 1950's, as to whether the German economic policy was correct, demonstrated the enormous success of the "socially responsible market economy" so convincingly that it deprived Western socialist programs of their appeal. Röpke stressed that the economic recovery of Germany was not at all the "miracle" by which it had become known but the logical result of a free market economy.

After the success of that economic system had been demonstrated in Germany, Röpke's friend and colleague Luigi Einaudi, the first President of postwar Italy, imitated the German economic policy in his country. It was so successful that even such men as the present President of Italy, Saragat, a Socialist, became admirers of Röpke. In France, Jacques Rueff proposed similar measures, which led to the recovery of France. Other nations in one way or another followed suit. A continent that after World War II lay dying recovered in freedom.

With all his success in realizing his ideas, Röpke did not rest on his laurels. He remained a warner to the very end.

When in the late fifties French tendencies toward "programming" and "planification" became known around the world and found disciples especially in the developing nations, Röpke denounced the "economocrats" in unmistakable terms. Wary about the situation in Germany, he continually warned that nothing could be taken for granted and urged the Germans always to remember to reapply the original formulas for success in the realm of economic policy. To the very end, Röpke saw the market economy threatened by interventionism, inflation, and the demagoguery of the welfare state.

And yet neoliberalism, of which Röpke was an outstanding exponent, by no means was opposed to all state action. As the name implies, it was not identical to the liberalism of the Manchester School, to a laissez-faire that permitted monopolies. A viable market economy, according to Röpke, requires an effective government to establish and maintain a stable monetary and fiscal system and secure competition by restraining monopolies. While the government should not interfere with the mechanism of supply and demand lest it induce a planned, collectivist economic order, it should intervene to defend the system against abuse. For Röpke, the state no longer had merely the function of a nightwatchman, as in nineteenth-century liberalism. Synthesizing the traditional antitheses of laissez-faire and planning, he favored an order under which the individual enjoys a maximum of freedom and respects the freedom of his fellow men. As he wrote a friend, Lord Acton stressed that power only *tends* to corrupt. Government is to be preferred over anarchy, including economic anarchy. In a humane society, there is no room for a *bellum omnium contra omnes*. A market economy is not an end in itself but a means for the welfare of the individual. It is a necessary, but not sufficient, prerequisite for a free, happy, prosperous, and just society: "The fate of the market economy with its admirable and absolutely irreplaceable mechanism of supply and demand will be decided beyond supply and demand." The market economy could survive only as *A Humane Economy*.

"Made to the measure of man," that economy would protect the individual against the masses. It would revitalize the culture of the West, which is threatened by a quantitative civilization, burdened by a soulless mechanization, and equalized by a faceless standardization. Röpke complemented neoliberalism with neohumanism. A great spokesman for a free society, he favored "measure and moderation" and was opposed to extremism and ideological exclusiveness.

Like his great predecessor, Adam Smith, Wilhelm Röpke developed; from being an advocate of free enterprise, he became a moral philosopher. Some of his liberal friends were advocates of a more exclusively scientific and technical approach and accused him of being too neoliberal. But perhaps Röpke, believing with Rabelais that "science without conscience means the ruin of the soul," actually came closer to the genuine liberalism that originally had been conceived as a humanist antidote against oppression of any kind.

When Röpke refused an invitation to join the International Political Science Association because in his opinion that association committed a *trahison des clercs* by accepting members from communist nations, he wrote: "For more than a quarter of a century I have devoted all my strength to the struggle against the plague of our time which is totalitarianism in all its forms and colors, brown or red, and you know that in this struggle I have not hesitated to expose myself to the greatest dangers and to prefer exile and the abandonment of my career to submission." Indeed he was, in Julien Benda's sense, a *clerc* who kept the faith. And his faith was opposed not only to totalitarianism but also to modern scientism, intellectualism, and moral indifference, to the trend of making intellectual activity an end in itself, of experimenting with men and treating them like raw material in the industrial production process.

Following Fichte's admonition that "the scholar must forget what he has done as soon as it is done and think only of what else there is to be done," Röpke became one of the most prolific scholars of his time. When he died, his never-ending courageous struggle against the *Zeitgeist* was lauded by personalities ranging from the President of Italy and the Chancellor of Germany to representatives of labor. In his *Admonition to the Germans,* Nietzsche wrote: "We want to be heard, for we speak as warners, and the voice of the warner, whoever he may be and wherever it may sound, is always right; for you who are addressed have the right to decide whether you want to consider your warners honest and wise men who only make noise because you are in danger and who are scared to find you so silent, indifferent and naive." When Röpke was heard, as in the adoption of a neoliberal economic policy, the results were conspicuous blessings to the poor and rich, the most successful wars against poverty that were ever fought. Now that the world has lost this great sentinel, it should always bear in mind the warnings of his work.

The following essays offer a cross section of that work.

GOTTFRIED DIETZE

October 10, 1969   *Johns Hopkins University*

Table of Contents

AGAINST THE TIDE

I

Weimar Republic,
Brown Totalitarianism,
and World War II

On the Transfer Problem
in International Capital Movements*

Some years ago one of the distinguished scholars to whom Dutch economics owes its excellent reputation published an article called "Das Geld als Quelle von Missverständnissen im internationalen Güteraustausch" ["Money as a Source of Misunderstandings on the International Exchange of Goods"].[1] It contains the following sentence, which I would like to take as a starting point: "One feels it would be nice to be a Communist, to live in a world that has no need of money, so as to be able to look in the simplest terms at so many economic problems that now are a source of numerous misunderstandings." How true this is! And never is this desire felt more urgently than when it is a question of gaining for oneself and conveying to others a clear understanding of the intricate processes of foreign trade. But although our, somewhat frivolous, wish has to remain unfulfilled, there is nothing to stop us taking a leap from reality into the realm of imagination and trying to clear our minds by working out how this or that process, encumbered by all the complications of our modern economic system, would take place in the idyllic simplicity of

---

* *Lecture delivered on May 21, 1930, at the Nederlandsche Handelshoogeschool at Rotterdam, subsequently published in* Jahrbücher für Nationalökonomie und Statistik, *Vol. cxxxiii (1930).*

[1] *A. van Gijn, "Das Geld als Quelle von Missverständnissen im internationalen Güteraustausch,"* Weltwirtschaftliches Archiv, *Vol. xix (January, 1923), pp. 81 et seq.*

Utopia's moneyless and marketless economy. An attempt to apply this method to the process of international capital movements, which is under discussion today and need not be described in detail to this audience, would give the following result.

Imagine two socialist economies, comparable to two giant corporations, and suppose that in consequence of some commercial or political debt a certain capital sum is to be transferred from one economy to the other. The first question would clearly be whether the debtor economy is able to raise the required sum domestically without prejudice to the present and future livelihood of the inhabitants. Even this question would take a simplified form in comparison with the actual state of affairs today, insofar as the state and economy are identical, whereas in our system on one side the state is an authority imposing taxation and on the other side the economy is the sum of individual economic units where the stream of national income collects and forms a pool on which the state draws by more or less imperfect methods. But more important in our context are the next questions, namely, in what form is the capital sum to be transferred and in what manner is it handed over to the recipient economy. Money is excluded by assumption. The capital sum can, therefore, only take the form of actual goods, to be selected by a commission of delegates from both countries on two criteria: first, according to whether the debtor country has a sufficient supply of this or that good and can spare it without detriment to a minimum standard of living for its own inhabitants, and second, according to what goods are most urgently in demand in the creditor country. There is not a shadow of doubt that the debt can be paid only in the form of goods (or services). The meaning of the transaction by which a certain volume of goods is to be withdrawn from one country and handed over unrequited to the creditor country is brutally and nakedly plain. But several other features of the process are likewise seen in a clearer light. It is, for instance, quite conceivable that the debtor country for its part can raise the required resources domestically, in the sense that it can set aside from its social product a certain amount of goods, say, wine and cigarettes, and make these goods available for transfer to the other country without detriment to its own future, except that the creditor country unfortunately happens to be the United States—which, as we may imagine without great flights of fancy, has banned not only drinks but smoking as well. What happens now? The commission reaches no agreement; it would have been possible to raise the resources, but their transfer was not feasible. The transfer problem, to use the expression of the Dawes Plan which quickly gained currency, has emerged as a separate problem alongside the problem of domestic procurement.

Consider yet another case. It would seem to go without saying that the free receipt of resources, like the receipt of a gift, can give rise to nothing but joy. Or are there not also gifts to be looked at suspiciously, like a Trojan horse? Here again our imagined economy without money and market helps us to greater clarity, insofar as it mercilessly demolishes the notion that a creditor country can gleefully pocket the resources to be transferred as it could a sum of money. If the creditor country wants to be paid, it has to accept payment in the only form in which it can be made, that is, in the form of goods. But once more we may imagine a constellation of circumstances that prevents the transfers working out smoothly. Suppose that the goods that the debtor country can supply are produced also by the creditor country in quantities sufficient to meet demand in comparison with the coverage of other categories of demand. Unless the debtor country can be induced to adjust its production accordingly in consequence of the creditor country's raising difficulties about accepting these competing goods—difficulties which have their parallel in the protective tariffs of creditor countries in today's conditions—such an adjustment will have to be made by the creditor country. Here is a new problem that should give us food for thought and that points to the actual difficulties we must be prepared to encounter.

A final set of complications arises if we drop the assumption that only two countries are involved and insert third countries into our imagined process. We may suppose, for example, that some especially rich third country advances the required resources to the debtor country and thereby postpones the moment when the latter inexorably has to begin transferring resources in the form of goods or services, at the price, of course, that the debtor country, in addition to the original sum, must now also repay its debt to the third country. But these complications had better not be followed through in all their implications here, so as not to spin out the overture to the point of tediousness. Instead, we turn at once to the question of how the whole process we have just considered on the simplifying assumption of a moneyless economy takes place in the real world, in which the complications introduced by money and the market have caused that special science to emerge that is called economics.

I

Given that in our economic order money is merely an indispensable medium of exchange, a transactions entry that disappears in the final accounts and in no way alters the fact that ultimately goods and services are exchanged against goods and services, we must expect today's international capital movements not to differ essentially from those discussed in the initial, utopian and socialist, setting. And this is indeed so with respect to the most important point, for it turns out at once that an international capital movement today, in the end effect, amounts to an equivalent volume of goods and services being transferred from the debtor to the creditor country.

In other words, every international capital movement

resolves itself in a transfer of goods and services and only thereby fulfils its real meaning of increasing one country's economic assets at the cost of those of another, provided, of course, that no capital flow moves simultaneously in the opposite direction. An international capital movement must, therefore, cause a deficit on the goods and services account in the originating country's balance of payments and a surplus in the goods and services account of the recipient country. If the goods and services account is taken to cover all visible and invisible goods that cross the frontier, the strict and inescapable conclusion is that the structure of the goods and services account is the mirror image of the structure of the capital account. The goods and services account is in surplus always, and only, when the capital account is in deficit, and it is in deficit always, and only, when the capital account is in surplus. If, on balance, more capital flows out of the country than into it, then the outflow of goods and services exceeds their inflow, and *vice versa*. The surplus or deficit on goods and services account, therefore, is always merely the expression and consequence of a corresponding deficit or surplus on capital account. The whole world's goods and services accounts would balance, and the theorem that ultimately goods and services are exchanged against goods and services would be fully substantiated, were it not that international capital movements canceled the equality of the two terms in the *quid pro quo*.

Anyone who has grasped these simple relationships will henceforth cease to be one of those who regard a trade surplus as auspicious and a trade deficit as ominous, nor will he be one of the countless number of people whose faces beam when the latest trade returns show the trade balance to be in surplus, only to assume a worried look when the press reports yet another trade deficit. There is no more room for the notion that a trade surplus as such is a good thing, and a trade deficit as such a bad thing, once it has been grasped that the structure of the goods and services account is a mere reflex of the capital account, that the goods and services account *must* be in surplus when capital exports exceed capital imports, and that it *must* be in deficit when capital imports exceed capital exports. A trade balance is in deficit not because the economy works at a loss and is "unviable" but because, on balance, it receives more capital from abroad than it disburses abroad. Similarly, a trade balance is in surplus not because the economy works at a profit and is bursting with health but because, on balance, it exports more capital abroad than it receives from abroad.

However, it does make a great deal of difference to an economy under what heading capital flows in and out. Four cases may be distinguished in this connection.

1. The case of a nation that does not use some portion of the regular export proceeds for imports, but leaves it abroad as capital investment and thereby *becomes* a so-called creditor country (the case of the emerging creditor country). Capital flows out of the country for the creation of a creditor position. The capital account is in deficit and to the same extent turns the goods and services account into *surplus*.

2. The case of a nation that, thanks to a steady increase in its capital investments abroad, eventually reaches the point where the sum of interest, dividends, and repayments exceeds the amount of new investments abroad (the case of the pure creditor country). Capital exports for the creation of a creditor position now bear fruit in the shape of a net inflow of capital, the capital account swings into surplus, and the goods and services account into *deficit*.

3. The case of a nation that incurs debts abroad and to the extent of its indebtedness can import goods and services from abroad without paying for them currently (the case of an emerging debtor country). The capital account is in surplus and correspondingly the goods and services account in *deficit*.

4. The case of a nation that, while possibly incurring further debts abroad, eventually reaches the point where the sum of its outgoings for interest, dividends, and repayments exceeds the sum of new debts, so that a portion of export

proceeds corresponding to that excess can no longer be used for imports but serves as a unilateral transfer to abroad (the case of the pure debtor country). The capital account is in deficit and correspondingly the goods and services account in *surplus*. This category includes the case euphemistically described as "political indebtedness," to characterize the case best illustrated by German reparations, namely, one where the creditor's claim arises not from prior credits for commercial and hence constructive purposes but from a mere political stipulation. The special feature of political indebtedness, therefore, is that it has not been preceded by a capital import that raised the economic potential of the debtor country, but, as in the case of reparations, that it is linked with a process that enormously weakened that potential.

No one who wants to avoid the pitfalls of crude amateurishness should ever lose sight of the above model in discussing questions of foreign trade. There are, then, four possible cases of surplus or deficit on goods and services account, and these in turn can be grouped in pairs from the point of view of an excess of capital imports or capital exports. But capital imports or capital exports are of very different character in the various cases. They are either provisional or definitive. Capital export is provisional in the case of the emerging creditor country and definitive in that of the pure debtor country; capital import is provisional in the case of the emerging debtor country and definitive in that of the pure creditor country. Accordingly, the surplus on capital account is either provisional or definitive. In the first case capital import carries the condition of subsequent repayment; in the second case it does not. The same applies to the deficit on capital account. From this point of view the various possible cases of surplus and deficit in the trade balance may be grouped as follows:

1. The trade balance is in surplus because the capital account is in deficit. This deficit may be: (a) definitive (pure debtor country); (b) provisional (emerging creditor country).

2. The trade balance is in deficit because the capital

account is in surplus. This surplus may be: (a) definitive (pure creditor country); (b) provisional (emerging debtor country).

To illustrate these four possible cases of surplus and deficit in the trade balance by concrete example of individual countries is extremely difficult, because the only reasonably reliable figures are those referring to the actual merchandise account, while those referring to the services and the capital account are mere estimates, which are all the more vague the further we go back into the past. Subject to this reservation, the following may be said about the development of the German trade balance, as the example closest at hand.

Germany's trade balance was in surplus until the middle eighties of the nineteenth century (case of the emerging creditor country). It then swung into deficit, which by 1899 had reached almost 1.5 billion and subsequently, until 1914, fluctuated around approximately 1 billion. How is this prewar trade deficit to be explained? Partly by the fact that Germany was by then running an appreciable surplus on services account (net receipts on account of international freights, banking, insurance, etc.), though this surplus was certainly not large enough to explain the whole of the trade deficit. It will have to be assumed, therefore, that Germany had a deficit on goods and services account before the war, for which there is only one explanation, namely, that Germany had in the meantime reached a stage in its development where gains from capital investments abroad—which by the outbreak of the war had grown to about 28 billion—exceeded each year's new investments (case of the pure creditor country). The war dispossessed Germany of these investments and turned it from a creditor into a debtor country. Just as before the war, the German trade balance was in deficit until quite recently, but it was the deficit, not of a creditor country, but of an emerging debtor country. The German trade deficit (which was partly offset by a surplus on services account) amounted to about RM 2.3 billion in 1925, to RM 2.8 billion in 1927, and to RM 1.2 billion in 1928; only in 1926 did the trade balance register a surplus of

RM 859 million, in connection with that year's economic crisis and the resulting turnabout in the capital account. In effect, Germany took up foreign credits of all kinds in an approximate amount of RM 12 billion between 1924 and 1928, and thus developed into the world's foremost debtor country.

Having thus successively gone through the stages of an emerging creditor country, pure creditor country, and emerging debtor country, the moment must inexorably arrive when the sum of payments due to abroad for interest, dividends, repayments, and reparations exceeds the sum of new credits contracted. In a gradually rising curve and subject to many fluctuations, such as we are already experiencing, the German balance of trade will move from equilibrium to surplus, and it will be a surplus that, to the extent that Germany is at all able to honor its commitments arising from commercial debts and above all the political debt of reparations, may reach an extent that perhaps we cannot quite imagine at present. But the great question, which constitutes the true content of the transfer problem, is whether that inversion in the balance of trade will happen with or without major disturbances, indeed possibly with disturbances so great as to frustrate the whole transfer of capital. This is the question that must now occupy us.

II

I hope I have made it clear beyond doubt that there are absolutely no grounds for believing, in connection with the above-mentioned trade-balance syndrome, that the transfer problem in international capital movements is a question of the trade balance in the sense that a prior surplus in the debtor country's balance of trade is a *conditio sine qua non* of any capital transfer. According to this extraordinarily popular transfer theory, the size of the trade surplus that can be achieved is to determine the extent to which a transfer is possible. Whatever efforts a country may make domestically to raise the capital sum, if the gods send unfavorable winds to the flow of goods across frontiers, this sum must rest and wait, like the Achaeans' army at Aulis, while the high priests of economics get busy with their hocus-pocus and implore the gods for the miracle of a trade surplus.

Is this theory really to be taken seriously and is it worth the trouble of taking issue with it in detail? I should think that before this audience it will be enough merely to state that the trade-balance theory simply stands the relationship on its head and forgets that an export surplus can appear only in the presence of a transfer no longer accompanied by net capital imports, and not one moment earlier. It is not the trade balance that determines the transfer, but the transfer that determines the trade balance. And with this we have demolished also another equally widespread view, to wit, that all the medieval weapons in the armory of foreign trade policy must be applied in an attempt to get the trade balance into surplus, and thereby to create the conditions for the capital transfer. The same goes for any attempt by the transferee country to mobilize its trade policy against the trade deficit that comes in the wake of net capital imports.

This latter case shows up especially clearly how untenable is the whole argument. For what can be achieved if a capital-important country applies its trade policy to an attempt at correcting its trade deficit? Since the trade deficit is an inescapable consequence of the import surplus on capital account, it can be diminished in no other way than by cutting down capital imports. To obstruct merchandise imports by customs duties therefore can only have the result of diminishing imports and exports in equal measure, while the surplus of imports over exports remains as big as it was before. The total volume of foreign trade decreases, but not the difference between the volume of imports and the volume of exports. The only thing that is achieved is that the inexorable import surplus will be due more to a decrease of exports than to an increase in imports. In all cases the question is not *whether* there will be a surplus or a deficit in the balance of trade, but only *how* either comes about—more by changes on the export side or more by changes on the import side. And on the occasion of future reparations payments by Germany the question, therefore, will be not "trade surplus or not?" but "more exports or less imports?"—the road of declining imports being undesirable precisely in the measure in which it is artificially induced by import duties or import restrictions.

Now that we have disposed of the trade-balance theory, the field is cleared for an investigation of the true transfer problem. The problem is this: What is the nature of the mechanism that brings about that altered relationship between exports and imports that is the necessary expression of an international capital transfer? Or, we may ask the equivalent question: What guarantees are there in the transfer mechanism to prevent the transfer from jeopardizing the stability of the currency by causing a disproportion between supply and demand on the foreign exchange market?

This mechanism has been described so often that the barest outline should be enough here.[2] Schematically simplified, the process may be imagined as follows.

1. The debtor country year after year accumulates a fund to cover its debt payments and does so by the ordinary means of fiscal policy, that is, without recourse to inflation.

2. This implies a contraction of the total money supply in the debtor country, and, for reasons that need not be discussed here, the same applies if the fund is accumulated by open market sales.[3]

3. This contraction implies a relative downward pressure on prices in the debtor country.

4. In consequence, the debtor country becomes a good market to buy in but a bad one to sell in, so that imports will tend to diminish and exports to expand.

[2] See *W. Röpke, in "Das Reparationsproblem" (Protocol of the Pyrmont Conference), 1929, pp. 329* et seq.

[3] See *W. Röpke, "Neuere Literatur zum Reparationsproblem,"* Zeitschrift für Nationalökonomie *(1930), p. 1.*

5. As a further consequence, demand for foreign exchange diminishes while its supply rises.

6. The foreign exchange market is thereby adequately prepared for a conversion of the capital sums due to be transferred abroad into the currency of the creditor country. The pressure this conversion exercises on the national currency automatically leads to a further considerable improvement in the already transfer-favorable situation of the foreign exchange market since other demand for foreign exchange will diminish and supply will rise.

7. The pressure to which the exchange rate of the debtor country's currency is thus subject, and which may push the rate of the creditor countries' currencies to the upper gold point, at the same time forces the central bank of the debtor country to protect its gold reserves by raising its bank rate, thereby to restrict the volume of credit and thus to reinforce the existing tendency for exports to expand and imports to contract.

8. The last stage is that the creditor country's currency units bought up by the debtor country's government are handed over to the recipients in the former country. This means a corresponding increase in the money supply of the creditor country, with a consequent tendency for prices to rise, imports to expand, and exports to fall, so that the market is automatically prepared for additional exports from the debtor country. Any possible imports of gold enhance this tendency just as does the state of the foreign exchange market, as described above, and the correspondingly liberal credit policy of the creditor country.

If the transfer mechanism so outlined works without friction, we would expect, therefore, that the sum raised domestically in the debtor country is reflected in an equally large decrease of the same country's total money supply, which decrease, in its turn, equals the shift in the proportion of Germany's visible and invisible exports and imports, equals the opposite shift in the exports and imports of the creditor countries, equals the sum which the creditor country receives, and finally equals the increase in the creditor country's total money supply.

The existence of relationships of the kind thus briefly outlined is seldom denied anymore in authoritative circles, especially since the theory is confirmed by experience, witness the most recent capital imports into Germany, which worked perfectly smoothly in spite of their gigantic proportions. There may be some doubt about the effectiveness of one or the other little wheel in the machanism as described, or one cog may be replaced by another, but the *principle* of the transfer mechanism in international capital transfers can surely be taken as agreed by now, at least among *scholars*.

This agreement on principles extends, in particular, also to the conviction that the monetary transfer problem, in the sense that the successful internal accumulation of the required sum might endanger the currency of the debtor country or—as has indeed been seriously suggested—that of the creditor country, is in fact a pseudo-problem that need not cause any headaches. But this does not dispose of the whole content of the transfer problem, nor is that problem itself exposed as a pseudo-problem that can be treated lightly. One major question that still has to be regarded as open and requiring an answer is whether the transfer mechanism is perhaps subject to friction and adjustment difficulties such as might put an additional burden on the debtor country beyond the nominal value of the capital sum to be transferred, or indeed might conceivably cripple the whole transfer mechanism. This is the question on which the discussion of the transfer problem really turns today, and we will take it up next.

III

The eminently important question in this context is to what extent is a special *price pressure* on the debtor country's goods necessary for the establishment of a new equilibrium in international economic relations in the case of international capital transfers?[4] Is it necessary for the debtor country, which needs to export more because of the capital transfer, to find an outlet on the world market by exporting at lower prices than the competitors, and thus to accept a relative deflation of its price level? Or, to use the language of foreign trade theory, is it necessary for the international terms of trade to shift against the debtor country in order that a new equilibrium may come about on the international product market? If this question has to be answered in the affirmative, far-reaching consequences must be expected, in two directions.

First of all, the deflationary pressure or what really amounts to the same thing, the deterioration in the debtor country's international terms of trade, means that in addition to the primary burden of raising the nominal amount of its debt payment, the debtor country is saddled with a secondary burden, which finds expression in the lower value attached to factors of production in the debtor country or, in other words, lower money incomes and especially lower wages. To put it briefly: For Germany to pay reparations, German workers must not only part with some of their income in the form of taxes, but the very income from which taxes are deducted is lower than it would be without the obligation to pay reparations. But this increase in the real value of the reparations would by no means accrue to the creditor countries; it would merely be the price for the disturbance of international econ-

---

[4] See *the following among recent literature: F. W. Taussig,* International Trade, *New York, 1927; J. M. Keynes, "The German Transfer Problem,"* Economic Journal, *March, 1929; B. Ohlin, "The Reparations Problem,"* Index *(Svenska Handelsbanken, Stockholm), No. 27 (March, 1928), and No. 28 (April, 1928); B. Ohlin, "Transfer Difficulties, Real and Imagined," and Keynes's reply,* Economic Journal, *June, 1929; G. Haberler, "Transfer und Preisbewegung,"* Zeitschrift für Nationalökonomie, *I, 4 (1930), pp. 547 et seq.; F. Machlup, "Transfer und Preisbewegung,"* ibid., *pp. 555 et seq.; W. Röpke, loc. cit.; B. Ohlin, "Transfer und Preisbewegung,"* Zeitschrift für Nationalökonomie, *I, 5 (1930), pp. 762 et seq.*

omic equilibrium due to the reparations payment. It would be yet another example of the case, not infrequent in economic matters, that one party's loss need not be the other's gain, or at any rate may be altogether out of proportion to it, rather like the case of a man who sets fire to his neighbor's house in order to cook his broth for dinner. If things are indeed as they are here assumed to be, the capital transfer, by the severe disturbances it implies for international economic equilibrium, does considerable harm also to the creditor countries as well as to third countries affected via the nexus of world trade. All the more important it is, therefore, to be quite clear on this question.

The best approach to a correct answer to the question of the *necessity of price pressure constituting a secondary burden on the debtor country as well as a disturbance to international economic equilibrium* is to distinguish two groups of views: on the one hand, a *quantitative* and a *qualitative* group of views; on the other, a *static* and *dynamic* one. A purely *quantitative view of the problem* leads to the conclusion that the decrease in the German money supply entailed by the reparations payment is matched by an equal increase in the money supply of the reparations creditors. It follows that, in terms of the total volume of demand, regardless of its qualitative composition, the question of where additional German exports are to find a market without causing havoc to the economies of the creditor countries is irrelevant. If we use the term *reception problem* for the problem of the effects of the capital export on the economy of the receiving country, there admittedly is no reception problem in this quantitative sense. This explains the barely concealed sarcasm often encountered in the receiving countries in response to any attempt to win acceptance for the view that these countries ill serve their own interests by insisting on reparations payments. Why, people ask, should it be such bad business to get something for nothing? They forget that apart from the quantitative reception problem, which has been shown to be an apparent one only, there may exist a *qualitative reception problem* in the sense that the additional demand of the creditor countries (or of third countries affected by triangular trade relations) may not coincide with Germany's *shortfall of demand in qualitative* terms, that is, that it may be directed to goods other than those that have become exportable in Germany as a result of the contraction of demand.

There is obviously no guarantee whatever for such coincidence, and this brings us to the heart of the whole, so often misunderstood, transfer problem in international capital movements. *The true problem in international capital transfer lies in the possibility of serious qualitative divergence in terms of composition between the minus of demand in the transferor country and the plus of demand in the transferee country.* And it is this possibility that provides a foundation for taking a pessimistic view of reparations developments, without any *sacrificium intellectus* and without denying the uncontested or at any rate uncontestable principles of the theory of foreign trade. *Whether such pessimism proves justified or not depends on whether or not a serious qualitative divergence in the relevant demand quantities can or cannot be shown to be probable.*

It is not possible here to go into this question in detail.[5] We are concerned with principles here, and from this point of view it must be stressed that what actually happens is likely to lie somewhere between *two extreme limiting cases*. The *most favorable limiting case* is that of a full qualitative match between the demand quantities. In that ideal case, capital transfer would cease to be a problem, and there would be no need either for a price war or a price fall. In Germany there would be less demand for, say, shoes, while the enrichment of the British or the French economy would show up precisely in an increased demand for shoes. There clearly is no occasion for any difficulties in this. At the opposite extreme there is

[5] See *W. Röpke, Protocol of the Prymont Conference*, loc. cit.

the other limiting case, which has already been touched upon in the introductory description of conditions in the socialist state, the case, that is, where the goods made available for export by the debtor country meet with no additional demand in the receiving countries such as would enable these goods to be sold without a price fall (or at any rate, without a price fall so large that the total proceeds do not rise in spite of higher sales).[6] In that case the capital transfer would clearly be altogether impossible. But while the first, most favorable, limiting case is quite conceivable, the second, most unfavorable one, is unimaginable. The second would require conditions that are most unlikely ever to obtain. It would have to be assumed, for example, that there are no other goods at all in the debtor country that could take the place of those not wanted in the creditor countries; it would have to be assumed, furthermore, that there are no services that could take the place of these goods; and it would, finally, have to be concluded that the goods offered by the debtor country could be transformed into others more acceptable to the creditor country via triangular trade, that is, by the intermediary of third countries.

By comparison the ideal limiting case is at least conceivable, but it is bound to remain a limiting case in the sense that it is likely to be the exception rather than the rule. The rule—at least in the case of such gigantic capital transfers as reparations and inter-Allied debt settlements—will be some qualitative divergence, greater or lesser, between the relevant demand on the two sides. But if this is what must be expected, it follows that *the transferor debtor country will not be spared some degree of downward pressure on prices, nor the creditor country and any third countries involved some degree of competitive pressure.* And the meaning of all this is that the transfer will be associated with painful readjustments and with disturbances of the economic equilibrium. This, I repeat, is the

---

[6] *The limiting case referred to in the text is one where the elasticity of demand for the goods in question is unity or less than unity.*

true aspect of the transfer problem: transfer is not impossible, but it leads to frictions and disturbances that add much to the burden of the debtor country and may well spoil the creditor countries' joy.

However, there is another point to consider, and this brings us to the second group of views. In the nature of things, any imbalances caused by the demand divergences will eventually even out by themselves, and at the end of the adjustment process there will be a new equilibrium, in which the additional exports of the debtor country can find a market without the sort of price pressure that is a burden on the debtor country and disturbs the world economy. *Being a solely qualitative problem, the reception problem is also solely dynamic,* whereas in quantitative-static terms, that is, with reference to the total volume of demand and in the long run, there is no problem at all.[7] In normal cases of international capital transfers this definition of the transfer problem may indeed be taken as belittling it, but not so in a case such as the German reparations, where the sums involved are so gigantic that the imbalance may be so great and last so long that there is plenty of room for pessimism. Equilibrium may indeed be so greatly disturbed that the creditor countries' fear of enforced competition by Germany need not be imaginary and might possibly in the not too distant future lead to another revision of the Young Plan.

No discussion of the transfer problem can be complete unless it takes due account of one more important factor. To this end I would recall my earlier distinction between *two kinds of capital export,* a *provisional* and a *definitive* one. The case of provisional capital export obtains when there is, in some country, capital that by a natural process looks for investment opportunities abroad and thus creates a creditor

---

[7] *This is overlooked by A. Cabiati, among others, in his otherwise so valuable book* 1919-1929 Da Versailles alla'Aja *(Turin, 1930), which has recently appeared in German under the title* Der Widersinn der Reparationen und die Internationale Bank *(Berlin, 1930).*

position for the country concerned. The case of definitive capital export obtains when a debtor country has to service commercial or political debts by transferring capital abroad for interest and principal and, contrary to the former case, has to do so definitively and without any claim for an eventual return of the sums concerned. It readily follows that provisional capital export is in all circumstances also voluntary capital export resulting automatically from a shift in the supply and demand schedule of capital, and that definitive capital export is in all cases imperative. For the sake of completeness let it be noted at once that, conversely, provisional capital *import* (on the part of the debtor country) is voluntary, and definitive capital import (on the part of the creditor country) imperative. Is there not a presumption that the transfer problem will differ according to whether the capital movements are of the *provisional/voluntary* or of the *definitive/imperative* kind? The difference is obvious enough, and can be deduced from the fact that in the case of provisional/voluntary capital transfers the transfer process itself is as natural and automatic as the whole process of capital seeking investment opportunities abroad. This is not so in the case of definitive/imperative capital transfers, where the capital movement simply has to be effected regardless of all transfer difficulties. But—and this brings us to the transfer factor still to be discussed—there is one circumstance that helps in overcoming these transfer difficulties and does much to mitigate the transfer problem even in the most desperate cases, and this is a new capital inflow into the debtor country. The definitive/imperative capital outflow from the debtor country is met by an opposite, provisional/voluntary flow of capital, the function of which is to replace an abrupt adjustment with all its losses and disturbances with a gradual process of adjustment. This happened recently on the occasion of the settlement of reparations payments, in the most patent manner and to an enormous extent. In the case of reparations it looks as though this counteraction of capital outflow and capital inflow is destined to continue for some time in the future, possibly with the assistance of the Bank for International Settlement, but it also looks as though Germany is approaching the moment where the amount of capital imports definitely no longer offsets the imperative capital export, so that gradually the present, spurious, credit transfer will be transformed into a genuine transfer of goods, with the result that, subject to inevitable fluctuations, the German balance of trade will run up a growing surplus.

IV

Those who have attentively followed my exposition will no doubt have sensed already how extremely awkward it is to treat the transfer problem as one and the same for all kinds of capital transfers. Their feeling is quite correct, and I have tried to allow for it by the distinctions I introduced between provisional and definitive, voluntary and imperative capital transfers. So far as the transfer problem as such is concerned, these distinctions are probably good enough. But when it comes to taking an overall view of international capital movements, we have to go further and give priority to the distinction between commercial and political capital transfers. A deep gulf divides the two categories. The one unites nations, the other divides them; the one is constructive, the other destructive. This fact cannot be altered by any attempt to bridge the gulf by artificially commercializing the political debts.

There is one aspect, though, that commercial indebtedness has in common with political indebtedness, namely, that they create the closest interrelations of nations in the sphere of money. In turn, these interrelations in the monetary sphere must, as we know, logically lead to equally close interrelations in the sphere of goods. Since international indebtedness in the world, both of commercial and of political origin, has grown tremendously in comparison with the past and shows every sign of growing still more, we cannot escape the conclusion that international economic relations in the world will not diminish, as some false prophets predict, but will, in defiance of all autarkic tendencies, continue to intensify. There is no greater or more exasperating contradiction than that between this irresistible development and the highly protectionist tariff policies throughout the world, which seems to be further removed than ever from any sort of economic reason. The sooner the nations become aware of this contradiction and the sooner their commercial policies draw the consequences from this immanent development, the better. Fortified by this inner logic of things we may hope that Friedrich Albert Lange, the nineteenth-century Marburg philosopher, may be proved right in the field of foreign trade policy as in others, when he said: "In politics the realist has the hour on his side, but great ideas command the support of centuries."

The Intellectuals and "Capitalism"*

No one capable of judgment can deny that "capitalism"—that economic system of the Western world that rests upon private ownership of the means of production, upon an extraordinary differentiation of production and a long list of "freedoms"— has, in the course of the century and more of its history, proved to possess a greater power of creating prosperity than any other economic system that preceded it. And no one was more eloquent in praising this power than Karl Marx in the *Communist Manifesto* he wrote together with Friedrich Engels— Karl Marx, that great "intellectual" who combined his panegyrics on the historical achievements of capitalism with an anti-capitalist philosophy of so far unexcelled vigor and thereby set an example to thousands of lesser men after him. We all know that with this he laid the foundations of the socialist mass movement of our day, but it is equally well known that criticism of capitalism has not remained the exclusive preserve of the socialist camp. It has also spread to circles opposed to the socialist economic ideal, and thus led to a now almost-unending series of reformatory government interventions of all kinds.

This criticism invariably became loudest in times of crisis and depression, when the most distinguishing quality of

* Frankfurter Zeitung, *Nos. 662–663, 675–676, and 681–682, September 6, 11, and 13, 1931, signed by the pseudonym: Ulrich Unfried.*

capitalism, its outstanding achievements in production, seemed called in question and the host of immediate victims of the crisis became a challenge subject of anti-capitalist criticism and at the same time its natural sounding board. There is, therefore, nothing special in capitalism once more being pushed into the defensive all along the line. What is special and really rather alarming in the present situation is that the barrage of criticism has never before been so violent, nor the aggressive spirit of the opponents so fiery. And—to come to the most dangerous aspect of the situation—the exponents and advocates of the present economic system have never before been so lacking in self-assertion and have never been more unskillful in defending themselves.

Increasingly we find, not only in Germany, but also in the United States and England, a nagging doubt as to whether capitalism can be maintained much longer in this greatest of all depressions, whether indeed it is right and expedient to maintain it. A growing number of deserters leave the capitalist for the socialist camp, which soon will be as motley as ever Wallenstein's was. There is mounting evidence of a distinct feeling of inferiority on the part of the capitalist world, of despondency and flirtation with socialist ideas of economic planning; openly or implicitly, the outward progress of the Russian five-year plan is taken as the yardstick for measuring the imagined and the real shortcomings of capitalism. And so that we should not be without that vicious circle that seems to be our fate in all spheres today, the crisis of confidence itself saps the efficiency of capitalism and thus creates the very substance on which it feeds.

There are some, and indeed more than a few, who see their dawn breaking and with barely concealed pleasure pour oil onto the fires of criticism and despair: some from selfless fanaticism and some because they covet the heritage they expect to come to them, but all without giving a thought to what we should put in the place of this economic system, on which the existence and civilization of the densely populated Western countries have rested so far and on which they alone can rest in the future. Nothing is easier than to find fault with this system, and no less a man than Owen Young, one of the leading personalities of the American economy, is said to have declared not long ago that he was second to no Bolshevik in his criticism of capitalism. After all, is our sense of justice satisfied with the distribution of income and wealth that we have today? Is it not disgraceful and provocative nonsense for millions to be idle and unable to find work to protect them from hunger and destitution, while at the same time countless machines are standing still? Who can really be at ease in the presence of the growing concentration in economic life, which goes hand in hand with the increasing dependence of the masses? Who can fail to see that our civilization is being destroyed by the progressive commercialization of things that are beyond economics, by the obsessive business spirit that confuses ends and means and forgets that man does not live in order to work, but works in order to live, and thus perverts all human values, by the empty bustle and sterile excitement of our time? Who, indeed, does not feel that all this is destructive of civilization, does not want to fight against it all? Who can fail to be shocked by the largely meaningless and uncultured extravagance of the rich, here in Europe as in America? In truth, we would not want for grandiloquence, lung-power, and acute observation in matching the critics of capitalism in this tune, and in our hymn of hate we would enjoy introducing appropriate allusions to bags of coffee dumped into the sea and corn used to fire locomotives. Any fool can do that, and there's no need for anyone to feel clever and superior just because he reads out for the nth time the long list of sins imputable to the modern economy, with the implication that we are too stupid or obdurate to see it for ourselves. This is only where the true task begins. It is a double task.

First, it would be an act of unexampled irresponsibility to go from criticizing the present economic system to pronouncing the death sentence upon it so long as there is not at least a probability that the economic system that is to follow will give more satisfactory results. The fact that the present economic system has defects that no clear-thinking person denies is not sufficient proof of the existence of a better one. But the economic system that is to replace the present one so far exists only in the more or less extravagant imagination of the gullible and the enthusiastic. We fully understand the despair that grips the victims of the present economic crisis, and we insist that this despair should be an incentive to clear-sighted leadership to take such measures as can be taken with any prospect of success. But despair itself can generate only forces of destruction, not of reconstruction. We understand that a man in despair wants to smash everything to bits, but we doubt whether that will improve matters. In heaping accusation upon accusation, the opponents of capitalism forget to furnish any proof that we shall do better with their brand of economy. There is so far no experience to prove it; even the Russian example does not prove it, for reasons to be discussed presently. On the contrary, all experience so far with any kind of economic planning measures overwhelmingly speaks against the latter's repetition and cumulation. On the other hand, our often so reckless anti-capitalists would do well to get thoroughly acquainted with the voluminous literature on economics, which demonstrates that in practice socialism must founder on the impossibility of economic calculation in a socialist community. Let them try their hand at a refutation which no one has yet managed. This is, of course, more troublesome and less rewarding than brandishing the hatchet, but it should not be too much to ask of men conscious of their responsibilities.

So much for the first task. Secondly, it is the duty of any serious critic of our economic and social environment to examine very carefully what defects and imperfections are to be imputed to the economic system as such, rather than to other historically more or less incidental circumstances. One point to note in this context is that the capitalist economic system has been saddled with burdens such as no other economic system probably has ever borne. Among them is a population increase unparalleled in history. It is the fault of that increase that the incredible growth of productivity has not done as much to raise individual welfare as might have been expected but has had, in part, to provide a means of existence for a larger number of people. But to hold capitalism responsible for that increase in population ill becomes those who fall over themselves today in blaming capitalism, and the alleged decay which it causes, for the steadily decreasing rate of demographic growth, or the "waning of the people's vital force," as certain circles are fond of expressing themselves. And then, let us ponder how very different the world would look today if capitalism had not been made to bear political burdens under which it nearly broke down. But capitalism cannot very well be blamed for the armaments race, the world war, the peace treaties, inflation, revolution, and political mass epidemics of all kinds, without exposing to utter ridicule the sociological approach underlying such an attempt. Were there no wars before capitalism ever existed, and did they not wreak destruction? And are Sweden, Denmark, the Netherlands, and Switzerland by any chance less capitalistic than Germany and England? And, surely, the first group of countries is the best demonstration of what peace signifies for the thriving of capitalism's welfare-creating forces. As we take a closer look at one feature after another that we don't like in capitalism, it turns out in very many cases that the complaint is misaddressed.

How much thought, for instance, is given to the extent to which the picture presented by quite a few capitalist countries is distorted by feudal and pre-capitalist vestiges carried over into the present time? Why does France enjoy such a happy balance, with a strong middle class and a vigorous peasantry? Surely it is because in 1789 that liberal revolution so busily ridiculed by the contemporary condemners of liberalism made a cleaner sweep of feudalism than elsewhere. And it wasn't the fault of capitalism, after all, that England is a country without peasants but rather, as in Germany, the fault of an agrarian policy devoid of sense and of any understanding for the importance of the peasant class. Another example of a misaddressed complaint is the whole set of unedifying aspects of big industry that are the favorite butts of anti-capitalist criticism, to wit, the individual's dependent condition, the threat to his satisfaction in work, and much else. Only careful sifting will show how much of all this is to be imputed to the big industrial enterprise as such and how much to the capitalist one, and it turns out that in a majority of cases there would be no less cause for complaint if the big enterprise were under socialist management. It may indeed be assumed that in a socialist state, where the workers are faced with only one employer, they would be a good deal more dependent and less free.

The decisive point in judging capitalism, finally, is that precisely in our days, when the system is being attacked so sharply, it is disfigured and distorted almost beyond recognition by alien elements. The direct manipulation of prices by the government, price ceilings such as still exist for dwellings, minimum prices for coffee, rubber, wheat or rye, an increasingly more complicated system of protection for domestic producers against foreign competition, regulations on the compulsory utilization of materials, regulations on consumption, "political" wage formation, the growing infiltration of public intervention in the field of production and trade, an endless string of premiums and subventions, the steadily increasing expansion of public expenditure—in short, intervention, collectivism, and economic "planning" all along the line. Can this still be called capitalism? Had we not better give it a new name, such as subventionism, interventionism, or pseudo-capitalism? What is so grotesque in this situation is that all these interventions and manipulations have lowered the efficiency of capitalism in a way of which we are only too painfully aware now, in the crisis, but that, on the other hand, they fit perfectly into precisely that pattern of economic policy that is advocated by the most vociferous critics of capitalism. And in order to refloat the economy whose functioning has been so largely impaired by past interventions, those same critics of capitalism clamor for more interventions, more planning, and hence a further emasculation of our economy. It is as though one poured sand into an engine and then hoped to start it up again by pouring in more sand. This is the admirable logic that bedevils us today.

Notoriously, the class of people somewhat loosely designated as "intellectuals" has long played a significant, perhaps even a decisive, part in the anti-capitalist *Fronde*. All the same, it is an astonishing spectacle, which needs some explanation, that today a mass wave of anti-capitalist sentiment threatens to engulf almost the whole intellectual class—at least in Germany but, to a lesser extent, also in the United States and in England. The consequences are incalculable. Whether they join the social democrats, the communists, or the national socialists, whether they side with Marx or swear by Spann and utter dark prognostications, none of them will have any truck with capitalism, and the younger they are, the less will they do so. It is worth looking a little closer into the background of this intellectual mass flight from capitalism.

The first point that comes to mind is that the economic and social changes of the last fifteen years have gotten the intellectuals into a situation that increasingly resembles that of the proletariat. We not only need to think in this context of the decimation of the old middle classes but also of the mass entry into the professions needing academic training, the prospects of which thereby become steadily poorer. In this situation people cling to the dream opportunities of escape and preferment that the anti-capitalist economic constructions appear to offer. Perhaps they hope that the planned economy of the future will need more lawyers and engineers than the market economy of the present, and it is thought a grave defect of the latter that it cannot always absorb the steadily mounting supply of intellectual workers without growing proletarianization, that is, without cheapening each individual. It must be obvious to any thoughtful person how big a danger this proletarianization of the intellectual middle classes, this constant erosion of the "bourgeois" concept, spells for the present economic system, and it must be equally obvious that the decimation of middle-class wealth by inflation is having to be paid for very dearly now and that it would be an unforgivable mistake to let the civil servants, in their turn, be swallowed up by the whirlpool.

But the intellectuals' anti-capitalism is by no means conditioned solely by their economic situation and, in many cases, perhaps not even decisively. Their attitude is buttressed by strong sentiments, noble and ignoble alike. Hats off to the philanthropists whom the sense of justice, compassion, and charity leads to champion the cause of the economically weak and ultimately to oppose an economic system that rightly or wrongly is regarded as the sole culprit. Hats off to the patriot who is prepared to sacrifice not the others but himself to the common weal. But it may well happen that our sentiments fool us when we give them too free a rein and let them become a soporific of the cooly calculating mind. The tremendous danger in any sentimental justification of meddling with the ruling economic system is precisely that we are over and again driven beyond the limits that we can recognize and would respect if our mind were not dulled by sentiments of the most honorable and noble kind. The free-trader is no less patriotic than the protectionist and no less concerned with the common interests, but his mind tells him that the common interests are damaged when the international division of labor is obstructed by obstacles that look patriotic only because of a failure to appreciate that an obstacle to imports is also an obstacle to exports. The social revisionist is no worse nor less social a man than his opponents; he, too, knows of no higher purpose than to replace mass poverty by mass prosperity, and he, too, has a profound hatred of exploitation, unfairness, injustice, and that "hardness of heart" with which men torment each other and make one another unhappy. But is it not a sign of his particularly acute sense of social responsibility that he does not let his sentiments obscure his recognition of the fact that some part, at least, of what for ten years or so has been extolled as social progress ultimately annuls itself and, beyond that, is destructive and in the end effect, therefore, unsocial? These are just examples to show that anyone who cannot refute our rational arguments has no right to cast doubt on our sentiments and motives.

But there are also sentiments of a morally less clear-cut kind, and they are today associated especially with the anti-capitalism of those intellectuals who stand aside from the real mass movement of socialism. It is a brand of anti-capitalism that at present finds particularly striking and, it would seem, effectual expression in the circle connected with the periodical *Die Tat*. The first impression the reader of this periodical gets is the frequency of doom and destruction articles, which, one would think, are bound to become wearisome to the public in time. But the contrary seems to be true; the economic and political ideas developed in the review every month by a number of contributors, especially by Ferdinand Fried (clearly a pseudonym), seem gradually to be accepted as gospel truth by an uncritical section of the younger generation. "The Road to Chaos," "The Crisis of Capitalism, " "Breakdown of the World Economy," "Getting Better?—Storm Signal!" "Blind Alley," "Exit the Old Economy," "The Road to Catastrophe" —these are just a few sample titles. Wallowing in pessimism, these apocalyptic visions seem to betray more than just the satisfaction Cassandra might have felt had she been able to gather a circle of readers around herself. There seems to be something else behind these effusions, and that is the all too human inclination to exaggerate the historical significance of present happenings, to feel as though one were standing on the Gaurisankar of epoch-making events, whereas it is maybe just a little molehill of history, in short, to believe "that as of here and now a new epoch of world history is beginning" and to add proudly: "I was there." To begin with, pessimism appeals to intellectuals because it is the mark of a certain lack of vitality, a certain escapism, and it suits people who, in their own way of putting it, have more "mind" than "blood." But perhaps it is also a mark of the German character, as *Die Tat* itself somewhere states, "to welcome even the most destructive phenomenon if only it fits into some theory." This is the only possible explanation for the unconcealed pleasure and satisfaction with which the *Tat* circle hailed the latest credit crisis in Germany as "a decisive and saving step forward."

What gives the anti-capitalism of our intellectuals, and especially of the *Tat* circle, its distinctive flavor and, I frankly confess, makes it so peculiarly unpalatable is the wholesale rejection of all those values and ideals that we subsume under the, admittedly somewhat discredited, expression of liberalism. These circles, it seems, have lost all feeling for the infinite and absolute value of individual freedom, all understanding of the truth that what the Age of Enlightenment and liberalism fought for, what men like Hume, Voltaire, Wilhelm von Humboldt, John Stuart Mill, Jefferson, or Mazzini as well as our classical poets extolled, what our grandfathers and great-grandfathers battled and suffered for, is ultimately mankind's oldest and finest intellectual heritage. All feeling for *humanitas* in the widest sense of the word seems to be dead to them and seems to have given way to a new enthusiasm for the omnipotence of the state, the subjection of the individual, for the militarization and tutelage that threatens to lead us back into another barbarism—until, fifty or a hundred years later, people will rediscover the truth that there can be no civilization without freedom, and this truth will prevail in another fearful struggle, as can be predicted right now in Italy. They are racing full steam ahead toward the termite state, and however much our friends on the other side prefer to call it the "total state," this does not make their ideal any prettier. Certainly, it is to be hoped that all those who still have a remnant of resistance against this barbaric social philosophy should oppose it with an unbending NO. Since one cannot very well argue about opinions, it can at least be pointed out forcefully how unrealistic is this *étatism*, which is here being resurrected in its most radical form. Has anyone stopped to think that the state, in practice, means bureaucracy, about which, after all, even *Die Tat* has its biting tale to tell? Have the red tape of our war economy and the corruption of our foreign trade controls after the war been forgotten? Has it been forgotten, for example, that for months during the war we had to eat turnip jam because some junior official in a position of responsibility confused turnips with beetroot? Or, to mention another example, has it been forgotten in the heat of the battle against the gold standard where we end up if we let the state handle and mishandle the currency at its discretion? All these experiences, which we would have expected to provide salutary immunization for at least one generation, must, indeed, have been forgotten, for otherwise this new enthusiasm for a war-time and planned economy would be incomprehensible.

The more tasks are assigned to the state, the more "total" it is made, the more emphasis is laid on its external position, and the more significance is attached to the national frontiers. It is only consistent—though we shudder at this kind of consistency—that our anti-capitalist intellectuals are ready to jettison economic freedom not only within but without, and that they want to achieve national autarky by means even more drastic than protective tariffs. Along with the social philosophy of mercantilism, its whole economic armory has thus been taken over. That no one makes even the slightest attempt to refute the simply overwhelming arguments that speak against such a policy is hardly worth mentioning, for economics is, after all, a liberal invention that need not be bothered with. Instead of anything like a real proof, we are fobbed off with a device that is extremely popular in this whole spiritual province of our country, namely, the use of emotional appeals of all kinds to create a certain atmosphere, to which the reader is then exposed. One of these emotional appeals is a sort of glorified nationalism, which so dominates the *Tat* circle in particular, that one almost gets the impression that the whole economic policy program is merely a means to some foreign policy purpose. Again and again we read how closely things national and social belong together. And this connection is made even closer by defining, if need be, the infinitely iridescent concept of "capitalism" in such a way that it coincides with the whole group of countries that are the bugbear of foreign policy, that is, Western Europe.

Another emotional appeal that is very effective in Germany is what I would call geographical romanticism, a brand of romanticism publicized linguistically by the frequent use of the word "space." Geopolitics, as such a very useful approach that we owe to the Swedish geographer Kjéllèn, though he was not to know what we would make of it, is thereby turned almost into a caricature of itself. With the finger on the map an attempt is made to prove to us that our salvation lies in a certain "space" (Southeast and Eastern Europe), without worrying about the consequences such self-encirclement is bound to have on our trade and foreign relations, however plainly visible these consequences have already become, and without considering that what counts is not square miles but purchasing power and capital wealth. The fact that small countries such as Denmark, the Netherlands, and Switzerland are doing very well without "space" is ignored. If they establish contacts with a view to defending themselves against regionalism in foreign trade, they are at once suspected of wanting to form a new "space," and this is used as an argument to justify more "space-building" of our own. If only all these things were for once discussed more soberly and without throwing around so many pompous words! But that is just what is so characteristic of the intellectuals' socialism in Germany, however much its representatives, such as the members of the *Tat*

THE INTELLECTUALS AND "CAPITALISM"

circle, may otherwise be perfectly articulate in the German language.

Verbal pomposity is something that applies in the first place to the very expression "capitalism," which, just like the expression "space," is used in countless nuances and compounds and is an indispensible prop in the written output of our intellectuals, where it has helped them to many a logical fraud. On closer inspection it is frightening to see how this seductively iridescent concept is manipulated at will to provide ever new justification for the eternal *ceterum censeo*. Western "capitalism," *rentier* "capitalism," creditor "capitalism," private "capitalism," state "capitalism"—all are concepts that elude precise definition and, hence, lend themselves eminently to whipping up a certain stylistic lather. By hook or by crook everything is pressed into the mold of the "crisis of capitalism" with a violence one is tempted to describe as "association mania," and this applies regardless of whether the thing in question has as little to do with the economic system as such, as, say, deficit financing in Germany.

The self-assurance with which our anti-capitalist intellectuals justify the *pereat* they hurl at the capitalist economy and with which they predict its demise by a sort of self-intoxication, by the course of some much-quoted "fate," is by no means matched (taking, once more, *Die Tat* as an example) by the sort of knowledge of economics one would have a right to expect. The statistics of which *Die Tat* makes copious and tendentious use cannot make good this shortcoming, for all depends on the interpretation of the figures, and that cannot possibly be done without economic theory. Ferdinand Fried, for instance, took a lot of trouble proving the inequality of the distribution of income and wealth in Germany, only to reach the conclusion, among others, that one third of the country's total wealth is in the hands of no more than seventy-nine thousand people. But then he adds: "The whole hullabaloo that goes on at present in Germany about the economy, private property, politics and parties in the end turns on just these seventy-nine thousand people—and that is nothing less than grotesque!"[1] That is the sort of primitive black and white approach we thought serious Socialists had outgrown by now. Not an inkling of the fact that in the debate about the economic system the fate of these people is totally irrelevant, but that any improvement in the situation of the have-nots to be expected from a more equal distribution of income and wealth would be so minute that this point is completely overshadowed by the question of the system itself, which is rooted in private ownership of the means of production. Not an inkling of the fact that arbitrary interference with the existing distribution of income and wealth, however much such interference may be desirable from a host of other points of view, has to be paid for with intolerable disturbances that would cause more hardship to the have-nots themselves. Not an inkling of the fact that "capitalists" really fulfill the function of social officials, who are selected on the strict principle of performance, who are responsible for the good management of the means of production and for this get paid a sum that, all in all, is probably less than the pay of officials in a socialist state in relation to their performance, and who must pay the penalty for their mistakes by the loss of their livelihood.

It is true that in the modern economy there is often a wide divergence between income and performance, but that does not affect the principle. On the contrary, we place the strongest possible emphasis on degenerative symptoms of this kind and differ from the anti-capitalist radicals only insofar as we do not allow our indignation to carry us away into an ultimately sterile negation of the whole system but draw from it the passionate demand for an economic policy that, to the extent possible, stops up the sources of fraudulent incomes (without corresponding performance) and unpunished mistakes. What is at stake here are questions of trade policy, monopoly control,

[1] Die Tat, *September, 1930, p. 442.*

reform of corporation law, monetary and credit policy, and this is the appropriate sphere for positive criticism of the existing system. That the capitalist economy is just as much a want-satisfaction economy as the socialist one should be self-evident to anyone who has ever stopped to think that the success of any business, that is, its profit, is determined by the sensitive scales of the market, and that means consumer demand. It is quite illogical to contrast the capitalist profit economy ("want-creation" economy) with the socialist "want-satisfaction" economy. Both economic systems aim at satisfying wants, and it is only the motives and organization of "want-satisfaction" that differ. The only logical contrast to the profit economy would be, say, "bureaucratic" economy. So far as I am concerned, I am inclined to think that this capitalist "want-creation" economy (profit economy), however much its equilibrium is upset by the present crisis, does not come off so badly by comparison with the Russian "want-satisfaction" (bureaucratic) economy.

Here is another example to illustrate where too bold an emancipation from economics may lead. Anyone familiar with the most elementary notions of economics knows that price determination on the basis of production cost has a profound economic significance, insofar as this is the means of achieving the best and most efficient possible distribution of factors of production in the economy. Ferdinand Fried is innocent of this. He obviously suspects[2] that he is here on the scent of some eccentricity of the capitalists, a psychosis contrasting to its disadvantage, as he implies, with the Russians' happy-go-lucky policy of dumping. This goes to show, once more, the pitfalls that await the amateur who wants to attack an economic system he has not thoroughly studied beforehand, were it only with the sort of love-hate that must have driven Karl Marx to such study. On the other hand, Ferdinand Fried seems to take a very poor view of businessmen's being interested in economics, and thinking, talking, or writing about the mean-

[2] *In his article "Der Umbau der Welt," Die Tat, May, 1931.*

ing of what they do. They can't do that, opines Fried[3] without giving away that their vital sap has become thinner. What would be his judgment if they responded with silence to all the attacks showered upon them is anybody's guess, but that his conclusion is quite absurd would be obvious even if so many of the businessmen who talk and write did not burst with vitality and energy. The sole example of Ford should clinch the argument.

The more deeply the capitalist world sinks down in the sulphurous vapors of catastrophe, the brighter rises the Russian star for our anti-capitalist intellectuals. To be sure, they make reservations of all kinds, but on the whole they look to Russia in a way that some years ago would have been called national bolshevikism, and that seems to arouse a good deal more sympathy today than it did then. After thirteen years the Russian system is at long last beginning to develop ideas that look constructive at least formally and from the technical point of view, and at the precise moment when the capitalist world is convulsively contracting after a gigantic wave of investment and is groping for a new equilibrium in the severest of all depressions, the Russians have embarked with tremendous energy upon an investment program of huge dimensions, with the result that all-out effort combines with relatively little unemployment in Russia at this time of depression in the capitalist world. For many people this is enough proof that the Russian method is superior to the capitalist one. More than just a few of those who only a few years ago admired the American "economic miracle" seem to have turned right about and now see a new "economic miracle" emerging in the East. All these widespread attitudes seem to be largely devoid of objective thought. The Russians may well succeed in building power plants and other things on a gigantic scale, but that really need not astonish us any more than the successful erection of the pyramid of Cheops. What is astonishing in both

[3] Die Tat, *July, 1931.*

cases is merely the tremendous social pressure and the remarkable compressibility of consumption, which alone make such investment projects possible, as well as the political and social system that can withstand this pressure. But a people's ability to stand impoverishment is no proof of the superiority of a system that uses this ability for the creation of durable investments. This applies all the more forcefully as the machines that are being installed in Russian factories have to be bought in capitalist countries, the best that only capitalist industry can produce, and are paid for with money procured by dumping, to the detriment of Russians as consumers and non-Russians as producers. And then there still remains the question not only of how much the Russians manage to do with these machines, but, far more important, of whether there is any chance at all of economic calculation such as would prevent at least the worst cases of misallocation of resources and faulty investment, and whether the incentives are sufficiently strong to guarantee some minimum of speed and quality of work. For an answer to this question, all the enthusiastic admirers of Russia would be well advised to read Boris Brutzku's extremely well-informed and instructive article "Planwirtschaft und Marktwirtschaft in der Sowjetunion."[4] What they can learn there about the increasing disruption of the Russian economy owing to the sheer impossibility of running an economy without a market should give them as much food for thought as the circumstance that, unlike the typical investment booms of capitalist economies, the Russian investment boom has not so far caused the slightest improvement in the general supply situation for the population—if anything, the contrary. (Ferdinand Fried, to be sure, seems to suggest that this is another special merit of the Russian investment boom, to judge from his article "Der Umbau der Welt," as indeed he is visibly at pains to belittle the terrible shortages from which the Russian population suffers according to all

[4] Der Deutsche Volkswirt, *May 8, 1931.*

reports.) But then, I hear someone object, surely Russia is free from the appalling unemployment of the capitalist countries. Well, during the inflation we, too, had no appreciable unemployment, but the price we would have to pay for a repetition of that experiment seems to us too high, and rightly so, because an economy cannot with impunity be subjected to such heroic treatment. That will become apparent in Russia as well when the investment phase comes to an end and a new equilibrium has to be found for the economy, which will be all the more difficult, just as in the case of a capitalist boom, the steeper was the climb of the investment curve. But these are considerations of economics that are far from the minds of our anti-capitalist intellectuals of the *Tat* species. They wax enthusiastic about the "anti-pole of Western private capitalism" (Fried), about the "total state" (for which in the interests of clarity, I continue to prefer the name "termite state"), they have no detailed program of their own but are thrilled by their belief that instead that can not only invoke "fate" but point to the Russian example. It is all a piece of dilettantism of the kind that cannot be censured too sharply, dilettantism interwoven with romantic enthusiasm for political dictatorship.

In effect the anti-capitalism of the *Tat* circle has one thing in common with old-style Marxism: it leaves us in the dark regarding its positive program. They throw out expressions like "state economy," "want-satisfaction economy," "organic economic community," "spiritualization, moralization and nationalization of the economy," "tied planning," "the mass of the unpropertied people growing into the state," "realization of the idea of true democracy," but these are all more or less lyrical catch-phrases that cannot give us any clear idea of the nature of the new economic system. The only clear intention is to close off the economy against the rest of the world even more than is already the case, if possible by a state monopoly of foreign trade. No attempt is made to discuss the real problems of socialization, not even in the August issue of *Die*

Tat, which was supposed to have published the positive program. Before we see that positive program, there is no possibility of a critical assessment that will carry further the general considerations already propounded in these articles.

The strong appeal of the Russian economic experiment as well as the whole intellectual socialism of our days, especially as represented by *Die Tat,* is, of course, like many another contemporary phenomenon that would find no echo in dispassionate minds, explicable only as an emotional reaction to the great economic depression of the capitalist world. It is this that helps to create a sort of chiliastic mood and creates the impression that we are faced with a crisis not merely of the economy but of the whole system, with the last great "crash," with the "crisis to end crises," when reason is out of place and fate takes its course, a fate to which we must blindly bow. It would be interesting to know today how this doomsday mood is going to be judged in fifty years' time, but my guess is that the chronicler of 1980 will find that mood very strange if he compares it with the technical feats achieved by capitalism during the ten years preceding the crisis, feats that had become one of the main causes of imbalance. He will note that history takes a longer view than our pessimists had assumed, and that it was premature to introduce such expressions as "late capitalism" so long as there was still a possibility that our economic system was not breathing its last. No doubt, he will see much in a different light than we do, and he won't be able to make head nor tail of much apprehension and hysteria on one side and of self-confidence on the other. He will be moved on seeing what efforts we made to get out of the pandemonium of the crisis, and, we hope, will go on to record that in spite of gigantic difficulties and unpardonable mistakes we did eventually find our way back to safe ground. But things may also turn out otherwise. The chronicler of 1980 may have to record, sadly, how badly we failed when there was still time to prevent a catastrophic regression into poverty and barbarism. Maybe he will have to record that the civilization and the economy of the Western world perished because people allowed an economic system of unparalleled strength and resilience to rot or threw it overboard. And not without bitterness will he recall not only those who sinned against the economic system but also the pessimists and amateurish activists whose prophesies based on secret desires came true, just because their propaganda was more than anything else responsible for undermining the intellectual foundations of the system. And his curse will also fall upon those who were indolent enough to succumb to that propaganda.

III

The Secular Significance
of the World Crisis*

I

Some branches of the economy are cyclically sensitive, some are not. The same distinction may be applied to branches of science. While astronomy carries on its work with the majestic calm with which the stars pursue their courses high above all earthly troubles and confusion, there are other disciplines, such as, say, constitutional law, whose tasks are more and more wholly dictated by the rapid succession of political events. Economics follows not far behind; witness the fact that the world crisis, being a world economic crisis, has radically disturbed and revolutionized the subject of our science. Unexampled confusion reigns in our ranks. Some seem to want to go so far as to invoke Article 48 of the Weimar Constitution even for economics, declare a state of emergency in the science, and suspend or, indeed, permanently abrogate all its fundamental laws. Judging by this extreme group, economics appears to be in a state of dissolution, to consist of nothing but policy proposals of the most radical kind and of political rhetoric. The results of 150 years of economic thought seem to be buried under the rubble of the crisis, or at any rate they seem no longer to exist for these desperadoes. It is a golden age for persons who never underwent the intellectual

* Weltwirtschaftliches Archiv, *January, 1933.*

discipline of studying the theoretical work of that century-and-a-half, and who now feel free to substitute a ready and melodramatic pen for economic knowledge. When big banks collapse overnight, and whole countries become insolvent, everything becomes possible in the realm of ideas as well. No opinion is so harebrained and no proposal so bizarre as not to find enthusiastic admirers—and indulgent judges among professional economists. For their ranks, too, are invaded by uncertainty and confusion. The shock of an unprecedented economic breakdown has largely undermined the firmness of their judgment and their convictions and so weakened their intellectual health as to allow entry to bacilli against which they used to be immune.

There can be no other explanation for the benevolent indulgence, not to say sympathy, with which economists nowadays accept ideas of autarky and economic planning. It is a widespread view that the unrivaled decline of the economy has invalidated some of the most important laws of economics and thus created a state of emergency matching the situation in national politics. Characteristically, this view is openly reflected in a recently published textbook by one of Germany's leading theoretical economists.[1] Is not this crisis maybe the beginning of a new epoch in economic history? Could it be that all our economics so far was a historically conditioned expression of the rise of capitalism, and that it now needs to be replaced by an economics of decline? What remains that is still valid? Perhaps the classical equilibrium theory of foreign trade? Or the common property of modern theories of capital and interest? Have machine techniques and rationalization made nonsense of economic progress? Are we not witnessing the merry resurrection of the mercantilist doctrine—that concern with the balance of trade and payments has to be the alpha and omega of economic policy? And, we may finally ask

[1] *O. v. Zwiedineck-Südenhorst,* Allgemeine Volkswirtschaltslehre *(Enzyklopädie der Rechts- und Staatswissenschaft. Abt. Staatswissenschaft, 33) (Berlin, 1932). p. 265.*

with some alarm, how many economists are there still who feel they are standing on firm ground amid all this confusion, and who are prepared to defend it against an overwhelming majority?

All these questions must be answered. But an answer to them can be found only by avoiding any flirtation with mass opinions and mass sentiments, and by managing instead to interpret the upheaval manifest in the current world crisis in terms acceptable to the intellect. This can be done only by shaking off the tyranny of the writers who dominate the field not only in Germany, to be sure, but more insufferably here than elsewhere. Their preferred method is to create a certain atmosphere by skillfully selected means, thus escaping the need to prove their theses. At a moment when in some countries output has shrunk to barely more than half what it was before the crisis, when throughout the world unemployment has assumed unimaginable proportions, at a moment when nothing seems to divide us from general bankruptcy except some open or disguised moratorium, it really does not take much to create the impression that this is the crash of a trunk long rotten within, and that the world is the victim of a destiny the fatal course of which had long been traced in advance. People have become receptive to such impressions and are only too willing to do without proof such as might convince the intellect, especially since those self-same writers do their level best to represent the use of the intellect as an incomprehensible aberration of the nineteenth century. Now, it is one of the peculiarities of these proclaimers of an era's end that the decline they announce seems to warm the cockles of their heart, and that they see emerging from it a new economic system that meets their desires and ideals. Some acknowledge the historical mission of capitalism in the international economy and hold that it has now come to an end. Others fairly fall over themselves with heaping abuse on this age.

Not long ago, for instance, Salin used the columns of this review to pour a conservative's full disgust upon the "nineteenth century, presumptuous in its arrogant hubris," which for him was also "a century of unprecedented horrors."[2] Nobody can and nobody will prevent his doing so, nobody is going to deny respect to genuine indignation of this kind, and there are few who would not agree with him that this unique century, which ended in the catastrophe and moral bankruptcy of the great war, represented a fatal aberration in more than one aspect. We would perhaps prefer to use expressions that are not so strong, would consider that there were greater horrors in other centuries, would ask whether the nineteenth century's unexampled population growth, which alone gave meaning, direction, and strength to the expansion of industry and world trade, is one of the "horrors," and whether the most unedifying phase of that era was not already behind us when catastrophe overtook us. But this whole question is of no interest in our context. What is of interest is that the execration of the past, the abysmally pessimistic judgment of the present, and the paean sung to the future sound a treacherous chord that makes us prick up our ears. Surely, we know that tune and know also who wrote it. Was it not Hegel's faithful disciple Karl Marx who developed in masterly fashion the method of wrapping up the quinine of economic policy aims in the neutral wafer of a philosophic interpretation of history? The success he achieved precisely in Germany, and the loud echo that our modern German doomsday prophets are arousing prove indeed that there is no better way to gain support for an idea in Germany than to endow it with the metaphysical consecration of being predestined and ineluctably prescribed by inflexible law. The German seems to have a special predilection for molding his thought to a historical and philosophic pattern, and for exulting in the feeling that he and his contemporaries stand on the threshold of a new era. Maybe this is the German's own way of saving his ubiqui-

---

[2] E. Salin, "Von den Wandlungen der Weltwirtschaft in der Nachkriegszeit," Weltwirtschaftliches Archiv, Vol. 35, No. 1, 1932, pp. 1 et seq.

tously threatened personality from being swallowed up by the void, and of preserving for himself some sort of significance when most of it has been stripped from him by modern mass civilization. Once more we are surrounded by a penetratingly chiliastic atmosphere, and millions are on the point of yielding to its narcotic influence. The aims of economic policy are something that can be discussed, and, indeed, we are doing so right now, but do let us be spared any attempt to smuggle the economic policy aim into the discussion as a *res judicata* and thus to cut short any further discussion.

Let us be spared, likewise, other means of evading discussion. The swaggering tone of a popular German monthly, in which we were actually told in black and white not long ago that instead of discussion we should rely on the sword and the fist, is something we will pass over in silence. We have not reached that point yet. For the time being the methods used are more subtle. One of them is the attempt to treat the ideological shift toward illiberalism, the spread of which during the present crisis could, in fact, acquire secular significance, as though it were already an accomplished fact, in the face of which nothing remains but to lay down the arms of intellect and the arguments of experience. We all know tactics of this kind from meetings, where a skillful chairman can quickly and imperceptibly steer the debate in such a way as to create an atmosphere in which initially doubtful premises are accepted as established, so that the timid are afraid to question them any more. These tactics of taking people by surprise and intimidating them are used against those who oppose radical illiberalism. When they explain, soberly and without excitement, the meaning and true significance of economic developments and try to remind people of the elementary facts about the functioning of the capitalist market economy, they are represented as men belonging to a lost world, as mummies that have no place in the progressive era of illiberalism, as dry intellectuals insensitive to the new, wonderful *ver sacrum* supposedly sweeping across Central Europe. Anyone who contradicts and has no use for the esoteric language bandied about is—well, a liberal—and it is obviously taken for granted and as requiring no further proof that this adjective amounts to a crushing condemnation, especially when it's used in the woolly form "liberalistic." The whole thing is an attempt to promote an opinion, which, like any other in the democracy of opinions, has to fight for its power of conviction, to give it a head start by ceaselessly repeating that "it marches." It is rather as though a government, based like any other on one political party, were to claim the authority of an above-party government. Among scholars, votes are not counted but weighed, and neither the circulation figures of illiberal books and periodicals nor any other symptom of the "awakening of youth" can ever take the place of valid arguments.

II

It was necessary to use plain, quite unmistakable words in order to place the discussion of the secular significance of the world crisis on a basis free from that atmosphere in which knowledge and purpose mingle, so that we can examine with detachment whether the distressing events that culminated in the world credit crisis of 1931 do or do not signify an abrupt break in economic history, and, in case we regard this as a catastrophe, whether it is one against which resistance is useless. To make our attitude clear: we are prepared for all possibilities, even the worst. It is perhaps unlikely but by no means impossible that the present crisis is the beginning of a most far-reaching process of disintegration, in which eventually the ultimate foundations of our economic and social system will be engulfed. Nobody can look into the future; nobody can, in a world taut with such tremendous tensions, guarantee that the world crisis will be overcome within the framework of the existing economic and social system. But how does this affect and alter our notions about the aims of economic policy? If we regard the idea of national economic planning as antagonistic both to the economy and civilization, is it not just, when we take the full measure of the dangerous strength of the disintegrating forces working in that direction, that we must multiply the counterforces and fight to the last ditch? For whatever the future may bring, it is we ourselves, in the last resort, who fashion the future.

My opposition to the economic policies and the ideas of social philosophy associated with the pessimism of our illiberals need not prevent my sharing their pessimism if I thought it justified. It certainly does not prevent me and should not prevent anyone like-minded from taking a detached look at all the circumstances that speak for or against the view that the present world crisis signifies a turning point in economic history.

In weighing these circumstances one against the other, we have to begin by conceding that in view of the developments since 1931, the world crisis cannot simply be regarded as the slump of a normal business cycle. Month after month it became less legitimate to compare this crisis with any of the great crises of the past; month after month it has been growing beyond any historical precedent. To put it in convenient, though not altogether unproblematical terms: the present world crisis has ceased to be a mere cyclical phase and has increasingly assumed the character of structural change, or perhaps better, of a whole set of structural changes. For the sake of a simple exposition, we might even concede that it is a case not merely of a crisis within the system but of a crisis of the very system itself.

But though we have to make this concession, its implications should not be overestimated. First of all, we may recall that the past, too, knew crises which defied comparison with any earlier ones, and that they led in the past to the same sort of doomsday mood that has developed today. Surely, every great crisis of the past equally had a structural character and called forth structural changes which by their nature ranged beyond the crisis, though without bringing to an end the system itself. The great crisis of the eighteen-seventies can furnish us with a wealth of material on this point. The whole history of capitalism remains incomprehensible unless it is appreciated that every great crisis of the past somehow closed one phase of development and opened a new one. The present crisis can hardly be an exception, seeing that it outstrips all preceding ones in intensity and extensity. The strikingly characteristic point, however, is that the breaks that the crises interposed in capitalist development left the constitutional features of the system unaltered and never interrupted for any length of time the trends corresponding to the essence of the system. These trends include in particular one that the present crisis is supposed to cut short for good, namely, the growth of economic interrelations throughout the world. More will have to be said about this presently.

Up to this point, the statement that the crisis has assumed the character of structural change means no more than that it is an economic crisis of unprecedented extent, and that it does more than any other has ever done to shake the foundations of our economic system. But the metaphysicians of the end-of-an-economic-era school go much further. They assert and, to prove their metaphysics, are forced to assert that the world crisis, far from being even originally and basically a cyclical crisis, was of structural origin to begin with. What they say is this: we are witnessing the collapse of an edifice doomed to collapse by virtue of long-period trends, that is, trends valid for the very distant future. In other words: the crisis is not the nemesis for the few preceding years of boom but the nemesis for a whole century.

We may ask whether anyone has yet managed to explain the world crisis in terms of one or more *structural causes*, in isolation from the mechanism of cyclical reactions. The answer is a conclusive No. Any attempts of this kind must, in fact, be regarded as unsuccessful. Even mere hypotheses of this kind prove untenable, though they would by no means involve anything like the end of an economic era or seal the fate of capitalism. This applies, for instance, to the hypothesis of structural causes of a monetary kind. Surely, nobody would any more seriously maintain that the primary cause of the world crisis is a structural *shortage of gold*.[3] This hypothesis was faulted from the outset by its failure to explain why, nevertheless, the volume of money and credit was able to expand so much immediately before the outbreak of the crisis. Nothing better can be said of another view, according to which one of the causes of the crisis is to be found in the serious disturbances in the mechanism of the gold standard, as evidenced particularly by the wrong distribution of gold and by the ineffectiveness of the proven automatic controls of the gold standard. The truth is that the crisis, above all insofar as it is a crisis of confidence, came first, and that the gold standard cannot work when its conditions have been removed by the crisis, just as the parliamentary system and democracy cannot work when a nation has lost its political health, with the result that a "wrong distribution" of votes temporarily invalidates the mechanism of parliamentary democracy.

While the hypothesis that the crisis is due to structural causes of a monetary kind would not, even at worst, involve the fate of capitalism, it is not impossible to conceive of other trends that would, indeed, have such dire implications. One idea, for instance, that plays a major part in the end-of-an-economic-era philosophy is that the *downward turn in the demographic movement* is a completely new structural factor that has made its appearance in the western economy with this crisis. This is a very popular idea and is worth examining carefully. The statement of the problem is favorable and promising for the end-of-an-economic-era philosophy, for the tremendous population growth of the nineteenth and twentieth

---

[3] *Gold production has, in fact, been rising ever since 1929, and there is every prospect that it will continue to do so.* See W. Sundheimer, *"Die amerikanischen Wahlen und der Gold-Standard,"* Währung und Wirtschaft. Mitteilungen des Währungsinstituts Berlin, *I, 1932, pp. 65* et seq.

centuries really was unprecedented and something necessarily unique, which had to come to an end sooner or later. Furthermore, there can be no doubt about this population growth having been one of the strongest impulses for the flowering of worldwide industrial capitalism. Is it, then, the implication that capitalism must follow the down-turn of the population movement? Now, it is a fact that the slowing of the population increase cannot have been a contributory cause to the present crisis. First of all, this trend is for the time being and will be for some years to come merely relative. Nowhere in the Western countries has the population actually decreased so far; all that has decreased is its rate of increase, and this is not preventing the population from still growing quite considerably. Nor is it easy to see how this trend should have toppled the last boom, and how this boom was at all possible. It always is a weakness of all cultural explanations of the world crisis that, after all, the structural factors on which they rely must, as such, have already been present during the preceding boom, which, with its rapid economic growth, was as unrivaled as the crisis itself; the sudden end of the boom thus remains unexplained, and there seems no reason why there should not be another upturn on the old conditions. One argument is that the slow-down in the population increase does, at any rate, make it extraordinarily difficult to get out of the present depression, because we now lack the automatic increase in the demand for housing that in former depressions led building firms to step up residential construction at an early date and thus to give the initial impulse to the recovery. Undeniably, this is a problem, but it is greatly overestimated and also viewed in the wrong perspective. First of all, it is overlooked that the sluggishness of the building trade is to a far greater extent attributable to other causes, especially to the fact that owing to a number of circumstances—in Germany, thanks to public works—the last boom was, more than previous ones, an investment boom in civil engineering, which in turn has much to do with the effects of the war. This is another point of

resemblance between the present crisis and the company promotion crisis of the eighteen-seventies. Secondly, it is wrong
to calculate the need for housing simply from a count of heads
and still more wrong to equate this need for housing with the
demand for housing. So, there is little left of the whole argument. Finally, there is the almost viciously stubborn belief that
eventually and in the long run the down-turn of the demographic curve cannot fail to narrow the margin for an expansion of production and markets, especially for the production
of capital goods, and hence to lead to the decline of capitalism.
What we have here is a common weed in the garden of economics, and it belongs to the large family of logical errors
which Whitehead fittingly calls the fallacy of misplaced concreteness.[4]

In our case this is how it works: because purchasing power
is, in practice, exercised by individual persons, the total volume of demand is taken to depend on the number of persons.
This is to confuse people with Reichmarks and dollars. It is
true that there are needs so inelastic that the total volume of
demand does in their case depend more or less on the number
of people, but in all other cases demand is independent of the
number of people—it is a function of purchasing power, which
in turn, as we all know, depends on production. The number
of Christmas trees that can be sold is determined, by and large,
by the number of families; this is a case of very inelastic demand, which, in combination with an equally inelastic supply,
usually leads to sharp price fluctuations either way just before
the holidays. On the other hand, the value and the amount of
presents laying under the Christmas tree vary from one family
to another in accordance with the bread-winner's income. If,
now, the population stops increasing, this will, indeed, put an
end to any further expansion of the production of goods the
demand for which is very inelastic. But what possible sense

[4] *A. N. Whitehead,* Science and the Modern World *(New York, 1926),*
p. 75.

does it make even to moot the possibility of a saturation point in the case of all other conceivable goods? Even if the production increased a hundred times, it would still fail to raise the incomes of the masses to a level that is regarded as necessary in the high-income brackets today. There can be no doubt that the regressive demographic trend will cause many and probably very painful adjustments, but to assume that these adjustments will seal the fate of capitalism can be described only as a neurotic flight of imagination. It definitely has nothing to do with the present crisis.

The category of fallacies of misplaced concreteness includes another, extremely popular view, of which there are the most diverse variants, namely, that capitalism has come up against insuperable limits in *space*, and that the present crisis is a first reflection of the exhaustion of the store of square miles still susceptible to being "opened up" by capitalism. In this case, *square miles are confused with Reichmarks and dollars*, just as people were in the case of the population argument. This confusion is at the base of all the misuse made nowadays of the word "space"; it is the cardinal error of the Luxemburg-Sternberg theory of imperialism and also the πρῶτον ψεῦδος of all the geopolitical and geo-economic aberrations, whether they refer to southeast Europe or some other seductive "space." Every kind of geographical romanticism draws on it, and so does the notion that the United States has an advantage over Europe in its fast "free trade space" (whereas, in fact, the very extent of their "space," which in the West is very thinly populated and unfertile, is more of a hindrance economically). It goes without saying that the size of the market depends not on the number of square miles but on the volume of purchasing power, and this, in turn, depends on (socially and economically correct) production. This puts paid to the idea that world capitalism is possible only if it can steadily expand in space. Its extent and intensity are determined not by space but by the world's total purchasing power, and this cannot be raised more effectively than by the unobstructed expansion of world trade.[5]

One point that is most unclear in the pronouncements of the end-of-an-economic-era philosophers is the part played by *technology* in their view of the world. On the one hand they maintain almost unanimously that the pace of technological advance has become much slower, so that even this source of capitalism's strength is drying up. On the other hand they make copious use of the popular notion that technology, machines, and organization have outgrown people. This tangle of thought is largely explicable in terms of still another case of the fallacy of misplaced concreteness. Technical inventions as such are confused with the economic *exploitation* of technical and organizational progress. It is true that the age of technical sensations has probably come more or less to an end, but this has not prevented the economic applications of existing knowledge (e.g., of the internal combustion engine) and its further technical and economic development, making the last boom a period distinguished by all the characteristics of a second industrial revolution. Without a simultaneous credit expansion of gigantic extent it would, of course, not have been possible; this has to be added for the benefit of those people, like Salin for instance, who blame the boom's overexpansion on the demographic down-turn and on the growing size of firms and thus try to transpose the dynamics of the cycle into the field of structural change. It is very difficult to predict anything for the future, but if we do assume that technical change will play a lesser part in the future than in the past, I personally can only conclude that future economic development will be

[5] *For this reason H. Ritschl, who, in his article "Wiederaufstieg der Konjunktur" (Der deutsche Volkswirt, V (Berlin, 2 1930–1931), pp. 1207 et seq.) made a praiseworthy attack on the errors mentioned in the text, cannot be followed when he concludes from the shift in the area of capitalist expansion that the main emphasis must now be placed on the domestic market. There are no grounds whatever for this assumption, which likewise rests on the fallacy of misplaced concreteness.*

that much more steady, which can do nothing but strengthen our economic system. In any case, it is hard to see how the slowing-down of technological process is supposed to be a factor in reshaping capitalism into autarky and economic planning. There is, however, one sort of technical invention that we can only pray to be spared. I have in mind those that make it economically feasible to produce at home substitutes for certain goods so far produced only abroad. Suppose that German technicians succeed in making rubber, copper, cocoa, cotton, etc., from German raw materials and to do so at a cost perhaps no more than fifty per cent higher than production cost abroad; to judge from our experience with, say, German gasoline production, we can be sure in that case that for the sake of the "balance of payments," and under the pseudo-patriotic slogan "Germans, buy German raw materials," every possible means of trade policy will soon be applied to make the domestic substitutes competitive. No doubt the same prediction can be ventured for other countries. In that case, technological progress really would become the pacemaker of autarky and, with it, of immeasurable impoverishment. It would be a new and odd contribution to the old subject of "progress and poverty."

But we have not yet come to the central assertion of the end-of-an-economic-era philosophy. It is that the *disintegration of international economic relations* is the most important of the structural changes that threaten the future of capitalism. The extraordinary contraction of world trade in the course of the present crisis and the related moves of countries to close themselves off from the rest of the world suggest, if we follow writers like Sombart, Salin, and Fried, that the crisis is indeed closing the era of the worldwide economy and bringing in a new epoch of more or less autarkic "national" economies. "The tower of Babel was built on firm ground—but the world economy at the turn of the nineteenth and twentieth centuries was built on intellectual and political foundations so brittle, that the first impact of creative or destructive events could turn them to dust and blow them away like shifting sand," states Salin,[6] and similar eloquent explanations have been proffered by other writers of the same ilk. It seems preferable to reply in a dry tone. Recalling earlier remarks in this paper, we would point out that no thoughtful person would dream of denying the possibility of a complete decline of international economic relations and thus of a relapse into a more primitive stage, but that it is an entirely different question whether this possibility has any great likelihood, and whether, if it turns into reality, it will do so in accordance or in contradiction with the inner logic of economic evolution. In the latter case, it must be expected that the inner logic of economic evolution will eventually prevail again. And it is still another question, finally, whether the possible decline of international economic relations is to be considered good or bad.

If the present decline of international economic relations is supposed to be an event of secular significance, then, surely, it must have been long prepared by prior economic developments, that is, it would have to be the result of forces that were not unleashed merely by the present crisis and will disappear with it. Otherwise, it would really be frivolous to philosophize *in saeculum* on the basis of what happened during the last year and a half—for the marked decline of international economic relations dates no further back than the summer of 1931. There is no need on this occasion to take issue with this kind of frivolity. Instead, let us turn our attention to those who seriously try to discover long-term trends of decline. Now, such attempts are contradicted by the sober fact that the present crisis followed a period of extremely vigorous expansion of international trade, by which the world economy explosively overcame the preceding disruption caused by the world war and inflation—another time of overhasty prognostications. A reaction was bound to follow. The thing to do at this point would be to examine in detail whether the relative

---

[6] Loc cit., *p. 11*.

importance of world trade in fact rose or fell up to the present crisis. This would require extensive special research and is impossible on this occasion.[7]

As a starting point, we have the calculations of the Kiel *Institut für Weltwirtschaft und Seeverkehr*, as published in the fundamental work *Der deutsch Aussenhandel unter der Einwirkung weltwirtschaftlicher Strukturwandlungen*.[8] The statistics do not bear out the *thesis of a falling export quota* having the validity of a general law. Between 1890 and 1895 world trade grew at the same pace as industrial production (measured by a carefully calculated raw material index), and between 1895 and 1913 slightly outpaced the latter; after the war the distance first widened and then diminished. The volume of world trade expanded more between 1925 and 1929 than it did between 1908 and 1913. However, for various reasons there is always a very wide margin of statistical error in calculations of this kind. Condliffe,[9] for instance, reaches the result that throughout the period 1881-1929 (with the exception, of course, of the years 1913-1921) the rate of increase in world trade was always slightly higher than the rate of increase in world production. Careful appraisal suggests the conclusion that there is no proof of any fall in the relative importance of world trade up to 1929, and that with the best will in the world no more than a very slight decline can be read out of the statistics. But this is still far from settling the question.

First of all, it seems surprising that the strong expansion of world trade since 1925 occurred at a time when trade policies

[7] See *especially M. Victor, "Das sogenannte Gesetz der abnehmenden Aussenhandelsbedeutung,"* Weltwirtschaftliches Archiv, *Vol. xxxvi, No. 2 (1932), pp. 59 et seq.*

[8] Der deutsch Aussenhandel unter der Einwirkung weltwirtschaftlicher Strukturwandlungen. *Prepared and edited by the Institut für Weltwirtschaft und Seeverkehr an der Universität Kiel (Berlin, 1932).*

[9] *League of Nations, Economic Intelligence Service,* World Economic Survey 1931-32. *Series of League of Nations Publications. II. Economic and Financial. 1932, II, A. 18 (Geneva, 1932).*

were already doing much more to cut the nations off from each other than before the war.[10] This speaks for the strength of the forces making for economic internationalism, seeing that they caused world trade to expand despite the steadily mounting obstructions to trade. This bears out once more what I recently had occasion to write elsewhere:[11] that in spite of all protectionist obstacles, economic interrelationships throughout the world have become denser, that the trend envisaged by the liberals has gained unimagined force, and that protectionism, insofar as its aim is to slow up the integration of any country's economy in the nexus of world trade, is much further from this aim than liberalism is from the opposite one. But even if all this were not so, even if the statistics unequivocably proved the thesis of a relative fall in the importance of world trade, nothing whatsoever could be concluded therefrom as regards the alleged structural "disintegration of the world economy." The point to remember in this context is *that the quantitative ratio between domestic and foreign trade in no way does full justice to the true economic importance of international economic relations.* Strangely enough, this point of view is usually overlooked precisely by the illiberal autarkists, whose whole social philosophy otherwise makes them recoil in horror[12] from every quantitative and mechanical approach. The mere existence of a world market and the mere possibility of substituting foreign for domestic sales and playing off the national against the international market are of immense importance for the rational conduct of the national economy, an importance that cannot be measured statistically. Similarly, industrial exports are of far greater economic importance than the bare figures suggest. To appreciate this point, it must be remembered that *the exported portion of in-*

---

[10] Ibid., *p. 152.*

[11] *W. Röpke, "Liberale Handelspolitik,"* Archiv fur Rechts- und Wirtschaftsphilosophie. *Vol. xxiv (1930–1931), p. 365.*

[12] See, *as one example among many, E. Salin,* op. cit., *p. 1.*

*dustrial output represents that peak margin of production
which, by virtue of the economies of scale, makes the whole of
mass production possible and with it the very existence of modern industrial concerns.* Lucien Romier[13] is right when he says,
in another context, that even the United States with its apparently secure independence could not stand the test of a block-
ade, because it would prevent the export of "peak output" and
would thereby destroy the country's social equilibrium. As
regards United States imports, A. Rühl[14] notes that barely
more than ten per cent of imports were goods produced
domestically in equal quality and sufficient quantity, whereas
almost ninety per cent of imports were supplementary to home
production, that is, goods that had to be imported because
they were not produced domestically in equal quality and
sufficient quantity.

It will be seen that the tissue of the world economy is rather
more dense and intricate than our illiberal autarkists imagine, and it is high time that they should cease keeping a double
set of books in which the national economy is presented as an
organism and the world economy as a mere mechanism.

But the greatest error committed by the illiberals in this
connection is that they keep making great play with the patent
contraction of world trade in the present crisis but overlook
that *this contraction is part of a general process of contraction.*
In point of fact, world trade has not, until quite recently, been
shrinking more than production, and until 1931 it shrank
less.[15] In other words: the relative importance of foreign trade
has been rising considerably, precisely in the crisis, in defiance
of all the hysterical measures by which countries are trying to
close their frontiers, and despite the fact, above all, that it

[13] *L. Romier,* Der Mensch von heute *(Freiburg im Breisgau, 1930), p.
46.*

[14] *A Rühl, "Zur Frage der internationalen Arbeitsteilung,"* Viertel-
jahreshefte zur Konjunkturforschung, *Special issue 25 (Berlin, 1932).*

[15] Der deutsche Aussenhandel, op. cit., *II, pp. 463 et seq.*

was only during this period that the new U.S. customs tariff, the Hawley-Smoot tariff, began to exercise its calamitous effects. Here again, of course, allowance must be made for the statistical margin of error, and the figures must be used with caution. The one point to grasp is that the decline of world trade in absolute terms during the crisis is no proof at all of the secular end of the international economy, because the absolute contraction of world trade has not diminished its relative importance. If the world market has shrunk along with domestic markets, why on earth should it not expand again with recovery in domestic markets? Are we to believe seriously that the forces making with ineluctable necessity for international economic relations will, in the future, not be strong enough to overcome all the obstacles that certainly are not to be underrated and that Salin and others rightly point out, such as England's departure from the gold standard, the decline of British financial supremacy, etc.?

But let us once more give the floor to the illiberal end-of-an-economic-era philosophers, just to be told that none of our arguments will stand up to the higher judgment of world history. I quote Salin:[16] "Only this once were the casual economic relations of the past combined by an apparently world-wide network of prices into a mechanism which linked the economic destiny of individuals and whole nations alike and made it dependent upon economic actions in all other parts of the globe—only this once did people and states place such blind trust in the indestructibility and durability of the artificial construction that they were prepared to cover even their vital needs by imports from across the frontier, if only they were cheaper, and to produce the most useless goods at home, if only there was a prospect of profitable sale." If this is supposed to prove that we must now finally bury world trade, it is merely another substitution of emotional atmosphere for

16 E. Salin, op. cit., p. 11.

proof. It may be true that nothing like the modern world economy ever existed before,[17] but the conclusion that something that never previously existed is by that very fact necessarily or probably doomed to ruin, and that this ruin must come about just now—that conclusion may be conservative, but it certainly is not convincing. Everything, after all, once happened for the first time. Perhaps some contemporary of Columbus thought that the existence of America was something novel and unique that was bound to disappear again. All we can say is that he was wrong, and the very fact that he was wrong is not the least of the reasons for the advent of the world-wide economy and for its remaining with us, so long as we do not revert to the belief that the world ends at the Pillars of Hercules.

No doubt it would be possible to discover evidence that, at the time when the Zollverein created the German national economy, there also were calamity-howlers who declared the economic integration of the separate German states to be an act of presumptuous originality. A man like Friedrich List[18] was more farsighted when he viewed the growth of the geographical sphere of economic integration merely as stages of one unitary process of integration, explaining: "Even now it can be predicted with certainty that a few decades hence the improvement in means of transport will cause the most civilized nations of the world to be no less, or even more, closely linked together by relationships both material and spiritual

---

[17] *The historical accuracy of even this assertion may be doubted. The economic network that covered the Imperium Romanum at the time of the emperors was really nothing else than a "world economy" in the modern sense. It might be objected that "world economy," too, collapsed. But was its collapse a matter of compelling necessity? And what followed its collapse at the time is surely in no way alluring. It does not make much difference whether barbarism breaks in "horizontally," as it did then, or "vertically," as it now threatens to do.*

[18] *Friedrich List,* Das nationale System der Politischen Ökonomie. *Reprint of the author's own last revised edition. Fourth edition (Jena, 1922), p. 210.*

than were the counties of England a century ago." Finally, those who put the stress on the historical primacy and uniqueness of the international economy overlook the fact that the tremendous population growth during the nineteenth and twentieth centuries was likewise something unprecedented. "Only this once" the population increased faster than ever before in history and thereby created an objective fact which simply cannot be evaded. If the international economy is the "most artificial construction," it will still have to be conceded that the millions of people whose very basis of existence was created by industrialism and world trade will certainly not put up with being described as artificial constructions that can be made to collapse and disappear for the sake of ingenious theories. These people have entered life in a very natural way; they certainly are not creatures of rationalism but products of the most irrational of all processes on earth, and they have every right to demand that they be respected as such. All this talk about the international economy being artificial, about industrialism, the telephone and the railways being destructive of civilization, about corporative, planned or otherwise, anti-capitalist and anti-industrialist economy rejuvenating the nation—all this talk remains empty and meaningless, so long as we are not told how the millions thereby uprooted economically are to be painlessly killed off, and by what selection criterion the necessary decimation and "cooliefication" is to be carried out. Naturally, we would expect the champions of these ideas to come forward as volunteers. So great is the mental confusion that only the bluntest language can help to clear the atmosphere. The disastrous effects of the first steps taken so far by Germany in the direction of autarky, which in the name of "food freedom" have already led to "freedom from food" for thousands of workers in the German export industries, give us a foretaste of what will be our lot if we turn our backs on the allegedly "artificial" world market. Whoever despises "economic-thinking" as the "mortal enemy of ethnical idealism," who prefers "blood" to "money" or dismisses the rational arguments against a "national" economy by some similar phrase of the kind that is so popular nowadays with public opinion, must accept the verdict that he has no right to claim as his motive the plight of the unemployed masses.

The international economy marches not against the inner logic of economic evolution but with it, as Friedrich List said in the passage quoted. And ultimately this is proved by the incontrovertible fact that the area of integration by trade and by the international division of labor has steadily grown during the last five hundred years and certainly has not shrunk. *This process of integration did not stop at national frontiers, just as it did not stop earlier at the frontiers of Länder and cities, and, indeed, one can see no reason why it should have done so.* Among the forces operative in this process of integration, there is one that indeed has the demerit of being of the material and mechanical kind, but for all that is all the more powerful and tangible, namely, the steady progress of communications techniques. Their latest branch, broadcasting, has already forged at least Europe into a unit the length and breadth of which can be traversed every evening, and in which no customs barriers, no import restrictions, no exchange controls, and no ethnical metaphysics can prevent people from switching from German lectures to Danish chamber music or Hungarian folk songs, or the other way around. Of course, no absolute force is inherent in this circumstance; of course, people can ignore the contradiction implied in their cheering the "Graf Zeppelin" and the trans-Atlantic flights, and in the same breath approving the economic and cultural isolation of their country, stripping railways and ports of their traffic and, as once before in history, between antiquity and the Middle Ages, letting the roads go to ruin. But it still is a contradiction, and it is of no mean importance that it exists and can be explained to people. Just how strong is the resistance which progress in communications opposes to the isolationist tendencies of nations is evidenced by the vigorous growth of world trade in defiance of mounting obstacles, as we had occasion to point out before.

All these explanations would still lack the ultimate power of persuasion if we did not deal with one more argument, to the effect that the *world's increasing industrialization* constitutes a mounting threat to the sales markets of the old industrial countries and thus forces them to *turn back to agriculture* and thereby to loosen the traditional international division of labor. According to this view, there is an ineluctable trend toward the industrialization of the countries that are primary producers both of agricultural commodities and raw materials and toward a revival of agriculture in industrial countries, so that all along the line every economy would contain a balanced mixture of industry and agriculture. As a result, world trade would be reduced to the exchange of goods produced at specially favored locations.

Now, first of all, there is not so far any evidence at all to prove such a trend. So far all experience with the industrialization of primary-producing countries points to the exact opposite. One country after another followed England on the road to industrialization, and the result was an unrivaled growth of world trade. To mention only the last of the major cases: the United States, too, was once an overseas supplier of raw materials, but here, as elsewhere, the result of industrialization was an enormous increase in the country's effective demand, not the least of which was for the industrial products of Europe, while the falling-off of American agricultural exports benefited both European farmers and, even more so, the not as yet industrialized agricultural countries (Canada, Argentina, etc.), whose rising farm exports in turn paid for growing industrial imports. During the last ten years before the world war these developments led to an appreciable rise in agricultural prices, that is, an improvement in the terms of trade between industrial and agricultural products to the benefit of the latter. Now things have long been going the other way, with the terms of trade steadily and strongly improving for industrial products. It can only be concluded that the world has not too much industry but too much agriculture or too little industry, and that the agrarian understructure of the world is too broad and the industrial superstructure too narrow—certainly not the other way around. This conclusion cannot be denied by anyone capable of abstracting from the present disturbances in the structure of industry and the efficacy of the credit mechanism. It follows that the present world crisis is no proof at all for the assertion that international economic relations are being undermined by increasing industrialization.[19] It should hardly be necessary to point out that the world agrarian crisis has been going on for more than ten years, while world industry as a whole has only just emerged from an unprecedented boom. And now we are told that never again can things be even approximately like that. Are we really to believe that within a few months the industrialization of the new countries created consequences that it never created during the whole of the preceding century?

The truth is, of course, that the catastrophe that overtook the world economy came from an altogether different direction, namely, from the disruption of the network of *international short-term credit*. It is this that led to all those symptoms of breakdown without which no one would have thought the "twilight" theory of international economic relations even worth discussing. It is this that led individual countries to vie with each other in putting up obstacles to trade—the debtor countries in order to protect their balance of payments and the creditor countries in order to keep out additional exports by the debtor countries. It was only the resulting general aggravation of the economic crisis everywhere that caused autarkic

---

[19] See E. Döblin, "*Internationale Konjunkturabhängigkeit und Autarkie,*" Archiv fur Sozialwissenschaft und Sozialpolitik. *Tübingen. Vol. LXVII (1932/33); pp. 303* et seq. *The train of thought outlined in the text does not exclude that the industrial hegemony of Western Europe is declining, just as the industrialization of Germany and the United States in their time broke the industrial hegemony of England. Apart from the disappearance of former industrial quasi-rents, this has the consequence that manufactures, both semi-finished and finished, are coming to account for a steadily growing proportion of world trade.* See World Economic Survey, op. cit., *pp. 148* et seq.

tendencies to spread through the world. The accumulation of international short-term debts, which in July of 1931 were estimated by the Bank for International Settlements to amount altogether to some 40 billion Reichsmark, and the sudden collapse of the short-term credit mechanism were calamities of unprecedented proportions, but they still remain historically unique calamities and not ones in any way inherent in the nature of international economic relations. These exceptional calamities in their turn connected with a series of other exceptional circumstances, among which we may mention the last aftereffects of the war, the enormous political debts (reparations and inter-Allied debts) combined with high protective tariffs in the United States as the main creditor country, the effects of the general adoption of the gold exchange standard (that is, the partial dethronement of gold, a practice so popular in the illiberal camp), the unsound financial policies of many countries, balance-of-payments difficulties as a result of the rigidities introduced into the economy of many countries by government intervention, the repercussions of the world agricultural crisis, unsound investment practices by the banks, and many others. The very fact that so dense a network of international capital movements ever came into existence at all is in flat contradiction with the autarkists' assertion that the international mobility of factors of production has been steadily diminishing up to the crisis.

Our present troubles stem precisely from the circumstance that the international mobility of capital has assumed proportions and forms that led to such extraordinarily severe strains.[20] Although, therefore, the dense network of international capital interrelations, which alone has, via an international liquidity crisis, led to the present symptoms of breakdown,

[20] *According to Sprague, of the Bank for International Settlements, more than 20 billion Reichsmark of the total 40 billion were mobilized internationally and transferred within one year; this surely proves the immense vitality of our economic system, not its decadence.* (Journal des Nations, *May 12, 1932, Geneva.*)

is in no way part of a necassary secular trend, it does raise the question as to what consequences it is likely to have in the future. As we all know there are some (e.g., Fried) who argue that the debtor countries' enormous foreign indebtedness hardly leaves them a choice other than to withdraw from international economic relations and, come what may, to stop all payments of interest and principal. This argument applied in the first place to reparations. Now that it is made inapplicable by the virtual discontinuance of reparations payments, attempts are being made to build up acceptance of the idea that Germany's foreign commercial debts, in their turn, are not genuine debts that have to be honored but are only another form of reparations. The proofs adduced for this idea are not convincing. We quite certainly have not paid reparations twice over; on the contrary, our commercial debts abroad have enabled us to create assets that are no more affected by the present crisis than are those financed by internal borrowing. Germany's foreign indebtedness has to be regarded as a reflection of inflation, that is, of the process that led to an immediate radical depreciation of Germany's war debts and to the depletion of German capital reserves. Any attempt to jettison the principle that *pacta sunt servanda* with respect to Germany's foreign commercial debts is to be sharply repudiated in our own most urgent interests, if we are not to burn our bridges and range ourselves alongside Russia, which surely no sensible person could suggest.[21]

[21] *It is just another case of the fallacy of misplaced concreteness to work out, as has been done, what "bankruptcy dividend" the German economy might pay its foreign creditors. This strange notion has been encouraged by the standstill agreement, but it is surely obvious that the foreign debts have been incurred not by the German "economy" but by individual debtors, of whom some are good and some bad. This new form of the fallacy of misplaced concreteness has the economically most questionable consequence that all the stress is laid on Germany's ability to transfer, while the question of the debtors' private solvency is neglected. On the one hand, solvent debtors are prevented from repaying their foreign debts, and on the other hand, debtors in need of economic protection are forced to repay theirs. See A. Lansburgh, "Die deutschen Stillhalte-Kredite," Die Bank, Vol. XXV (1932), pp. 1528 et seq.*

This is not to imply that things can go on as they are. Every day it is becoming more urgent to consolidate international short-term debts, and, as regards total indebtedness, the disproportion between the volume of output and trade and the price level, on the one side, and the volume of indebtedness, on the other, has become so great that some adjustment has become inescapable. It would probably be more rational to adjust the volume of output and trade and the price level to the volume of indebtedness, rather than the other way around. Nothing could be more out of place than to deduce therefrom an argument for autarky in the sense that we are allegedly at a turning point of history, from which onward we are predestined to follow the way of autarky, and it is all the more out of place as the problem arises for internal just as much as for external indebtedness.

III

We return to our starting point. We said that the present world crisis cannot simply be regarded as the slump of a normal business cycle. It certainly has assumed the proportions of a major break in economic history, and thereby has assumed secular significance. On the other hand it has been shown that every attempt to trace the crisis back to any causes of secular structural change has to be given up as hopeless. The two statements can be reconciled only by saying that what caused the crisis was a cyclical reaction to the preceding phase of credit expansion and overinvestment, which phase in its turn is to be interpreted as an immense effort of capitalism to overcome the loss of wealth caused by the war as well as to take advantage quickly of all the numerous technical inventions during that time. That the crisis should have become so severe and so stubborn can be explained by four circumstances.

1. It happened to occur in a world full of tensions and unassimilated structural changes, among which the worst is the agricultural, and especially the wheat crisis. Among these ten-

sions and unassimiliated structural changes there is another
that probably ranks as high as the wheat crisis, and that is
excessive government intervention of all kinds and, in connection with it, the formation of monopolies.

2. The credit expansion and overinvestment are now seen
to have assumed such exceptional proportions that a strong
reaction was to be expected even in ordinary circumstances.

3. When we already had a crisis so heavily loaded in advance, another one broke out right in the middle of it, namely,
the international liquidity crisis that caused so much havoc.
The international liquidity crisis cannot simply be regarded
as a logical link in the chain of events, for the credit structure
did not really collapse before a new element appeared in the
shape of the ultimate repercussions of the political crisis that
emerged in September, 1930.

4. There was the circumstance that, for reasons which it yet
remains for business cycle theory to explain convincingly, the
crisis eventually gave rise to a cumulative downward process,
a process of "self-deflation," which pushed the economy more
and more deeply into a dead end.

That is the point at which we still are, even though deliberate credit expansion and stimulants of all kinds now seem
to herald the moment when this secondary, cumulative decline is approaching its lowest point. The present crisis, therefore, probably has to be interpreted as a special constellation,
namely, the collision of a strong, cyclical reaction with a series
of historically "random," non-recurring accidents.

This interpretation detracts nothing from the severity and
gravity of the crisis and does not preclude that it has secular
significance. But its secular significance does not lie in a total
breakdown of the system as the result of a long-term process
of disintegration, nor in the crisis presenting us with accomplished facts that dictate the direction of our future economic
policy and invalidate or make inapplicable the basic principles of economic policy which rest on a century's work of
economic and social analysis. We need neither a new social

philosophy nor a new economics, and we need not refashion
the foundations of our economic system. "Destiny" plays no
part in this, and neither an "era" nor the "economy" is at its
"end." The less talk there is of such things, the better. Nothing
has happened to make the system of equilibrium theory irrelevant or even needful of revision, and the same applies to the
theory that a differentiated economy, based on division of
labor, is infinitely superior to an undifferentiated economy
made up of more or less autarkic, separate, economic areas.
Nothing can excuse the lack of discipline with which some of
the leading spokesmen of the illiberals violate economics in an
attempt to adapt it to their radicalism in economic policy.

The secular significance of the world crisis lies in an entirely
different sphere. Its historical mission is not that it confronts
us with accomplished, objective facts, but that it is a crisis in
the original, medical sense of a condition in which the decision has not yet been reached but is still to come, in which the
patient is in danger of his life, and it is uncertain whether he
will overcome the fever or succumb to it. This original meaning of the expression "crisis," which has become dim, must
be restored in the economic context if we are to take the true
measure of the present crisis. Our economic system and with
it our whole social system are still on the danger list, in spite
of all the symptoms that suggest that the fever may be abating.
Only with reservations can this condition be described as a
crisis of capitalism. It may be so described if we mean thereby
to indicate that capitalism is in danger of its life; it may not be
so described if we mean thereby to suggest that the present
crisis with all its severity has been caused by some inner defect
of the capitalist system as such. Everyone knows or should
know that the war, the peace treaties, reparations, inter-Allied
debts, political radicalism, government interventions of all
kinds, socialist experiments, and many other things subjected
capitalism to tests so severe that none but as resilient an economic system as capitalism could have withstood them. It is
only apparently paradoxical if we say that nothing proves the

astonishing vitality of our economic system better than the very fact that in spite of these tremendous stresses we can still speak merely of a crisis, and not—unless we happen to need an attractive book title—of the end of capitalism.

And so there is every justification for expecting capitalism eventually to stand the test of this crisis, just as it has stood the even greater test of the world war. In any event, the crisis has already done much to ease the strains and clear the atmosphere. Reparations are, to all intents and purposes, out of the way, and there is legitimate hope that they will soon be followed by the inter-Allied debts. Considerable flexibility has been reintroduced into the price and cost structure made rigid by government intervention. The credit system of the major countries has regained much of its former liberty of action and functional efficiency. It even looks as though the world is about to learn a few lessons from the extravagances and exaggerations of the last ten years. It could be that the secular significance of the world crisis is that the world had to be hurt to learn wisdom, that there had to be a crisis to redress the balance after the long list of distortions and exaggerations. Perhaps this will be our considered judgment in a few years' time.

But in the meantime we still have a long and difficult road ahead of us, a road so fraught with dangers that it will need our utmost effort to overcome them. The greatest danger of all lies in the psychological state of people who cannot grasp that the economic system is merely part of the whole social system, and that one cannot make experiments with the social system without destroying the roots of the economic system. It is impossible to rouse the masses against reason, freedom, and peace without the sorry ending of thirty million unemployed in the world. These three elements make up the air vital to our economic system, and it is impossible to pollute its air and then, when it cannot breathe, say that it is no good. No one can expect to reap reasonable results when he sows a storm of destructive and undisciplined emotions. Nothing spells greater danger to our entire social system than the "revolt of the masses"[22] emancipating themselves from the leadership of an intellectual élite. Never has the world been more thoroughly ruled by vapid catchwords resting on mass moods and sentiments and throwing up as leaders of the masses those who excel in interpreting these mass sentiments. "Liberalism"[23] has never had any appeal for the masses; among them, tolerance, discussion, *humanitas*, reason, and fair play do not prosper, but all the more propitious is the field for violence, resentment, emotional fog, and destructive action. Instead of "live and let live," we get "die and let die." The easiest victim of these developments is trade policy. The masses readily lap up catchwords that appeal to the emotions but are shy of the critique of reason, such as "protection of national labor," "food freedom," "Buy home-produced goods!" and other half-baked emotional arguments. By contrast, free trade, unless tangibly in the interests of the masses, has always been an aristocratic matter appealing only to the élite, since it requires serious thought and control of the emotions by reason and independent judgment; this is why free trade eventually fell victim to the rule of the masses.[24] Seen from the angle of the free trader, therefore, we have the paradoxical situation that a trade policy that serves the well-being of the masses against the interests of individuals or groups is supported by an élite, whereas

[22] *J. Ortega y Gasset,* The Revolt of the Masses.

[23] *It might be well to use Benedetto Croce's term "liberism" instead of "liberalism," so as to make things easier for those who imagine liberalism to be all sorts of things except what it really is, namely, a social philosophy to which we owe all the few somewhat brighter periods of world history, from antiquity to our age, from the Stoa to Spinoza and Goethe.*

[24] See *W. Röpke, "Liberale Handelspolitik,"* Archiv für Rechts- und Wirtschaftsphilosophie, *Vol. XXIV (1930–1931), pp. 354 et seq. The same line of thought can be found in A. Rüstow, "Interessenpolitik oder Staatspolitik?"* Der deutsche Volkswirt, *VII (1932–1933), pp. 169 et seq. and, above all, in W. Eucken, "Staatliche Strukturwandlungen und die Krisis des Kapitalismus,"* Weltwirtschaftliches Archiv, *Vol. XXXVI, No. 2 (1932), pp. 297 et seq.*

the masses back a trade policy that runs counter to their own interests. However, even here things are so arranged that even the longest rivers come somewhere to the sea, and so we may justifiably hope that, once a cyclical economic expansion is under way and the spasm in international payments and capital movements has been overcome by the consolidation of short-term debts, there will be a reaction against the present orgy of protectionism. We shall still be left, however, with the great problem of the international agrarian crisis. The crisis of the agricultural processing industries may, of course, be expected to solve itself with the rise in industrial purchasing power, but the wheat crisis will remain with us in all its severity so long as there is no drastic reduction in the cultivated area in the world as a whole, and this, in turn, depends on the industrial countries of Europe coming to understand that all their "grain battles" have ended in terrible Pyrrhic victories.

The present world crisis should teach us also that the rule of the masses threatens our economic and social system at another, closely related point. I have in mind the *bellicism* and *nationalism* of our age, which, with the support of the inflamed masses, have created an inconsistency, intolerable in the long run, between the areas of economic and political integration.[25] An economy on the world scale in a world in which, barring a few praiseworthy exceptions, nationalism is at a boiling point as never before, in which people are told they must reckon with the possibility of another war and at the same time know that this is going to mean Europe's suicide— that is indeed a blatant contradiction, which cries out for a solution. There are only two alternatives. One of them is to adapt the degree of political co-operation among nations to the degree of their economic co-operation and thus to supplement economic integration by political integration. This is the way of peace, prosperity, civilization, and the continuance and rise of Europe. Or else we fail in building a new system of

[25] See *W. Eucken*, op. cit., *pp. 309* et seq.

international security and peace and in cooling down nationalism in all countries. In that case, political disintegration will be
followed by gradual economic disintegration. The secular
significance of the world crisis is ultimately this—that the
economic, political, and hence also the cultural future of
Europe depends upon whether the first alternative can be
achieved soon enough. Success turns on our being able to
break the front of unreason, mass hysteria, ruthless egoism,
and emotional fog and to confound nationalism by the motto
that Friedrich List placed at the head of his *magnum opus*:
Et la patrie et l'humanité.

IV

End of an Era?*

The more the day's political and economic events crowd one upon another, the more is it essential to grasp the wider and deeper context of these disquieting developments. Let us forget for a moment about Hitler and Hugenberg, about East Aid, lard duties, and injunctions, and let us ask ourselves: Where do we stand? Whither are we going?

Many of our contemporaries will answer that we are standing at one of history's great turning points. In view of the last few years' events, it does indeed require the serenity of a philosopher to avoid being influenced by the "end of an era" catchword. But it should help us to keep our calm if we reflect that every period of slump has its ideological superstructure just as every period of boom, and that the very individuals who during the boom cannot believe that good business will ever come to an end are often the ones who now, in the slump, cannot see how we shall ever get out of our troubles. The inflation euphoria of the boom is matched by the deflation hysteria of the slump; there can be no doubt about it. In the past, too, people used to say that no earlier crisis was ever so severe and obstinate as the one at hand; sometimes they were right, and as often they were not. It cannot be gainsaid that the present world crisis outranges all standards of the past. But it is equally uncontestable that the world war, which is

* *Lecture delivered at Frankfurt am Main, February 8, 1933.*

ultimately at the source of all the trouble, in its turn over-shadowed everything that came before it, and that the last period of credit expansion and investment boom was equally unprecedented. There are no objective, no material, grounds for supposing that the current world crisis heralds the decline of the existing economic and social order and the dawn of a new historical era.

But this is cold comfort. The current world crisis could never have grown to such proportions, nor proved as stubborn, if it had not been for the many forces long at work to under-mine the intellectual and moral foundations of our social system and thereby eventually to cause the collapse of the economic system indissoulubly connected with the social system as a whole. Notwithstanding all the harshness and im-perfections of our economic system, which cry out for reform, it is a miracle of technology and organization; but it is con-demned to waste away if its three cardinal conditions—*reason, peace, and freedom*—are no longer even thought desirable by the masses ruthlessly reaching for power. We merely need to recall that the international liquidity crisis of 1931, which was the beginning of the real catastrophe, was unleashed by the German Reichstag elections of September, 1930, an event, that is, which world opinion interpreted as the signal herald-ing the collapse of the intellectual and political foundations of the Central European economic system. Since then, the National Socialists' unrelenting drive for internal political power has never allowed the Central European economy to come to rest, and the destruction of the economy thus caused is not mitigated by describing this ruthless struggle for power as "ethnic idealism," "Germany's awakening," or "the purifi-cation of the German soul," and by blaming the defenders of our social system for the economic crisis. The masses simply cannot be mobilized against reason, peace, and freedom with-out eventually landing in economic catastrophe. It is not pos-sible to want to run back into the virgin forests of Germania, to preach mass stupidity, and to unleash a storm of destructive and unruly emotions at a time when the machinery of mass supply has become so complicated that it makes increasingly higher claims on people's intelligence and discipline. Catastrophe is unavoidable if people get more and more stupid and barbarous, while the economy's technology and organization become more and more refined.

This is exactly the situation in which we are now, and that is the immense danger that threatens us. If this process of intellectual and political dissolution goes on, there is indeed no hope left, neither for our social system as a whole, nor for our economic system, and the fate of an historic era is sealed. But this is not a destiny to which we have to submit helplessly; it is not a social catastrophe with the inescapability of an earthquake. History is not a predetermined, mechanical course of events, but ultimately the result of everything that men think, want, and feel. There is a possibility that the sad old spectacle of the decline of a prosperous civilization is being re-enacted with us, but this possibility should not paralyze the forces of resistance, but call them forth in irresistible strength. If, against all expectations, this possibility does become reality, let us hope that no one will need to reproach himself with having been lukewarm, lazy, and cowardly in the hour of utmost danger, with having been an obfuscated worshipper of the childish twaddle of the day!

THE REVOLT AGAINST WESTERN CIVILIZATION

If we are to do battle in the way the times require, we must first grasp what is really going on behind the curtain of day-to-day politics. Well, what is going on is nothing less than a mass revolt against reason, freedom, humanity, and against the written and unwritten millennial rules that enable a highly differentiated human community to exist without degrading individuals into slaves of the state. We had forgotten, and now have to learn again, that to be civilized simply means that society again and again musters the strength and the will to keep clear of the two poles of barbarism, of anarchy, and the barrack square. To perform this feat, men must be inspired by certain ideals of community life, they must have learned to dominate their instincts by reason, they must have the unshakeable conviction that every human being has the same claim for respect of his humanity, and they must have a sense of the infinite value of the individual's personality and of the inviolability of its spirit. All these conditions, as well we know, are on the wane, at least in Germany. A great political movement can count on the acclaim of broad classes of the population when it tramples the ideal of personal freedom underfoot, and one of its leaders was bold enough not long ago to describe freedom as something "inhuman." A nation marching to the steady beat of a military parade is the new ideal; a state slavery more Asiatic than German is naively and cheerfully extolled under the scientific-sounding name of "total state." Humaneness is thrown on the scrap heap, and its place has been taken by brutalization and ruffianism such as would have made even our Germanic forebearers blush with shame.

Up and down the countryside today, all the old ideals have become the butt of universal contempt and execration because they are "liberal." But while it is amusing to see what a caricature ignorance has made of those ideals of community life that we call liberal, the caricature that malice has made of them is outrageous. It seems that every political mass movement needs certain tangible opponents against whom the masses can be stirred to hatred, certain cockshies at which everyone is encouraged to let fly to his heart's content. Favorite figures of this kind are "freemasons" in Italy, "Jews" in Germany, "Marxists," "hereditary enemies" of all kinds, and, above all, "liberals." The cockshy-labeled liberal that the German illiberals have manufactured for themselves hardly needs to be specifically described: a dry pedant, ankle-deep in the asphalt of metropolitan streets, without faith of any kind and without any ideal higher than making money, a man of dissolute mentality and way of life, a professional traitor to his country, unprincipled, incapable of enthusiasm, a nineteenth-century mummy. And liberalism generally is equated with the nineteenth century, to which every conceivable abomination is attributed. The fact that the bulk of Goethe's work belongs to that century seems to create no difficulties. All the same, the embarrassment with which the anniversary of his death was celebrated throughout Germany last year was proof of the fact that, try as one would, he was not to be claimed for the cause of illiberalism but most decidedly stands on the other side.

WHAT IS LIBERALISM?

If it amuses people to describe as liberalism all sorts of unappealing and eminently perishable features of the nineteenth century, one could let that pass, if it were not that the term is pre-empted for something much wider and more lasting, and that the misuse of the term is a means of attacking the imperishable through the perishable. Today's rebellion against liberalism is not a mere rebellion against perishable ideals and modes of thought of the nineteenth century, but one against the ultimate and imperishable foundations of that unique flowering in the history of mankind that we call Western civilization. But then, what's in a name? If anyone feels that the word "liberalism" is too discredited by associations and can no longer carry the precious cargo stowed in its holds, he is at liberty to save the cargo by transhipping it to some other word. "Civilism" or "Westernism" are not very felicitous neologisms, but they may serve the purpose. What is much more important is that we should be clear in our minds as to what constitutes the precious cargo itself.

First of all, we must realize that liberalism, in the broad and profound sense in which alone the word is here used, is not an invention of the nineteenth century and is not to be equated with that century's political or economic liberalism.

Liberalism is at least two thousand years older. It signifies a cultural energy center that has been operative in all periods of the flowering of Western civilization and drew its sustenance from the thought of the best men of all times, however much our uncultural age may forget it. The manifestations of this energy center are of great variety, but it seems to me they can all be reduced to three basic elements, as follows.

1. The idea of freedom, of *liberty*, which gave liberalism its name. "A splendid word for who would understand it right!" But how little is gained by the word alone is shown by the fact that every movement that rebels against any situation whatever invariably talks of freedom, even if its aims are poles apart from everything we call liberal. Think only of the use of the word "freedom" in the vocabulary of National Socialism. Whether a movement talks of freedom depends in the first place only upon whether or not it has already come to power. The decisive question is whether it talks of it afterward and acts accordingly. Everything, therefore, depends on the use to be made of freedom, on the positive content it is to be given. What matters is not to be "free from something," but "free for something." The essence of liberalism is that it strives for liberation from old authority not in order to replace it with new authority, new suppression, and new intolerance, but in order to liberate the individual from external authority, suppression, and intolerance and thus to give him a chance of free development. The liberal program is this: tolerance, freedom of thought, opinion and the press, fair play, discussion. It is in this demand and in the historically proven power of giving effect to it that lies the immense civilizing mission of liberalism, for there can be no genuine civilization without that "civil liberty," as defined by John Stuart Mill in his immortal essay "On Liberty," of which every line is now as burningly topical as it ever was.

To question the absolute value of this liberty is to question the ultimate foundation of Western civilization, no less than the very air without which Europeans cannot breathe. The

mere circumstance that many among the so-called educated
élite of today assail the inviolability of this principle or even
merely suggest that it is open to discussion proves how shifting the foundations of our civilization have become. The conviction that true creative power can prosper only in liberty
and not in the graveyard silence of prescribed opinions, that
without intellectual individuality society and the state must
eventually wither, that man has a right to protection against
arbitrary power and the abuse of power, that the crushing of
every divergence of opinion and of any individual cast of mind
must eventually lead to a boredom in which the nation's intellectual life is stifled, which lacks the happiness of laughter,
every sign of humor, and the spice of life, and in which nothing
flourishes but the brutish earnestness of the fanatic—that conviction, and nothing else, constitutes the liberal's much-
maligned and much-misunderstood *individualism*. Most
illiberals take it for an expression of smug materialism. They
are often the self-same, prize philistines who think it so
wonderful of Italian fascism that it has made the trains run
on time, swept some of the beggars off the streets, drained
marshes, and generally done quite a bit for external order
and material progress. Could any materialism be cruder than
this? It is not sheer perversity to fling the accusation of
materialism at the liberal who thinks punctual trains are too
high a price for the loss of freedom? Let everyone stop to think
how philistine and materialistic an attitude lies behind
the widespread German overestimation of things "going
smoothly" and of external order and stop to think also whether
a certain measure of relaxation in external order may not be
the price that has to be paid for the infinitely valuable preservation of an individual sphere.[1] The French or Austrian
"sloppiness" has a thoroughly positive reverse side, and no
doubt the ancient Romans equally regarded the Greeks as

[1] See *the striking remarks on this point by Hermann Keyserling, in*
Das Spektrum Europas (*Heidelberg, 1928*).

decidedly "un-Prussian." It is impossible to overestimate the danger to European civilization that consists in our being over-whelmed by the sergeant-major's ideal of the faultless march-past and the soundless rifle drill. But, naturally, such a state of smooth external order and the forcible exclusion of any disturbing dissonance is the paradise of the smug, of the materialists, of the "bourgeois."

This liberal program has found its reflection in the most varied fields of public life. Presumably, few of those who de-cry liberalism are aware of the decisive part it has played in laying the foundations of our modern society. Liberalism recognized that there must be a generally accepted and un-breakable rule of law in order to protect individuals from arbitrary power and thereby, in the last analysis, society from the barbarism of lawlessness and "inner" anarchy. We sense how shaky this rule of law has become today, and this gives us a measure of how far we have already departed from the lib-eral program and come closer to barbarism. All the most important principles of our criminal law—"*nulla poena sine lege*" ("no one may be withdrawn from the jurisdiction of the regular court of law"), no "lettres de cachet" but public ar-raignment and trial proceedings, the institution of a public prosecutor and of counsel for the defense, and many others—originate in liberal ideas, as cannot be emphasized too force-fully in this context. But it equally needs to be stressed that these liberal achievements are already largely a thing of the past in such pronouncedly illiberal countries as Russia, Italy, and Yugoslavia. The right to legal action against the agents of the state is another institution that should be mentioned here. But these examples should be enough to make my meaning clear.

On the other hand, it is a misconception to believe that economic freedom is, as a matter of course, part and parcel of liberalism in the comprehensive sense here under discussion. It cannot be denied that the claim for economic freedom is close to the heart of the liberal and closely connected with liberalism, but in fact experience has taught us that economic freedom is perfectly compatible with an illiberal system of society. Italy is well endowed with economic freedom and advocates the liberation of world trade from customs barriers. On the other hand, the example of England shows how a country can remain the paragon of liberalism even if it infringes the principles of economic freedom at many a point. Of course, there are limits. An illiberal country may conceivably practice economic freedom, but there can be no question of a liberal country's making a principle of economic unfreedom, especially in questions of foreign trade. The complete economic and social bondage that socialism would necessarily introduce seems altogether incompatible with the principles of liberalism. Liberalism and private property are probably inseparable, and hence the future prospects of liberalism no doubt depend on whether we succeed in broadening the sphere of economic and social freedom within our economic system and in diminishing the "proletariat" by augmenting the property-owning class. But this, in turn, presupposes the fullest development of our production potential, and that cannot be achieved otherwise than by an individualist economic order.

Finally, there is *political liberty*, to be distinguished both from civil and from economic liberty. Political liberty is a natural ingredient of liberalism, since, in resisting authority imposed from without as well as arbitrary power, liberalism inevitably demands political self-determination. Ultimately, the liberal idea merges into the democratic idea, although this gives rise to possibilities of serious conflict, about which more will be said later.

2. Intimately connected with the idea of liberty is the idea of *reason*. The chorus of its mockers and despisers has become steadily louder, perhaps because they have in mind such "reasonable" things as a marriage of convenience and imagine that liberalism is out to reduce everything to reason. Reason is suspected of making a man philistine, pedantic, and hard-

hearted. Who can fail to agree with those who rebel against it? *Dulce est desipere in loco*. No lad in fine fettle wants to have anything to do with the sensible staidness of the boy who is top of his class, nor with the horrifying sobriety and utilitarianism of those who can consider sex only in terms of population policy and eugenics, the mountains in terms of electricity generation, and the birds in terms of the good or harm they do. No one wants to have anything to do with that inferno of progress and utilitarianism that Aldous Huxley conjures up in *Brave New World*. But there is another inferno to which we are much closer, that of brutish unreason and wretched barbarism.

But, of course, the liberal idea of reason is something very different from this ridiculous caricature. It means the emancipation of the mind from any heteronomous authority, the absolute pursuit of truth, and the rejection of every obscurantism, myth, and bias of any kind. It rests on a mental attitude of the nobility of which our modern mystagogues have no inkling. For it also demands that we should deceive neither ourselves nor others and strive for that intellectual integrity that is the very opposite of the humbug so popular today, of the rank jungle of thought and style. Discipline of thought and style instead of the indiscipline staring at us in every line of illiberal literature, truthfulness instead of obscurantism, clarity instead of hysteria, the advancement of knowledge instead of sensationalism for the masses, logic instead of wallowing in moods and emotions—that is the program. It is only the liberal ideal of the use of Reason in the service of truth that has engendered science—science that we cannot imagine as absent from Western civilization and that alone has liberated Europe from the stupor and wretchedness of barbarism. To have created the foundations of science is the greatest, the millennial, contribution of the Greeks to Western civilization. Science was born, no doubt, at the very moment when Thales first had the courage to think without preconceived ideas about the world and what it is, in essence, made of. Science is a liberal invention and as such is in great danger today. Anyone who rejects liberalism must jettison science as well and return to the stupor of the mythological age. There is no way of closing our ears to the trumpets that today in Germany blare out the signal for this retreat into a new darkness. A good many of our scholars blow the same tune for all they are worth, even though science stands or falls by Reason, and this tragi-comic spectacle would be really funny if it did not have such extraordinarily grave consequences. Rarely in history has a group of people been so busy helping to saw off the branch on which they sit. For the rest, it is a striking fact, which needs some explanation, that German professors are so prominent in today's mass revolt against liberalism and thereby against the breath of life of Western civilization.

The cultural heritage of antiquity was, as we all know, buried by that distressing process that we call the decline of antiquity. One of the essential characteristics of that decline was that the sun of Reason once more disappeared below the horizon. What we call the modern age is really nothing else but the rediscovery of Reason. The beginnings go back to the thirteenth century, when Marsilius of Padua deduced democracy and pacifism by reasoning, and when in England Roger Bacon declared war on "undue regard for authority, routine, popular prejudice and a false conceit of our own wisdom." But it was not until the flowering of the Italian Renaissance that there began the great movement of emancipation that continued well into the nineteenth century and went from strength to strength. Renaissance and humanism, reformation and Anglo-Saxon nonconformism, English rationalism and French enlightenment, political and economic liberalism of the eighteenth and nineteenth centuries, and the classical philosophy and poetry of Germany—all these are essential stages of this secular process of liberation. Pascal, Descartes, Spinoza, Leibniz, Kant, Voltaire, Goethe, and many others are the stars that rose to illuminate the darkness.

Science prospered and, without this being its purpose, created the foundations upon which rest the technical machinery of modern mass production—but how long will it continue to do so? Mankind awakened and rubbed the sleep from its eyes; it acquired consciousness and began to reflect and to look to Reason as the incorruptible arbiter. Institutions and processes that had hitherto been taken by the mass of the people as God-given and ordained by destiny now became the subject of rational criticism. War, formerly regarded as a scourge of God, was now examined to see how it could be restricted, and modern pacifism emerged as a mass movement. Economy and society were recognized as the work of man and thus became subject to rational investigation, a change to which economics, sociology, and political science owe their origins. Authority was no longer submitted to as God-given; philosophers debated its origin and justification and thus caused the idea of democracy to germinate. Critical reason probed the difference between rich and poor and examined private property, and thus the trunk of liberal rationalism eventually sprouted the bough of socialism. Everything was lifted into consciousness, not only in the case of a few leading personalities—that would have been nothing new—but in the broadest strata of the population. Even irrationalism, mysticism, and romanticism were forced to make use of language, and what had been a matter of naive spontaneity thus became one of alert awareness and literary reflection. Even the illiberal re-enthronement of violence is accompanied by theories; Fascism and Hitlerism look to Georges Sorel as their spiritual forerunner and Bolshevism to Karl Marx. The present time furnishes us with what is probably the sole historical example of barbarism that is not a spontaneous outbreak and practice, but the conscious elaboration of a literary program. It all goes to show that however hard we try, we cannot escape being intellectually alert.

Liberal rationalism leads by a direct way to economic liberalism, or at least, to that minimum program of economic liberalism that demands that no decision of economic policy be taken before the underlying relationships have been examined, down to their ultimate implications, rationally and without any emotional obscurantism, nor before all the pros and cons have been conscientiously weighed, including the question of possible repercussions contrary to the desired aim. If tariffs are introduced, it must be done only in full awareness of the implied loss of productivity and national wealth and may not be justified in terms of the sluggish emotional approach of economic nationalism that cannot see or, for reasons of mental inertia or vested interests, does not wish to see that the reasons customarily advanced for protective tariffs are unworthy of a thinking human being. Thanks to this minimum program, economic liberalism in effect coincides with economics, which likewise is not out to propound any economic policy aims, but would be betraying itself if it were to budge an inch from the rational examination of economic relationships. It should not be forgotten that economics as a science has its origin in rational criticism of the naively unscientific government practices of mercantilism.

3. Resting on the ideas of liberty and reason, finally, the third of the basic elements of liberalism is the idea of *humanity*. This means the unquestioned and absolute respect for every individual's human dignity, the rejection of the pessimistic doctrine of mankind's original sin, the profound conviction that man must never be degraded into an object, and the rejection of oppression of any kind, be it of individuals, classes, races, or nations; it means tolerance, protection, and respect for minorities. The genealogy of this idea cannot be traced here,[2] but certainly its origin, too, must be sought in pre-Christian antiquity, and its philosophic home was mainly in the Greek and Roman Stoa. Too few of us are aware that the humanizing of slavery in the West was essentially the achievement of pre-Christian humanity. Christianity (especially Catholicism and Calvinism, the position of the Lutheran

---

[2] *There is much about this in the works of Ernst Troeltsch.*

church being less clear in this respect), natural law, and eighteenth-century philosophy are the subsequent milestones of this development. The abolition of torture and cruel, physical punishment are some of the results that, for the time being, we still take for granted. The idea of humanity is seen in all its full significance when conceived as the rejection of the principle of violence in favor of the principle of reason. Violence is relegated to the very bottom of the scale of values; its use is admitted only as a last resort and with the utmost reluctance. This, ultimately, is the essence of civilization. "Negotiations, standards of behavior, courtesy, considerations, justice, reason! What were they all invented for? Why all this fuss? Well, all this makes up the conceptual content of the word civilization, which displays its origin in the concept of *civis*, the citizen, and it serves to make possible the *civitas*, the community, people living together. Anyone is as uncivilized and barbaric as he is inconsiderate toward his neighbor." This is how Ortega y Gasset puts it in his challenging book *The Revolt of the Masses,* and he hits the nail on the head.

The same principle of peace is ultimately served also by *liberal democracy* insofar as it incorporates in the highest degree men's determination to live together in communities. By tolerating opposition and offering every opposition party the chance of gaining a majority over the ruling group and thus replacing it in power, liberal democracy creates a safety valve that makes revolution redundant. This highest form of social organization naturally presupposes that all groups are willing loyally to apply the rules of the game, which means that their attitude corresponds to the liberal philosophy. Opinion and counter-opinion must be given free play; everything must be geared to "discussion" and "negotiation." This is where the institution of parliament finds its place. What it signifies, and how far even the worst parliament is superior to the dark room of an authoritarian régime under the sway of uncontrolled forces, is something the Germans will have to learn the hard way, and we can only hope that by then it will still be possible to regain political liberty without violation of the principle of peace. "Discussion" serves the principle of peace and with it the idea of humanity, but it presupposes the ideas of liberty and reason. Discussion is possible only where opinions may be expressed in complete freedom, but even then only on condition that both sides accept reason as the common denominator of all opinions. Where reason clashes with inarticulate, emotional intent, there can be no discussion. As a result, people hysterically shout down each other and eventually bash one another on the head. Thus, contempt of reason leads to contempt of man and humanity, to intolerance, violence, bellicism, and destructive action. Goethe knew what he was doing when he let the devil exult: "Reason and Knowledge only thou despise, The highest strength in man that lies! Let but the Lying Spirit bind thee, and I shall have thee fast and sure."* And thus we have arrived at the devil's own present day.

THE TRIUMPH OF ILLIBERALISM

If we measure the present by the yardstick of the liberal program, we see at once without further explanation how far we have already sunk into illiberal barbarism. The spirit of the barbarians, which the Western peoples thought they had tamed by centuries of struggle, is abroad again and threatens to destroy the civilizing work of all these centuries. The tide of nihilism, which Nietzsche foresaw, has been rising and already engulfs us up to the neck. In terms of the three basic elements of liberalism, the destruction wrought by illiberalism to date can be described as follows.

1. The idea of liberty has been replaced by a renewed will to subjection of the personality and a longing for state slavery. Thus, the first element of illiberalism is *servilism*. Men are

* *Translation by Bayard Taylor (London, Ward Lock, 1911).*—Ed.

gripped by a desire to be told what to do and to be ordered about, to the point almost of masochism. The state has become the subject of unparalleled idolatry, and it remains idolatry however much Protestant theologians may try to deduce it from the will of God. With giant tentacles the modern state encompasses all spheres of private life and society, strangles individuality, and eventually drains society of its vital sap. More deadly than all the despotisms of the past, and more inescapable, looms the "total state" of the future, and the servile illiberal, it would seem, can hardly wait to kiss its whip. The modern state's technical instruments of power have become so annihilating that any revolution from below is condemned to failure from the outset, and the only possible salvation lies in a coup d'état from above. The machinery of administration and police has been perfected to the point where the omnipotence of the state has virtually no limits any more except self-imposed ones, and the illiberal state is not inclined to accept any. The breakdown of prohibition in the United States and the current spread of smuggling are comforting proof that there still are some natural limits to state power, but they certainly have been moved out very far. I use the word "comforting" deliberately and without the slightest cynical intention, for in all truth there is no greater danger to the continuation of our civilization than the modern state's total claim to power, which, in the event of its becoming reality, is bound eventually to wither all intellectual life and thereby to block the state's own last source of energy. Servilism is followed by *nihilism*.

Closely connected with servilism is our era's *nationalism*. The more emphasis is laid on the state, and the more every individual becomes a serving member of the state mechanism, the more pronounced becomes the frontier dividing one state and nation from all others. This is in blatant contrast with liberalism, whose three basic ideas inevitably generate a feeling of inner bonds with other nations as well as the conviction that if a nation seals itself off from others internally or externally, it is acting against all the traditions to which we are bound by the development of Western civilization. And when national isolation eventually combines with blind hatred of everything foreign, when servilism combines with brutalism, then hardly anything is left to divide mankind from naked cannibalism. This kind of nationalism has, of course, nothing in common with the natural feeling and inclination of solidarity that we call love of our country, but such as it is, it is destructive of culture, as must be clear to anyone who stops to think that what we call national culture has been created only in constant interaction with European civilization as a whole, whose roots reach down to Athens, Rome, and Jerusalem. In the course of the centuries, cultural dependence has steadily grown rather than diminished, and this is why the leading spirits of all nations have never felt national frontiers to be as confining as today. Cultural nationalism leads as inescapably to provincial Babbittry as economic nationalism leads to material impoverishment and political nationalism to war.

2. Against the idea of reason the illiberals have set up *irrationalism*. The success of the counteroffensive of unreason against reason is well known to anyone in the least familiar with the political and intellectual trends of the present. "Myth," "voice of the people," "primordial soul," "blood," "*Reich*"—these are some of the words from the vocabulary of the modern illiberal jargon that every self-important ass thinks he has to throw around. Confusion is preferred to clarity, obscurity to light, excitement and sensationalism to logic and proof. Stupidity and stupor are being inculcated in a way that beggars description and must cause us to fear the worst for the future of the society falling prey to them.

3. The humanitarian idea of the liberal, finally, has its counterpart in the illiberal's *brutalism*. The situation this has led us into today needs no description. The beast of prey in man is extolled with unexampled cynicism (Spengler), and with equal cynicism every immoral and brutal act is justified by the sanctity of the political end. The liberal principle of

"live and let live" is opposed by the illiberal "die and let die."
We should not fruitlessly bewail this but conclude soberly
that a nation that yields to brutalism thereby excludes itself
from the community of Western civilization.

THE REVOLT OF THE MASSES

Servilism, irrationalism, and brutalism—that is the program
of today's arrogantly strutting illiberalism. Having looked
upon this Medusa's head, we are doubly crushed on hearing
what the movement pretends to stand for. It speaks, we are
told, in the name of "inwardness," "idealism," "order," and,
above all, in the name of youth! It could be taken as a grim
joke, were it not that we know only too well how honest and
sincere most people are about it. They do not know that in the
name of youth they are drawing up a program which, instead
of leaving the past behind and pointing to the future, is going
to turn the wheel of world history back at least several centuries. They do not know that they are the champions of a
barbarism into which mankind has once before relapsed in
the course of its history. For liberalism is younger than illiberalism, which has become so fossilized that it ill suits our
illiberal youth so arrogantly to treat liberalism as senile.

Illiberalism as such, therefore, is nothing new, but a much
used disk. What is new is that this revolt against civilization is
at the same time a revolt of the masses under the leadership
of those so-called educated individuals whom Ortega y Gasset
exposed as the typical mass man—a special merit of his above-
mentioned book, which altogether says everything that is
worth saying on this point. Ortega y Gasset showed, too, that
the advance of the masses is a main cause of illiberalism.
Almost by definition, mass man is intolerant and disinclined
to enter into discussion, follows his heart more than his head,
and has little more than a disdainful smile for the idea of
humanity. This mass man, who exists especially among the

lower-middle classes and, paradoxically, among the intellectuals, is now about to seize power. We all know the symptoms of
his domination, which are in all essentials identical with those
of the ruling illiberalism: hot air, slogans and a confused
stutter, glorification of "direct action," violence in dealing
with all those of different opinion, rabble-rousing in every
sphere, empty rhetoric, and deceitful stage effects. Mass man is
not used to thinking for himself; he likes to let others do his
thinking for him. That would not matter much if the ready-
made ideas he consumes were those of the best in the land, but
unfortunately they are simply the ideas of those who are most
skillful in pandering to mass moods and emotions. And the
mass is about to trample down the garden of European civilization, ruthlessly and uncomprehendingly. No conservative
could be more deeply convinced than the liberal that the mass
can never be constructive, but only destructive, and that the
tyranny of the masses is the worst there is, because it is by
nature incapable of even a glimmer of understanding for individuality. When liberalism advocates democracy, it can therefore do so only on condition that democracy is hedged in by
such limitations and safeguards as will prevent liberalism's
being devoured by democracy. "The limitation, therefore, of
the power of government over individuals loses none of its
importance when the holders of power are regularly account-
able to the community, that is, to the strongest party therein."
(John Stuart Mill.) This is the purpose of all those uncomprehendingly much-maligned institutions of liberal democracy,
the meaning and origin of which are so widely forgotten. Mass
man fights against liberal democracy in order to replace it by
illiberal democracy. His model is not Pericles, but Cleon, the
predecessor of all nationalistic philistines. He reviles the
French Revolution without knowing that he is an epigone of
Robespierre. At all times the Cleons and the Robespierres
have been the curse of mankind.

II

Reconstruction
and Red Totalitarianism

V

The Centenary of British Free Trade*

I

This summer it is a hundred years since the day when the abolition of the corn duties sealed the victory of free trade in Great Britain. Few of us can really take the full measure of what came to pass then; for its contemporaries it was an event that, however prosaic its subject may have seemed, burst with dramatic impact upon the scene of England's public life and was charged with the tension of a great historical moment. Anyone who is familiar at least in outline with the motive forces of the last century's history in general and of its economic history in particular knows the consequences of that day in June, 1846, when the Repeal Act became law after having been passed by both Houses of Parliament. But what does this breakthrough of free trade in the pioneer country of industrialism mean today for us, and what does it teach us, for better or worse? This is a question that, no doubt, everyone will admit is important, but answering it appears easy and simple only to the die-hards.

The antecedents of June, 1846, are indeed among the most fascinating episodes of the economic and social history of modern times and also constitute one of the most important chapters of British Parliamentary history. Its heroes, Richard

* Neue Zürcher Zeitung, *June 17 and 18, 1946.*

Cobden, John Bright, Sir Robert Peel, Lord Russell, and the rest of them have repeatedly attracted biographers and occupy a permanent place in the imagination of the British people. There is much to tell: how the seed of economic liberalism sown by Adam Smith, Ricardo, and others slowly germinated in the period following the Napoleonic wars; how amid the universal poverty of the English masses the idea steadily gained ground that the protectionist system signified an absurd burden on the whole economy; how among the multitude of merchants, bankers, manufacturers, and publicists clamoring for economic freedom the figures of Cobden and Bright emerged and with their Anti-Corn Law League gave the world the rare spectacle of a mass propaganda campaign conducted with intelligence, dash, and noble sentiments; how the great political reform of 1832 gave the middle classes their due influence; how the Chartist riots reflected the growing distress of the masses and the rising fever of social unrest; how Peel, the Tory, was slowly converted and with his budget reform of 1842 and bank reform of 1844 established the cornerstone of the liberal system in England; how Prince Consort Albert influenced the queen with the liberal economic philosophy he had acquired in Germany and thus by a rare irony of history caused Adam Smith's triumphal march, which had started in Edinburgh, to make the strange detour via Coburg, Bonn, and Göttingen—all this and more should be told. The story would approach its climax when it came to describe how at the beginning of August, 1845, the historic rain set in "that rained away the corn laws," how Ireland was suffering famine and England scarcity, how in December, in circumstances woven into a romantic fancy by Meredith in his novel *Diana of the Crossways, The Times* published the sensational news that the repeal of the Corn Laws was imminent, and how, eventually, they were repealed in June, 1846, in one of the most dramatic sessions in British Parliamentary history. England literally had had to choose between revolution and free trade and took the course that had become inevitable.

All that happened a hundred years ago, and to many it may seem a thousand years away. So unreal does it appear to our generation that there should once upon a time have been a country that, against the opposition of powerful interests, and after a free and passionate debate by democratic procedures, decided, without any countervailing concessions from abroad, to stand up to all foreign competition without tariff protection such as historical tradition has made to seem almost an attribute of sovereignty and is virtually taken for granted by the lay public. In now celebrating the centenary of British free trade, we not only should recall its remarkable birth, but also the almost more astonishing fact that the subject of our celebrations very nearly reached the biblical age of a hundred years—after prolonged ailments and several paralytic strokes, British free trade died in the great year of crisis, 1931. The vast body of literature on this subject notwithstanding, we are still waiting for a sociologically and economically trained historian to make us understand how this unique experiment, which was in flat contradiction to all the unedifying laws of political psychology, could be started with a postulate of economic reason and carried out for almost a century. Today we know how many conditions had to meet at that time in a historically rare combination so as to work the miracle of British free trade, conditions of a psychological, economic, social, and political nature. To the jubilant contemporaries and to several generations thereafter it appeared as the natural and lasting triumph of reason, of peace, of harmony among nations, and of the forces of material progress. "Free Trade, Goodwill and Peace among Nations"—that was Cobden's battle-cry, and its nobility stifles any attempt to smile it off with the sophistication of one above such naiveties. We have heard other battle-cries since then that wiped the smiles off our faces.

In a certain sense these sanguine expectations of our liberal forebears were not really exaggerated. To be sure, it was not the dawn of the golden age of peace, and the social philosophy that regarded free trade as the guardian of international concord, rather than as one strand in a unitary overall development, seems to us as faded as the paper on which it was printed. But it is equally true that British free trade was an essential foundation of the world economy such as developed, in all its impressive strength and breadth, and with all its intricate institutions, in the course of the nineteenth century. It needed British free trade for the world to take this course of international trade, industrialism, the gold standard, prosperity, the rising tide of population growth, and commercialization, and it then had to pay the price from which we would gladly knock off something today. That is why this world collapsed together with British free trade, a catastrophe which conditions our own present and imposes upon us the gigantic task of building a world that, while it may not be a mere copy of the old one, must allow for a network of relations more international than ever.

We spoke of the faded social philosophy of the men of 1846. But that does not mean that we have any right to suspect their motives, as has become fashionable on the continent since Friedrich List and others, or to impute to them the hypocritical hardness of heart and the dry egoism that many associate with the Manchester School. If at all, such an injustice can be excused only by ignorance of the time, of its leading personalities, and of its ideas. What really happened is no doubt well described by Alexander Rüstow in the novel interpretation he puts forward in his important treatise *Das Versagen des Wirtschaftsliberalismus als religionsgeschichtliches Problem*.[1] He is right when he says: "Uncouth disciples of Friedrich List, himself not overly discriminating to begin with, thereupon declared the whole Free Trade propaganda as a devilish trick of the English, who, like a wolf in sheep's clothing, wanted to get the other sheep to throw open their doors themselves to British trade expansion. In the meantime it has become clear

---

[1] *"Istanbuler Schriften," No. 12 (Oprecht, Zürich, 1946).*

that these people were looking for others behind a door behind which they themselves wanted to hide" (p. 55).

This analysis in terms of the history of thought needs to be supplemented by recalling the facts of British economic and social history, with which not everyone may be familiar. Generally speaking, in the early decades of the nineteenth century the poverty of the English masses had been dire beyond belief, and the burden that the corn duties imposed upon a rapidly growing population more and more depending upon industrial exports had increasingly been recognized as one of the principal causes of the distress. Cobden and Bright were perfectly honest in crusading for a cause that today we would describe by the slogan "the century of the common man." Developments after 1846 proved them right, and the broad masses of England thanked them for it. Free trade was their anticipated answer to the *Communist Manifesto*, in which Marx and Engels in 1847 tried to interpret the poverty of England's proletariat in their own fashion and with German metaphysics. And the answer was to prove convincing. It was probably in some part due to it that the seed scattered by the *Communist Manifesto* never germinated properly in the very country that was its authors' main concern.

II

What lesson does the imposing English venture of free trade hold for us today? Is it a perpetually valid model or a warning example still to be heeded? This question has been hotly debated by protectionists and free traders for a century, but today we can see that it is wrongly posed and hence sterile, and that is perhaps the most important reflection suggested by the centenary.

First of all, it may be pointed out that the whole question has lost its topicality today, because there is hardly anyone

left even in the free trade camp who thinks it is enough to
remind the world panegyrically of Cobden's achievements and
arguments. It is inconceivable that Cobden's slogans should
today launch a mass movement for free trade and lead it to
victory. Our worries are not those of 1846, and today's champion of a liberal trade policy must be prepared to answer
problems far from Cobden's and Bright's mind. And as our
tactics must be different today, so we have also learned to be
more modest in our expectations, and the old free-trader's
counterpart in the modern world is a man who would be happy
if only the different countries' trade policies were content with
protective tariffs as low and stable as possible and restored
multilateralism to international trade by the abolition of import restrictions, exchange control, and clearing agreements.
But such modesty is more than mere resignation. In most cases
it certainly rests on the more or less definite feeling that integral free trade not only would today be utopian, but in the
present world situation hardly justified. In practice, no one
would have the courage to be so radical as long as "goodwill
and peace among nations" do not look rather more secure than
they actually are, and a good many other conditions are fulfilled as well. Nor is this all. We always knew, of course, that
the victory of free trade in England rested on a principle that
opened the way to the mass civilization of industrialism and
commercialism, but today even the most determined liberal
can no longer fail to appreciate that this principle in many
ways contradicts a natural order, the political rationale of
which transcends the mere economic. Uncomprehendingly we
stare at Macaulay's lines in his essay "Southey's Colloquies on
Society" (1830), where he poured all his scorn upon an author
who thinks the old rural cottages look prettier than a cotton
factory, and who makes the ugliness of the cotton-spinners'
houses one of the standards by which to judge the new manufacturing age. Our sharper hearing has learned to distinguish
sounds to which the age of Macaulay and Cobden seems to
have been deaf, and we sense that for us the decision is not as

easy as it was for them. We may still defend as relatively more reasonable than others the principle that the decision as to what individual nations produce or not should be left to free international trade. But we do so without enthusiasm, because we know the other side of the balance sheet, and hence in the best of cases we make reservations, qualifications, and conditions.

But it is not only the free-traders who could usefully avail themselves of this birthday for reflections on their philosophy. Those others who from the outset made free trade the target of their attacks should, in their turn, give proof that they are prepared to learn something rather than gloat over the moderation of their opponents. If they regard British agriculture as the chief victim of free trade, they should not overlook the fact that this measure hit an agrarian economy whose sound structure had already been largely destroyed by the enclosures of the eighteenth century. They should also remember the extent to which agriculture, the fate of which, after all, is the main subject of the whole debate, has in other countries been disadvantaged precisely by industrial protectionism and hence renounce the doctrine that the interests of agriculture are necessarily served by tariff protection. As Professor C. von Dietze recently once more demonstrated in his interesting article "Bauernwirtschaft und Kollektiv,"[2] it is ". . . precisely the decades of the most complete domination of economic liberalism . . . [which brought with them] . . . an unprecedented flowering of agriculture in all parts of the world." Even though outside England that age was by no means governed by free trade, it was at least under the influence of a basically liberal trade policy, which was incomparably less at variance with free trade than with the autarkic system of protection that many countries today think they owe their farmers. The example of Germany shows with nothing less than heartbreaking

[2] Schweizerische Zeitschrift für Volkswirtschaft und Statistik (June, 1946).

forcefulness what disintegrating economic, social, and human effects such a system is bound eventually to exercise upon peasant agriculture. Professor von Dietze describes them in his above-mentioned article, and the voices of other experts that reach us from across the northern frontier confirm the impression that the German peasantry has suffered the most serious damage to its health in the last twelve years of autarkic protectionism and now, weakened to the marrow, has to face the salf-same tasks of adaptation and conversion from which an escape was sought in autarky in the first place. We are told of the blind alley into which the policy of autarky and subsidies has led German agriculture and of the task of guilding it back to the right path of world market orientation and competitiveness. It may be that radical free trade, such as no one still seriously advocates, is unwholesome for agriculture; certainly autarkic protection is for it a sweet but eventually fatal poison. Since the old controversy between free trade and protective tariffs has now taken the new shape of opposition between the traditional policy of tariff protection and the new one of planned autarky, today's successors of the old free-traders still uphold the liberal principle as superior even when, or rather, precisely when they adopt the new aims of a natural order and outdo all others in their insistence on a healthy farming community.

And this brings us to the crucial point of our reflections. Resistance against a liberal trade policy, of which free trade is the most radical form, is understandable enough as a defense against the encroachment on a natural order of society and economy with the justified intention of preserving it from the excesses of modern industrial and commercial mass civilization. But it is an error, and one that has repeatedly had to be paid for dearly, to believe that this dangerous process can be stopped by obstructing it with an official prohibition at only one point, that is, at the national frontier. It is wrong to hold England's free trade and the liberal trade policy of most other countries responsible for the disastrous development of economy and society during the last century, instead of blaming that overall development itself, and of asking oneself whether free trade would have been any serious disturbance to another, more natural, more balanced, and more human development. But developments did take that fatal course, and in that given setting, liberal trade policy on the whole did more good than harm. If, on the other hand, things had developed after the event in the way we now wish, with fewer large towns and industrial centers, with a smaller proletariat, less monopoly, and less of all the other ingredients and philosophies of industrial-commercial mass civilization, then free trade would have been seen as a mere command of reason; it need not have collided with a much healthier development and would probably not have been taken as a serious threat to people's more firmly grounded and more natural existence. Just as it is wrong to single out international economic relations from among the overall developments and make a scapegoat of liberal trade policy, so it is groundless to expect that exchange control and customs officials can make any decisive impact on the unnaturalness of our civilization as a whole. On the contrary, it is just then that the worst disturbances and distortions must be expected, and things are bound to go from bad to worse.

This should make clear what was meant earlier in saying that the problem was stated in the wrong terms. We know now that the question no longer turns on free trade or protective tariffs, but on the contrast between essentially free international economic relations and the shackles of planning and autarky. Of the two opposing parties, one is primarily after international economic freedom, the other, among many other things, after protection against the anonymous forces of a worldwide mass civilization. Both, I think, are wrong—the first when it believes that its aim can still be achieved without at the same time solving the whole problem of our mass civilization, and the second when it overlooks the fact that the desired protection can only be found in that same solution of the general problem, and that to shackle foreign trade is harmful in any event. If both parties were made up only of philosophers and not of vested interests as well, they should have no undue difficulty in agreeing on a joint program. It would be the program of a natural order, in which freedom of economic life, both national and international, is logically connected with a policy designed to preserve and promote values and institutions to which, no doubt, Cobden and Bright gave little thought, or if they did, slightly contemptuous thought, when a hundred years ago they had their moment of triumph in the English Parliament. But this program would lack the most important ingredient if it were not at the same time inspired by the universalism and supra-national attitude of these men, who, with all their errors, had the saving grace of deep longing for peace and goodwill among nations.

VI

"Repressed Inflation":
The Ailment of the Modern Economy*

INFLATION PLUS COLLECTIVISM

Recent experience in many countries enables us to draw the picture of a strange distortion and stasis in economic life and to diagnose an economic ailment that, more and more, is proving to be the worst of all, and that to a very large extent explains the persistence of Europe's distress. I have in mind that cross between collectivism and inflation, for which I have suggested the name of "repressed inflation"—first in my essay "Lehren des deutschen Wirtschaftsmarasmus"[1] and later, more systematically, in "Offene und zurückgestaute Inflation"[2] Typically, what happens is as follows. As a result of the war and of postwar mismanagement, serious inflation developed in the sense that the means of payment are increasing strongly, while the production of goods stagnates. Were the government to permit an "open" inflation, this disproportion between the volume of money and the volume of goods would lead to the consequence we all know, namely, a general rise in prices and incomes. To its credit, the government in question does not wish this to happen. However, it cannot make up its mind to dam back the flood of money, either because, as in countries

---

* Neue Zürcher Zeitung, *June 14 and 15, 1947.*
[1] Neue Zürcher Zeitung, *Nos. 1931 and 1939, October 26 and 27, 1946.*
[2] Kyklos, *1947, No. 1.*

111

governed under the paralyzing three-party system, it lacks the political strength to do so, or because it does not wish to give up an economic policy that is incompatible with sound money (full employment, cheap money, or a socialist economic policy).

Now, what does a government do in such a situation? It prevents excess demand from working itself out in a rise of prices and exchange rates and replaces the regulating and stimulating functions of price by a system of rationing at fixed prices, together with the inevitable controls—a system well known from the war economy and, within its limits, useful and indeed indispensable. If the inflationary surplus of money pushes up prices, costs, and exchange rates, the increasingly comprehensive and more and more elaborate apparatus of physical controls tries to oppose this upward movement of values by a sort of police counterpressure. This is how open inflation has come to be replaced by another type, repressed inflation, which might also be called "forbidden inflation."

It is this repressed inflation that is associated with our present age of collectivism, and associated in the double sense that collectivism is at once a cause of inflation and an instrument of its repression. A host of subtle questions are connected with this, but it would lead us too far to discuss them here. One might analyze the different degrees and types of repressed inflation, and one might also argue about whether, and in what circumstances, a temporary and moderate repression of inflation is the lesser evil. The question I ask, however, is this: Where does repressed inflation end, if, in today's more normal peacetime conditions, it becomes a system dominating economic life?

There is only one answer to this question, and it can be found in the economic marasmus of several European countries, of which Germany is the extreme case. The longer the system of fictitious, controlled values is continued, the more fictitious these values become, in the double sense of corresponding less and less to the real scarcity relations and of serving for fewer and fewer exchanges of goods. The distortion of all value relations, the co-existence of "official" and "black" sectors, and the contradiction between the directives of the market and those of the authorities desperately fighting for their power eventually lead to chaos and to the virtual absence of any economic order whatever, whether of the free-enterprise or the collectivist kind. So long as the government succeeds at least in the negative purpose of preventing transactions from being switched to a gold or foreign-exchange basis, the economy relapses into the stage of primitive barter and payments in kind, but at the same time into a correspondingly primitive, low level of productivity. Eventually, as in the final stages of open inflation, money loses not only its function as a means of exchange and yardstick of value ordering the economic process, but also its other, and no less important, function as an incentive to produce and market as many goods as possible. The more the persistent inflation pushes up values, the more the government strengthens the counterpressure of controls, but the more fictitious becomes the system of controlled values, the greater the economic chaos and the general listlessness, and the more threadbare either the government's authority or its claim still to be democratic. There can be no doubt that unless repressed inflation is stopped in time, it will increasingly cause forces to develop that lead to the dissolution of the economy and even of the state itself.

Half a year ago or so, I had occasion in this newspaper to discuss the German case of repressed inflation. I tried then to distinguish what was typical and what was peculiar to Germany, which is the worst case of all because the disproportion between the repressed volume of purchasing power and the volume of goods is bigger than anywhere else, and because the disrupting effects of advanced collectivism are here combined with the well-known disturbing factors of politics. Despite all the warnings, nothing significant has been done in this half year toward a comprehensive currency and economic reform, such as would stop repressed inflation by removing the quantitative disproportion between purchasing power and goods through a drastic reduction in the volume of purchasing power, and by overcoming the chaos of paralyzing, collectivist policies through the re-establishment of a free-market economy. Failure to do so must in large part be held responsible for last winter's dismal misery, and it is, at least in part, the fault of socialist ideology. This is true in the two senses that, first, those responsible could not bring themselves to get out of the chaos at the cost of sacrificing socialist doctrine, and that, secondly, this selfsame doctrine paralyzed the decision to carry through a currency reform that, in view of the attitude of the Russians, demands independent action on the part of the Western allies in their respective occupation zones in Germany.

But many non-socialists, too, have so far resisted the necessary currency reform. Their argument has been that it would be more expedient to remove the excess of purchasing power by an increase in production rather than by a diminution of the money supply; meanwhile, they have thought it best to carry on with the present policy. They overlooked that it is precisely the continuing repression of excess purchasing power, with all its consequences, which again and again prevents the increase in production needed for the removal of the disproportion—assuming it can be removed at all from the side of production—because it deprives the economy of the required incentives. The longer the delay in breaking out of this vicious circle, the further recedes the desired end of production's growing into the outsized money supply. The truth of this is proved in the most distressing manner by the way the German economy has been going these last few months. It has confirmed the prediction that complete collapse was to be expected unless repressed inflation were stopped with all possible speed. After things were just left to drift for two years, the German economy lost so much blood that salvation now seems hardly possible without an all-out and very costly operation to bring in food, raw materials, and manufactures from abroad.

The longer the Western allies hold back from doing this, the larger will be the sum that they will eventually have to decide must be sacrificed. Thus ends this experiment in repressed inflation. But it ends also with the allied military authorities' stealing the thunder of the Russian threat to use military force for taking food away from the farmers. In so doing, they not only display singularly little understanding for the laws of economics but also prove the utter collapse of the whole system of controls on which repressed inflation rests.

As the German example demonstrates, the principal error of the champions of repressed inflation consists in their being unable to shed the idea of a more or less given deficit of goods, which, on the pattern of the war economy, have to be distributed as equitably as possible. They cling to the dismal idea of a "poorhouse socialism," and they defend their system with the argument that at least all are equally bad off (or even, as in England, venture the strange assertion that the masses are indeed better off under the rationing system than they were before); they gain a cheap success with the rhetorical question of how the masses are supposed to live if rationing were discontinued. But they do not see the essential point or do not want to see it. They disregard the fact that the repressed inflation they defend makes sense only in the presence of a major disproportion between the volume of purchasing power and the production of goods; in other words, their defense of controls rests on the assumption of inflation. Unless, being socialists, they perhaps harbor the secret wish that this disproportion would last forever, so that they can always justify socialism as an instrument of repressing inflation, their aim should not be the most equitable distribution of an insufficient amount of goods, but its increase. And they should aim at an increase such that, for example, all the inhabitants of so rich a country as France should be given their fill once more by the former, proven methods of the free economy, except for those who, then as now, need special assistance. It is astonishing that so reasonable a man as the French Prime Minister M. Ramadier, who, it is to be hoped, agrees with us on this point, will not admit also that the very system that he stubbornly defends against the mounting storm of public protests prevents ample and appropriate deliveries to the market by paralyzing production and withdrawing from the official markets a growing proportion of such goods as are still produced. France, too, can break out of this circle only if it gets rid of inflation and socialism together.

All those countries of Europe that suffer from the paralyzing, hampering, and disruptive effects of what I have called "repressed inflation," a combination of inflationary pressure and economic controls, are, like France, impoverished countries—with the sole exception of Sweden, where it needed the activities of doctrinaire socialists to create a similar situation artifically and, finally, to turn a "hard" currency into a "soft" one. Everywhere impoverishment is invoked to defend the collectivist inflation, and nowhere is it realized that this system of fictitious, controlled values perpetuates and aggravates the disproportion between the supply of money and of goods in the name of equitable distribution, while even this latter is turned into blatant injustice by the irresistible triumph of the "black" markets. Impoverishment is precisely what makes the return to the market economy and monetary stability a compelling necessity. How else except by the system of collectivist inflation is it to be explained that the soil of France, which is as fertile as it used to be, no longer seems to be able to feed that country? Is it not almost grotesque when the French prime minister tries to save the battered prestige of socialism with the bogey of the rich, who, if the market economy were to return, would snatch the most savory tidbits away from the mouths of the majority of the inhabitants of "la douce France"? When Henry IV promised the French the proverbial chicken in the pot, he certainly did not have in mind that mixture of meat coupons and inflation that is today vaunted as a means to the same purpose. And when, at last, will it be understood everywhere how absurd it is in the long run to keep price controls that discourage production exactly in the measure in which maximum production is wanted? When indeed will anyone even have the courage to admit that this is, in effect, what today's system of repressed inflation amounts to?

THE CASE OF ENGLAND

The vicious circle in which this system moves can be clearly observed in England as well. The country emerged from the war so impoverished that it was obvious it would be constrained for some length of time to lower the standard of living and produce more than ever. But the more time goes by, the less plausible does it appear that the deficiencies the British still suffer should solely be due to their initial impoverishment. One is led to the heretical idea that England is so bent on consuming less that it neglects to produce more, and a growing number of people are coming to blame this neglect of production on an economic system that, all over again, is that combination of socialism and inflationary pressure known to us as "repressed inflation." In this sort of poorhouse socialism the tightening of the belt, "austerity," becomes a permanent state of affairs that one would accept with resignation, were it not that here, too, it is associated with a steady deterioration of the economic situation and with a race between increasing controls and decreasing law-abidance. There is a credit expansion that, under the somewhat faded banner of "cheap money," causes investment to exceed saving, deficient as it is because of underproduction, overtaxation, and artificially low rates of interest. As a result, the British economy is under constant inflationary pressure, which the government curbs with the counterpressure of controls. But, as J. H. Jewkes and E. Devons remind us in an article eminently worth reading,[3] this suppression of inflation is bound, in its turn, to curtail production. "We succeed merely in preventing the vicious upward spiral of prices at the cost of having a vicious downward spiral of productivity." Thus are our English witnesses. They add that this downward pressure on productivity heightens the inflationary pressure, to which the government must react by still further restrictions on the use of consumers' purchasing power, which, in their turn, again depress productivity. The vicious circle is closed, and it seems that the British economy is moving around and around in it, notwithstanding the nervous protestations of the authorities. As Jewkes and Devons rightly observe, it is no use trying to break out of this circle by moral appeals to producers. "It is futile to expect individuals to work harder unless each one feels that his own standard of consumption depends on his own efforts and that he will get a greater share of the total cake as a result of his efforts." Like others, the British socialists will have to learn to make a distinction between the climate of war, which justifies a high degree of collectivism, and that of peace, which forces us to take account once more of normal human nature. But the costs of this lesson are borne by the whole country.

Nor is this the worst. If our English spokesmen note that success "in preventing the vicious upward spiral of prices" has to be paid for with a "vicious downward spiral of productivity," they do not name the full price, nor does it follow that success is assured. Heavier even than the loss of productivity entailed by such a system is the sacrifice of elementary liberties imposed upon the British people even now, together with the certain prospect of having to sacrifice more and more in the future. The country of habeas corpus, of the Bill of Rights, and of the proverb "My home is my castle" has become a country where the government is entitled, in

[3] Lloyds Bank Review, *April, 1947.*

peacetime, to enter your house with a search warrant at any time, where an economic secret police spreads its tentacles, where the rights of the Parliamentary opposition are curtailed in a unique manner—and where all this promises to be only the beginning. To quote the excellent weekly *Time and Tide* of March 8, 1947: "The present Government is composed of men who, we are convinced, would not wittingly take advantage of the power they have; unwittingly, they have already done so. But the fact remains that the physical basis of our liberties has been cut right away. The Government controls it all. The Parliamentary basis is fast going. The mechanism for the total destruction of freedom is already complete. It is too late to say 'it can't happen here.' It has happened."

Although there are no doubt a good many people in England, too, who do not take Professor Hayek's warning of the "Road to Serfdom" seriously or who regard it as a reactionary intrigue, there are various signs that suggest that the moment is not far off when those who govern will have to decide between what *Time and Tide* in another remarkable article calls "the cherished ideal of the Planned State" and the "equally cherished ideal of liberal humanism." And there are signs in England, too, that the high price that has to be paid for repressed inflation in the form of the loss of liberties formerly regarded as inalienable is buying a success that is rendered more and more doubtful by the steadily decreasing respect for the majesty of the law. We have a vivid memory of this process in the case of prohibition in America, and we know that legislation of this kind in the end becomes a poisonous source of corruption. Can anyone seriously believe that what did not succeed in the case of drink is likely to succeed in the case of inflation, that is, simply to forbid it? The recent open rebellion against economic controls in France has rightly caused a sensation, but it is only one among many symptoms of the war against the forces of the free economy on which such a country's government has embarked and which

it can hope to win even temporarily only by adopting the
political methods of Hitler or Stalin.

FRANCE AS AN EXAMPLE OF MISSED OPPORTUNITIES

All these considerations prove that under a system of repressed inflation time works against the government. In returning once more to the example of France, we see that on
this road there is one particularly critical moment that it is
fatal to miss. The above-mentioned April issue of *Lloyds
Bank Review* contains another very interesting article called
"The Economic Regeneration of France," in which the author,
Paul Bareau, rightly points out that France had at the time
of the liberation a unique opportunity of getting rid of
repressed inflation. If at that time, when the control mechanism was still effective in holding back the inflationary pressure, and when the psychological climate was as favorable as
could be for an energetic "monetary purge," repressed inflation had been stopped by getting rid in one sweep both of
inflation and controls, France would have been spared much
suffering and disorder. As soon as the provisional French government announced a general wage increase of forty per cent,
immediately after the liberation of Paris, it was a foregone
conclusion that a vicious spiral would now set in, by which
repressed inflation was bound to turn into open inflation to
the accompaniment of all the well-known phenomena of
economic disintegration and paralysis. The French have
always argued so far that things could not be put right from
the monetary side, but only from the side of production. But
this is just a convenient excuse, the faulty economic foundation of which we have demonstrated with the help of the
German example. In France, as elsewhere, everything of
course depends on producing more and on supplying the
market with the additional output, but one of the principal
conditions for that is the liberation of the economy from the

shackles imposed upon it by repressed inflation. The removal of repressed inflation implies two things: the end of the restrictive measures and the end of inflation. It is misleading, therefore, of the French prime minister to raise the bogey of more-than-ever runaway inflation in order to frighten those who call for the removal of controls, for no one can reasonably desire the end of controls without at the same time demanding the end of inflation. And the latter must be the aim of the prime minister. How is he going to achieve it if he makes no effort to break out of the vicious circle of repressed inflation? Nothing is more dangerous than socialism's becoming an end in itself at a moment when the most elementary considerations and unequivocal evidence prove that there is only one choice left, namely, to continue on the socialist course or to overcome the economic calamity.

The lessons that other countries can learn from the French case are plain. Think of Belgium as the example of a country that patently took advantage of the right moment for getting rid of repressed inflation and that is now reaping the fruits of its clear-sightedness. Or think of the Netherlands, which made earnest efforts to follow the Belgian example, but perhaps made the mistake of concentrating too much on sound money to the detriment of the removal of controls and, while doing its best to eliminate inflation as one part of the dangerous combination of repressed inflation, kept the controls. And, in conclusion, think once more and above all of Germany, where time is running out fast—the time, I mean, during which repressed inflation can still be removed before the price-wage spiral gets going, notwithstanding all the controls of the occupation authorities.

VII

Marshall Plan and Economic Policy*

THE EUROPEAN SIDE

The great idea of a joint aid program for the western world, as proposed by United States Secretary of State George C. Marshall in June this year, seems to be sharing the fate of so many of the ideas of our time once they are caught up in the vast apparatus that churns out the written and spoken words for the general public. The more that is written and said about them, the more confused and primitive they become. Finally the time comes to ask the classical question: *de quoi s'agit-il?*

The straitened economic circumstances of Europe have two causes: the war has destroyed so much, and the economic process is in disorder. The devastation wrought by the war is bad enough, but it would probably not have led to the present catastrophe had the economic process not fallen into a disorder which paralyzed the forces of recovery in the countries most plagued by the disorder. In its turn, this disorder of the economic process is the result of a certain economic policy that created chaos in the name of planning, confusion in the name of guidance, retrogression and autarky in the name of progress, and mass poverty in the name of justice. It is fairly generally known today what sort of economic policy this is, and even many socialists, who really should defend it as an outcome of

* Neue Zürcher Zeitung, *November 23, 1947.*

their own philosophy, now turn their back on it, because it has simply become impossible to defend. I have in mind the combination of direct controls and inflationary pressure that I have called "repressed inflation." Where it was introduced by a prosperous country spared by the war, such as Sweden, the same pathological symptoms soon developed as in other countries. Where, on the other hand, a poor and war-devastated country, such as Italy, allowed sufficient elbow room to the market economy, there was momentum, reconstruction, speedy recovery, and hope.

Once it was realized that what was required in Europe in the first place was to overcome an internal functional failure in the economic process with American help, and both Marshall and Bevin indicated that they knew it, then it must have been clear what the committee that met in Paris during the summer should do and what it should not do. It was not simply to draw up a list of holes into which the United States was to throw further billions. It was to diagnose the sickness of the European economy and propose a treatment to combine the promised blood transfusion with the patient's own inner recovery. There was only one possible diagnosis: more or less advanced repressed inflation. And the treatment to be prescribed was this: Get rid of repressed inflation by a simultaneous diminution of inflationary pressure and controls, at the same time wisely using the American blood transfusion so that the patient can recover his own strength.

It did seem for a while as though the responsible statesmen had a reasonably clear grasp of this task of the Paris Committee of European Economic Co-operation. There was an impression that the committee would avoid compiling mere statistics of shortages and would instead work out a serious recovery program. Unfortunately it was a false impression. Today it has to be admitted that the Paris Committee did precisely what it should not have done and what, I believe, the more farsighted of its members initially did not want to do. The report had nothing to say about a real diagnosis of the trouble nor about a serious treatment, and it eventually turned out to be what it was not meant to be, a shopping list. Nothing much is altered by the fact that the committee, in its embarrassment as to what constructive proposals it might make, retreated into the higher regions of well-meant recommendations for better international economic co-ordination. These recommendations are so ineffective precisely because the individual countries' collectivist economy policy is the strongest driving force of economic nationalism.

It must not be passed over in silence that those who had assumed the great responsibility of being Europe's spokesmen when America was offering help have failed. It probably means that one of history's great opportunities has been missed. To be sure, it is to be expected that America will go on handing out charity to hungry Europe, but perhaps it will be said later with bitterness that Western Europe, at the moment when it mattered, did not grasp that America was to be presented not with a letter to Father Christmas, but with a genuine and serious program for the inner recovery of the European economies. And the blame will fall upon a mentality prompted by collectivism and the contempt of economic freedom.

It is imperative to talk about these things openly, if only because a display of satisfaction might make the misfortune irrevocable. The Paris Committee had a unique opportunity to work out a bold and serious recovery program by which to inspire the U. S. Congress to a great gesture of solidarity and at the same time to give all European governments their cue for a reversal of their economic policy. This opportunity has been squandered. Nevertheless, the Marshall Plan can still be shunted onto the right track if the things left unsaid by the Paris Committee are now said by others in such words as to command the attention of the European governments and their advisers or, at least, of the people upon whom they depend. But what matters is that the European governments act accordingly and resolutely turn their back on the disastrous course of inflationary economic controls. Such a reversal, which derives from a clear knowledge of the causes of the economic paralysis and confusion, does not depend on the wisdom of international committees nor, for that matter, on American advice, excellent though some of it is. It is Europe's own business, the business of every single European government and every single European nation. Should, therefore, the U. S. Congress decide on a generous aid program in spite of the obvious weaknesses of the joint report of the European governments, it will still be up to every beneficiary country in Europe whether or not to avail itself of this unique opportunity for liberating the economy from inflationary controls. Unless this is done, however, it is to be feared that the new American billions will trickle away just as the old ones did.

With American aid forthcoming in rather impressive measure, European governments will be able to deny even less convincingly than before that the responsibility for the economic recovery of their countries lies with themselves and nowhere else. Once, however, a government understands what has to be done and has the intention of doing it, then it is up to the country's political forces to see to it that the government succeeds. What is meant thereby is best illustrated by the example of Italy. Here is a European country, poorly endowed by nature to begin with and one of the chief victims of the war, which would have fallen into chaos and misery without American aid, but also a country that knew how to use that aid for instilling new life into the economy, for, unlike other European countries, it allowed sufficiently free play to the regulatory and incentive forces of the market economy. Under the leadership of Luigi Einaudi, the doyen of Italian economists, the De Gasperi government's economic policy follows the general line required by the situation, by using American aid in support of efforts to diminish inflationary pressure and dismantle controls. It is clearly intended to create in Italy a genuine market economy resting on the foundation of monetary stability. Having already succeeded in removing one of the two causes of inflation, namely, an overexpansion of bank credit, it now remains to plug up the other source of inflation, that is, deficit spending. Whether the government will succeed in this second task depends mainly upon whether it can hold out against the sabotage policies of the extreme left. Italy's policy of using American aid for economic rehabilitation blazes a trail for the whole of Europe, but it also offers an example of the political, social, and psychological conditions in which the same policy will have to be carried through in Europe.

THE AMERICAN SIDE

As regards the European side of the Marshall Plan, it may be said that while the report of the Paris Committee has started it off on the wrong track, everything may still turn out aright provided the individual governments of Europe have enough good judgment and energy to take on their own initiative the road which the Paris Committee should have recommended. There is no salvation for a collectivist Europe; that much is clear. It is only as a plan to overcome economic planning that the—ambiguously so named—Marshall Plan can succeed. How, then, do things look on the American side? Do they, over there, have the clarity of mind that Europe lacks?

To judge by the bitter criticism rightly meted out to the Paris report and by an analysis of American opinion, it might be concluded that an obdurate patient can count on a wise helper. This conclusion is incorrect as regards the helper's superior knowledge. It is not sufficiently taken into account that over there, too, there is a conflict of different trends of thought. Yet suspicions should be aroused by the mere fact that in the part of Europe for which the Americans are directly responsible, the American-occupied zone of Germany, they have for two-and-a-half years applied economic principles that cannot be described otherwise than as collectivist. But, above all, it should not be forgotten that many of the theories and trends that gave Roosevelt's economic planning its determining impulse are still operative in America. A whole generation of American economists, after all, has been brought up to think of the permanent inflationary pressure implied in the "full employment" policy as an ideal and indeed a necessity. It is an easy step from there to accepting the idea of "guidance" that goes beyond the mere manipulation of money, especially for those who themselves sit at the steering wheel of bureaucracy.

Since Roosevelt, an economic policy dictated by the fear of deflation has become traditional, and it is this policy that is largely responsible for the inflationary pressure from which the American economy suffers today. The main trouble is that, as in Europe, this policy was continued in the United St̲a̲ even when it should have been obvious that it was n̲ flation but inflation that had to be fought. The accelerato̲ kept being pressed down long after one should have stepped on the brakes. It is, of course, not an easy task in the first place to get the better of this inflationary pressure, and it will become a good deal harder if unrequited American exports expand in the future to the extent implied by the execution of the Marshall Plan. But this also makes the task all the more pressing, since a further growth of inflation in the United States would be bound to deprive the aid program of a considerable portion of its efficacy and would spell the gravest dangers for the American economy itself.

When it comes to mastering this task, the United States is basically in the same situation as so many of the countries of Europe, in the situation, that is, of an overstrained economy that reacts to the strain by inflationary pressure. The European countries concerned were so weak and so much in need of help for the very reason that they tried to tackle this inflationary pressure with the deceptive means of collectivist controls. They are rightly told by America that the help offered to them will lead to recovery only on condition that they at long last give up this attempt of keeping down inflationary pressure by

police methods. But what conviction can such recommendations carry when the American government itself is about to
embark on the same road of repressed inflation, as announced
by President Truman in his message to Congress on November 17? If collectivist Europe is today at its wit's end and has
demonstrated where repressed inflation leads, how is it possible
in good conscience to advise the United States to go the same
way?

The consequences of this step would be so perilous that it
would be hard to understand if Congress were to approve the
government's proposals without further ado. But since inflation should certainly not be allowed to go any further, the
United States, in its turn, would have to adopt the course it
recommends to Europe and already adopted by Italy, namely,
to diminish the strain and inflationary pressure. The problem
is that European demand for goods, for which under the Marshall Plan the American government or other American
authorities issue assignments in the form of dollar checks, has
to compete with the rest of demand for America's goods. Some-
body must give way. If American inflation continues un-
checked, the price rise will curtail the amount of goods that
Europe can get, and at the same time internal American
developments will take a highly dangerous turn. President
Truman rightly warns against that. But then there remain
only two ways. Either the demand of the assisted countries is
protected against the competing claims of domestic American
demand by the power of the police and the threat of imprison-
ment, or else aggregate domestic demand in the United States
is reduced by as much as new demand is added by the imple-
mentation of the Marshall Plan.

What the Truman administration is now asking of Congress
is a mixture of the two methods, alleviation of the inflationary
pressure combined with the compulsion of what in English is
called by the dangerous euphemism of "physical controls."
But in this combined program the element of controls is much
stronger. Both inside and outside Congress the proposal has

met with sharp criticism, and unfortunately one cannot but agree with it, for the reasons indicated. The experiment of repressed inflation will be no more successful in the United States than in Europe, and slapping controls on the scarcest goods will only make them more scarce, as we should know from experience and reflection. And this means that the American economy, in its turn, will get its dose of the disorder and confusion that we know so well in Europe. Worst of all, perhaps, is that America's example will have a very bad effect on Europe. Will America really get itself into a position where it must say, with Gretchen: "How scornfully I once reviled. . . . And now a living sin am I!"?* It needs thinking through to the end what this would mean. America is prepared to shoulder heavy sacrifices in order to help Europe out of its economic crisis. Better than any one else, Americans realize that the European economic crisis can be overcome only by liberating Europe from inflationary controls, and they have been at pains to convince the governments of Europe of this truth. Is America now seriously thinking of going over to inflationary controls itself so as to make possible its help in Europe?

It is hard to believe this. But if America rightly refuses to take this path, then there remains only the other way of a genuine and energetic fight against inflationary pressure far beyond the President's proposals in his message. This would entail a break with a monetary and credit policy dominated all too long by the idea that everything that increases aggregate demand is good, and everything that diminishes it is bad. To do the right thing today, all that is needed is to do the opposite at critical points from what was thought right for the last ten years. Above all, this means abandoning the cheap money policy, and furthermore it would probably be well to consider to what extent an increase in indirect taxation (especially by means of a differentiated turnover tax) would serve the Truman administration's goal better than physical controls.

* Faust, *trans. by Bayard Taylor (London, 1911), p. 116.*—Ed.

Such a reversal of policy is exceedingly difficult for many reasons, especially in a country where the banking system has been overloaded with low-interest-bearing government securities during ten years of reckless deficit spending. But it has long been clear that sooner or later such a policy reversal would become necessary, even without the additional inflationary push deriving from the Marshall Plan.

VIII

Set the Rate of Interest Free*

If an individual constantly violates all the elementary and proven rules of good health, if he disregards all warnings and thinks he can just go on living on his physical reserves, he will indeed for some time be able to laugh at the admonitions of his friends and ridicule them as pedantic fussbudgets. For years he will have astonishing achievements to his credit, and as there appear to be no visible harmful consequences, the classical rules of reasonable living seem to be contradicted. But the day will come, after some prior warning symptoms, when his reserves are used up and suddenly the bill has to be footed for all the sins of the past. His health gives way at the weakest point, and since this usually is the circulatory system, he will feel the concentrated consequences of his former life in a pathologically high blood pressure with all its further effects. Once more the eternal laws of life will triumph over human foolishness.

Things are not very different in the case of society's social organism, which is no less intricate than that of the human body. Here, too, we may in a happy-go-lucky way sin for a long time, often an astonishingly long time, against the proven rules of reasonable economic conduct and laugh at the warners as "reactionaries" who do not appreciate that we now live in an

* Zeitschrift für das gesamte Kreditwesen, *1948, No. 1.*

inspired age when everything is different from what it was before. But if there is anything that we can learn from the present, it is how alarmingly ephemeral are such triumphs over sound common sense. Think of all the promises of the national-socialist economic futurists and of the pitiful collapse that followed. Think how they and their distressingly numerous followers in other countries took an altogether childish pleasure in standing economics on its head and making fun of the "liberalists." But again it has been shown that he who laughs last, laughs best—provided he feels like laughing in such tragic circumstances.

FINANCIAL "HYPERTONY"

At first, the reckless futurists seem to be right in economic life as well. Even though the promised beneficial effects of their "new economic policy" do not always materialize, the adverse effects expected by the level-headed are often astonishingly long in coming. Here, too, the hidden effects of irrationality keep accumulating at first, until all the reserves are exhausted, and they suddenly come out into the open. What happens then is much the same as what happens to the human body. Here, our liabilities are usually debited to the account of the circulatory system, until eventually the body has to be declared bankrupt; in the economy, the consequences of our constant sins against economic reason usually devolve upon public finance, when all other resistances have crumbled. Just as a steadily rising blood pressure insidiously registers our careless way of life, so does the steadily mounting pressure of public finance register our careless conduct of the economy. The result is a sort of financial hypertony that ends up in increasingly open inflation, possibly after an increasingly totalitarian government has tried to repress inflation by price, wage, capital, and exchange controls and thus to postpone the breakdown[1]—rather like the pathological thickening of the walls of our arteries in the case of high blood pressure in the human body.

It seems to me the time has come when we must draw the balance sheet of the sins against economic reason and do so without mercy according to the biblical saying: "By their fruits ye shall know them." It would have to be shown how we are having to pay the price for our contempt of proven principles in hunger on the one side and an alarmingly overheated boom on the other, in growing insecurity and shrinking profit margins, and not least in the race between the state's mounting tyranny and the piling up of economic and social calamities. It would have to be illustrated in detail where it has led us to smash one form of economic order, the market economy that rests on free price formation and has proved its worth, without being able to replace it with another economic order, that of collectivist compulsion. It would have to be demonstrated at length that the sensitive mechanism of prices and costs has been upset more and more, and that we are continuously creating conditions which paralyze men's voluntary effort. Taking one country after another, it would have to be proved that the economy's violation by an ambitious government leads to ever-new absurdities and to ever-new violations of the economy, which such a government then has the presumption to blame on the market economy and to take as an excuse for yet more violations. And we would have to draw the picture of a world in which wages and public expenditure seem to be mobile only upward and the rate of interest only downward, and we would have to point to the immense dangers of such a policy. But the warning is addressed to an age in which an alarmingly large number of people seem to have forgotten that the economy not only does not need the commands and punishments of

---

[1] Cf. my article "Offene und zurückgestaute Inflation" in Kyklos, Vol. I, No. 1 (1947), as well as my later article, in English, "Repressed Inflation," ibid. Vol. I, No. 3 (1947).

bureaucracy but is merely hampered and disturbed by them, and that bureaucracy itself eventually becomes the chain by which the Leviathan of the modern state shackles mankind.

INTEREST AS A PRICE

This is the broad setting in which we must test one of the favorite dogmas of the modern economic futurists. I have in mind their opinion, which really has become almost an article of faith, that everything must be done to keep the rate of interest as low as possible and thus to make a permanent fixture of what is known as cheap money policy. Seen in its true light, this modernistic dogma is tantamount to the demand that interest should cease to be an important instrument of monetary, credit, and counter-cyclical policy and thus of the control of the economic process. More than anything else, it was the influence of the late Lord Keynes that helped this revolutionary view of the nature and function of interest to win through and gain growing acceptance as a basis of practical policy. It was he who outdid all others in his advocacy not indeed of completely inactivating the lever of interest, but of blocking it in such a way that it serves only expansion, not containment.

This is, of course, one of the most difficult and most controversial questions in the whole of economics. We therefore have to limit ourselves to saying the essentials in the most concise form possible. We begin with an elementary statement. Interest is the price of a certain scarce good, namely, the use of capital. If it is, like any other price, to fulfill its function of ensuring the most rational allocation of a scarce good, it must accurately reflect the degree of capital scarcity at any given moment. If a government or a central bank, which nowadays is more or less the same thing, is asked to pursue a cheap money policy, this really means asking it to make the good concerned as inexpensive as possible. But this presupposes that this specific price (interest) is entirely at the discretion of government.

Just how strange this assumption is will be seen at once if we imagine the same clamor being raised for the government to adopt a "cheap butter policy." It is instructive to compare the two cases, because they clearly bring to light the peculiar quality of capital and interest. Leaving aside the fact that butter-producers are likely to put up a much stiffer defense against a cheapening of their product than the politically as-good-as-powerless producers of capital, that is, the savers, a policy of "cheap butter" appears ridiculous for the mere reason that it presupposes an appropriately abundant production of butter on the part of the government. If, therefore, interest is the price for the use of capital, and if the government promises a cheap money policy, this presupposes that the government can produce capital. Is it true?

REAL AND MONETARY FACTORS

It is. The government, or, in more general and better terms, the authority ruling the credit system in a modern economy, can in fact produce capital within certain limits and at the price of certain consequences, and that is the peculiarity of capital and interest that has to be grasped. In theoretically somewhat unpretentious terms, this can be expressed by saying that capital not only can be produced by the savers but also by the credit system, in other words, not only by individuals' curtailing their current consumption and putting the means of payment so released at the disposal of the capital market but also by supplying the capital market with means of payment created additionally (credit creation). Butter scarcity depends upon conditions determined by demand and supply; it is a "real" phenomenon. Scarcity of capital, as registered by the rate of interest, does not depend only upon the conditions determined by demand for capital and by saving, that is, by the willingness of individuals temporarily to forgo the consumption of real goods. Capital scarcity is at the same time influenced by the economy's largely arbitrary supply of money, which is the prime manifestation of capital. Capital and interest are not a "real" phenomenon, as classical theory maintains, nor are they a "monetary" phenomenon, as modernistic theory maintains. They are both simultaneously a real and a monetary phenomenon. The volume of capital and the level of interest depend both upon the "real" factors that are the concern of classical theory from Adam Smith to Böhm-Bawerk and upon the "monetary" factors of monetary and credit policy. The merit of having been the first to expose with full clarity this difficult double nature of capital and interest belongs to the Swedish economist Knut Wicksell. It is on his shoulders that rests the whole edifice of subsequent research, including the Keynesian school with its exaggerations and confusions.

The essential point for a correct understanding of the problem and for a sensible credit policy is to grasp that double aspect of capital and interest and to avoid exaggerations in either direction. It must not be overlooked that capital can be increased by credit creation and in certain circumstances should be so increased, nor, on the other hand, must it be overlooked that credit creation has its limits in the "real" factors of demand for credit and the volume of saving. Which particular circumstance merits most attention at any given moment depends upon whether the economy is moving more in the direction of deflation or more in that of inflation. In the first case, the right monetary and credit policy is one that does not feel unduly constrained by the real factors, in the second case, by contrast, one that accepts that constraint. From this follows an important consequence. While we shall be well advised to leave the butter market to the regulatory forces of free price formation, the capital market is the one point in our economic system that requires continuous control governed by definite principles. The reason is that capital is not only a "real" but also a "monetary" phenomenon. Nobody knew that better than the English liberals who a hundred years ago created the repeatedly proven foundations of all our thinking in questions of money and credit. The peculiarity of money is the reason for the absence, in its case, of the autonomous regulatory forces on which everywhere else, where "real" goods are concerned, we can on the average rely much more safely than on the wisdom of bureaucracy.

However, in correspondence with the double nature of capital and interest, this need for continuous and deliberate control works both ways. Too little control is to be avoided no less than too much, deflation no less than inflation. The Great Depression of the early 1930's was an unusual time when, in view of the plethora of unutilized factors of production, we were justified in almost forgetting for a time that there are limits to credit expansion. At that time it made sense to enlarge the volume of credit by every possible means and, among them, to put the greatest emphasis on a cheap money policy. It was what the situation urgently required. But there is no point today in still worrying about how to get out of the Great Depression of 1931-1933. However, that is precisely what those who think and talk in the terms formulated at that time by Keynes have been doing until recently, until they could no longer refuse to admit that the situation has changed radically. Today it is not merely meaningless, it is outright dangerous to pursue such a policy, because, in the belief of still having to fight the ghost of deflation, it leads straight into inflation. The danger is especially great in those countries where gigantic foreign loans combine with a generous wages policy to push up prices and costs in any case (United States, Sweden, and Switzerland).

INTEREST RATE AS A CONTROL INSTRUMENT

It has long been predictable that the situation after the war would be the exact opposite of that catastrophic depression which fifteen years earlier had given birth to the dogma of

cheap money policy as a permanent practice presumed beneficial.[2] The "real" factors (demand for capital on the one hand
and the formation of savings on the other) have long unmis-
takably pointed to a period of considerable capital scarcity,
when the rate of interest has a natural tendency to rise. If,
nevertheless, one insists on the doctrinaire policy of cheap
money and continues to hold the rate of interest down to ab-
normal levels, this can be done only with the help of a credit
expansion that at present, unlike the time of the Great Depression, does not have a salutary compensatory effect, but a
dangerous, inflationary one. There are only two cases in which
these effects can be avoided, either when the bureaucracy succeeds in curtailing the demand for capital by deliberate economic policy measures, or else when the formation of capital
by saving rises. Fifteen years ago it was right to stress the
monetary side of capital and permissible to neglect its real side.
Now the opposite is true. Now it must be pointed out that the
monetary increase of capital is brought up short by the real
factors. The question is no longer whether governments and
central banks decide, at their discretion, on a higher or a lower
rate of interest and in so doing weigh the advantages of a low
rate for debtors, especially for the state as the biggest among
them, against the disadvantages for creditors. The question
now is whether they can go on doing without the rate of interest as an instrument for controlling the economic process
and getting the better of the dangerous inflationary tendencies.

If there is one lesson to be drawn from today's situation, it
is that to refrain from using the rate of interest as an instrument leads to consequences that force governments to employ
increasingly bizarre means in their battle against inflationary
tendencies. They are means that encroach more and more up-

[2] *So that this should not seem as* vaticinium post eventum, *I refer the
reader to the beginning of my book* Internationale Ordnung, *which was
published early in 1945 (Eugen Rentsch, Erlenbach-Zurich).*

on what little freedom is left in the economy, and that threaten to become more and more reckless and indiscriminate without thereby gaining in efficacy. One of the characteristics of these means is that they keep on putting some new calamity in the place of an old one, and then take the latest calamity as an excuse for another odd form of intervention. As one watches this pulling this way and that way in all its abruptly changing phases, the expression "vaudeville of economic policy" comes to mind, and it does not seem to be too harsh.[3] The worst is that in the course of all this the economic order disintegrates and gives way to increasing anarchy. Everything is tried, except one thing: to pull the lever of interest sharply upward, as would previously have been done as a matter of course and as Wicksell only thirty years ago insisted in a famous article under the title "Up with Bank Rates."

The trouble is that, in view of the enormous public debt and of the flood of government stock in the credit system, it has become very hard to reverse course—a public debt, incidentally, which, as in the case of the United States, is largely a legacy of the time when it was thought that deficit spending could merrily go on forever. The first condition for reversing course is to understand that the Great Depression's formulas and dogmas—which Keynes seems to have had in mind when he contemptuously spoke of "modernistic stuff" in his posthumous article[4]—are now not merely inapplicable, but dangerous. The reader will be left, on this occasion, to draw his own conclusions in regard to monetary, credit, financial, and wages policy.

Most of the utopias and works of political fiction known to

---

[3] *The most blatant case is that of Sweden, where cheap money policy was largely responsible for plunging a prosperous economy, and one rich in capital, into a series of catastrophes and for solving in a jiffy the difficult problem of how to convert a "hard" currency into a "soft" one and how to create a balance-of-payments crisis.*

[4] Economic Journal, *June, 1946.*

us describe a strictly collectivist economy. Today, when so much of this has come true, they bore us, and we marvel at their naiveness. But who will write us a new "Retrospect from the Year 2000," in which one of our great-grandsons tells of a wonderful world in which all prices are free, and the government regulates only the discount rate, according to Wicksell's rules?

IX

Austerity*

THE INTERNATIONAL CRUSADE AGAINST LUXURY

Not long ago I wanted to buy a new briefcase in a shop in Copenhagen, because my old one was too worn, and I felt it was not a bad idea to buy good quality leather goods in a country famous for its cattle. The shop assistant said he was sorry, but he did not have what I wanted; all he could offer me was a rather dubious substitute, since articles made of genuine cowhide were not sold in Denmark. When I asked with some surprise what happened to all the Danish cowhides, I was told that certainly they were used for the manufacture of briefcases, but that these were a luxury which Denmark could not afford today. Hence they were all exported, and I would surely have no trouble at all buying the best Danish briefcases in Geneva.

Now, as an economist I ought to have known that to begin with. I should have been professionally familiar with the odd game that is being played at present in international trade, in which I had joined in my modest little way by vainly trying to buy a briefcase in Copenhagen. It is not a very new game, since it was fashionable centuries ago in the age of mercantilism. It can be described roughly as follows. Every country takes pride in manufacturing quality products of all kinds, which are not absolutely essential but which we rightly value. Everyone, the

* Neue Zürcher Zeitung, *March 21, 1948.*

rich and the poor, likes these so-called luxury goods and is prepared to work and to save in order to acquire them. But more and more governments take steps to withhold them to the extent possible from their own subjects—I rightly use the word—by exporting the country's home-produced luxury goods and not admitting any foreign ones. The end result of this international practice is that there are few countries left nowadays where the world's "luxury goods" can be bought freely or in reasonable quantities. They are not necessarily rich countries, such as the United States or Switzerland, but include also a country like Belgium, which was impoverished and ravaged by the war but, unlike other war-devastated countries, took the road of sound common sense and matter-of-fact hard work.

The reasons usually marshaled to justify this international crusade against luxury look quite plausible. Our country, it is said, is too poor to afford things that are not absolute essentials. Houses and wheat are more necessary than Swiss watches: thus runs this simple philosophy. People accept it all the more readily as—although the demagogues invariably fail to point it out—the good things of this world are in any case so rare that they can be enjoyed only by a minority against whom it is always easy to mobilize envy, suspicion, and self-righteous virtue. And thus nations can only too easily be persuaded not to contradict their governments openly when they do their best to export all the home-produced luxury goods and keep out those produced abroad.

A FEW BASIC MISCONCEPTIONS

All this sounds plausible enough, as I said. No doubt, therefore, many people will be surprised when they have to be told that this philosophy of "austerity" is all wrong. It rests on very insecure, logical arguments, and it leads to measures that are harmful and contradictory. Today's crusade against "luxury" is one of the strongest among the forces that deprive our civilization of its finest fruits, take the inner mainspring out of life, and pull the nations down more and more to the level of dreary drudgery and "controlled poverty." For this anti-luxury and big-brother philosophy is unfortunately one of the most effective means by which a bureaucracy suppresses everything, as during the decline of antiquity, and seeks to prove its indispensability and to extend its grip. Yet it is this very bureacracy that constitutes the real luxury that nations can no longer afford, but there are few who have the courage to say it.

Where is the fallacy? The first objection that comes to mind is that it is impossible to define objectively what is a luxury good. Swiss watches are today one of the chief victims of the international crusade against luxury. But who can maintain that first-class timepieces are a luxury in our age that owes so much to the correct measurement of time? Decisions of this kind are the thin end of the wedge for arbitrariness, and, of course, it is common knowledge to what extent the trade policy of governments is today based on arbitrariness.

But the real error lies deeper. It does not really matter whether the government calls something a luxury or not, so long as it is left to *us*, as adult human beings, to decide whether we can afford it or not. But it is precisely the presumption of modern collectivist bureaucracy that deprives us of this freedom of decision when it bars or restricts the import of certain products with the justification that "the nation" cannot afford this or that. The whole argument against importing "luxury goods" presupposes that bureaucracy knows better than the consumers what is good and useful for the latter, and that it therefore has to take strict measures to make sure that a particular quantity of wheat is imported rather than some other quantity of oranges, or a particular quantity of paper (in large part used by the bureaucracy itself) rather than a certain number of good quality shoes or watches. In other words, the government has the astonishing audacity to require of us that we should prefer its arbitrary list of priorities to our own. It

relies on people's not thinking about such things, simply forgetting that no hungry man or woman would rather have
coffee than groats or that consumers wanting new houses above
all other things are likely to put their money into dwellings
and not into automobiles. When we ask whether a country can
"afford" Swiss watches, fine textiles, refrigerators, or good
shoes, we are really asking something quite different. What we
are really asking is whether the demand for these products on
the part of the country's consumers as a whole is an expression
of their preference for these products rather than for others of
which the consumers already have enough, or which they regard as less essential. To put it differently: the fact that, in
response to the consumers' orders, private trade imports
oranges indicates that a broad class of people, who really ought
to know whether oranges are something they want, has come
to the conclusion that they can "afford" oranges. These peculiar people are called consumers, and it is for them that provi-
dence has caused this delicious fruit to ripen.

All this, I fear, may sound almost improper to persons who
specialized in what might be called social prudery. They will
wax indignant and inquire how we can claim to equate the
interests of the rich with those of the country as a whole, which
certainly is poor.

I am very sensitive to this reproach and hasten to repudiate
it as unjust. First of all, it has to be said that if the "luxury
goods" under discussion are to make any difference at all in the
national accounts, they cannot possibly be only goods of interest to the "rich." But this correction is not enough. It has
to be granted, of course, that in the case of a *very* unequal distribution of income, it is perfectly possible for some people to
go hungry in a country while others buy imported oranges.
But it is a common fallacy to believe that by prohibiting the
import of oranges or refrigerators we feed the hungry, clothe
the naked, or give shelter to the homeless. So long as the
government does not apply *internal* social measures that have
the effect of correcting the unequal distribution of income and

simply skims off the purchasing power standing ready to purchase luxury goods, so long is the prohibition of luxury imports a useless attempt to cure an illness by treating its symptoms. Instead of buying foreign luxury goods, people will now spend their money on home-produced ones. If a British consumer cannot buy a good Swiss watch that will last him for a lifetime, he will turn to, say, whisky, cigarettes, the dog races, or the movies. That this is actually happening is probably common knowledge. It is a fact that under the system of socialist consumer regimentation more money has been spent in Great Britain in recent years on drink, tobacco, and entertainment than ever before.

If restrictions on imports of luxury goods are supposed to force the nation into greater thrift, such a policy is bound to fail because it does not do away with the purchasing power available for the purchase of nonessentials, but merely diverts it into other and most often less desirable channels. To give a really elementary illustration: if a man wants to give his wife a watch for Christmas but is prevented by import restrictions from doing so, it is most unlikely that he will offer her a savings book instead. He will try to get hold of some other luxury article, with which both of them will be less happy. As far as the nation is concerned, the end result will be luxury expenditure in at least the same amount, but with less satisfaction and a less economic use of the national resources.

"BALANCE-OF-PAYMENTS CRISIS"

Up to this point the reader has no doubt followed us readily enough, but perhaps he will think that the real problem has not yet been touched upon. Although import restrictions on luxury goods can hardly help a nation to a more economic use of its resources, is it not the chief merit of these restrictions that they lead to the conutry's scarce foreign exchange reserves being used as sensibly and economically as possible? This argument, I fear, appears self-evident and irrefutable today to most people, and yet it rests on incomplete and over-simplified conclusions. Any child can understand that if coffee imports are restricted there will be more foreign exchange available for wheat imports, or less exports will be needed for "squaring" the balance of payments. If economics were as simple as that, all the clever books that have been written in the last two hundred years about this problem of the "balance-of-payments crisis" could be pulped. The only trouble is that we have forgotten what is written in those books and what practical experience in these two centuries should have taught us. A little more knowledge of these relationships is needed to understand that mere import restrictions can do just as little to cure a "balance-of-payments crisis" as bloodletting can do for a serious internal disease. To explain this, we will confine ourselves to the following three points.

1. At the time of the great German inflation, economists in Germany talked with justified scorn of the "God-given balance-of-payments deficit." A so-called balance-of-payments crisis is, in fact, not an isolated accident that suddenly befalls a country's international economic relations, but, as is at long last being rediscovered today, it is the result of an imbalance in the economy as a whole. It is the external expression of the economic overstrain from which a country suffers, because the simultaneous claims of consumption and investment on productive capacity are too high. This excess of claims is identical with inflationary pressure, which tends to drive up all prices and, hence, also the price of foreign money (the foreign exchange rates). If the government neither prevents this inflationary excess of claims nor allows the price rise to re-establish equilibrium at a higher level, that is, if the government's policy is one of "repressed inflation," as we call it, the balance of payments, in its turn, will be subject to heavy strains and *in these circumstances* (inflationary excess of purchasing power without a new price equilibrium at a higher level) will display the well-known symptom of a scarcity, especially of those for-

eign currencies that are not as yet subject to the same manipulation ("hard" currencies). The cause of the "balance-of-payments crisis," therefore, is an excess of claims on national output, an inflationary excess for which the government, and it alone, is responsible. The right treatment for the "crisis" is not to restrict imports, but to cut down on the government program that is responsible for the excess, or else to let foreign exchange rates rise until they fulfill the inherent function of all prices, namely, to balance supply and demand. This is the only effective method, but modern bureaucratic governments like it the least, because it diminishes their bureaucratic establishment and their power.

2. Import restrictions have repercussions that the more ingenuous of their advocates are apt to overlook. The most immediate and important repercussions are felt by exports. Reciprocity is of the essence in trade, and any restriction of imports must sooner or later lead to a fall in exports. This applies to all kinds of goods, essential and inessential alike. When the British government prevents Englishmen from buying a Swiss watch or going to the Alps for a holiday, this measure tends to prevent certain Swiss from ordering a suit of English cloth. This repercussion on exports is instantaneous nowadays in the case of economic relations between soft-currency countries with bilateral economic agreements. In the case of a hard-currency country like Switzerland, the repercussion takes a more roundabout way. But it most certainly will take place eventually. Many governments seem to think that they can go on indefinitely acquiring Swiss francs or gold by free exports to Switzerland, while at the same time keeping out a large part of Swiss export goods under the pretext that they are "luxury articles." But obviously such a hard-currency country must finally get into a position where it is forced in self-defense to curb imports in its turn, so long as the other countries carry on with their practice. This would mean great hardship for the export industries of such a country, which depends so largely on the export of high-quality goods, and it

will be worth remembering at that time that the country owes its plight to an ideology dear to the hearts of collectivists and to the import practices of governments that are keeping out "luxury goods" on principle, as an essential ingredient of their socialist program. It is the height of fatuity to talk of the "chaos of capitalist crisis" in connection with possible difficulties for the Swiss watch industry, as a social democratic paper recently did with hardly veiled glee.

3. There are yet other and highly important repercussions which leave scant grounds for hoping that compulsory import restrictions can overcome a "balance-of-payments crisis." Most of the war-devastated countries of Europe are basing their reconstruction on the simple idea that, with the help of a gigantic and comprehensive control apparatus, imports are to be compressed to a minimum, while everything that, in the government's view, the nation can do without should be exported. The idea is that this is the way to reconstitute the country's real capital as fast as possible. This is the philosophy of "austerity" with which we are concerned here, and we have already mentioned two reasons for its likely failure. Import restrictions and export promotion do not necessarily imply a corresponding net saving on the part of the economy as a whole. Unless the controls are turned into a truly collectivist and total tyranny, which among other things completely abolishes freedom of consumption and work, they will not achieve their purpose. It has to be remembered, furthermore, that the reconstitution of the nation's real capital depends not only upon what part of a given total product is absorbed by immediate consumption and what part allocated to investment, but it also depends just as much upon the size of the total product. Nothing could be more pointless than a policy that prevents people from buying what they want and at the same time paralyzes their willingness to work, their initiative, and their inclination to save, which cannot thrive except in an atmosphere of freedom, confidence, and optimism. This is precisely the

effect of all these European systems of officially dictated "austerity."

There seems to be a growing awareness today that the countries that put their trust in this all-too-simple reckoning of rigorous import restrictions and artificial export expansion have not been well advised. Why should anyone work hard when his earnings will not buy anything more than the bare necessities and when, therefore, he cannot see what good it will do him to save? This is the sort of reasoning that people are bound to adopt, and quite understandably so. The result is that the country continuously loses on the production account what it may temporarily gain on the foreign trade account. There are, indeed, good reasons for assuming that in the long run the losses on the one account outrun the gains on the other. Except in wartime, when people, too, are in a state of emergency, all efforts to raise output by moral appeals, posters, decorations, or propaganda plays will yield disappointing results. The spectacle of a government conducting a useless publicity campaign for more work or more saving is enough to characterize the country concerned as one in which collectivist economic policy turns the nature of things inside out. Posters like "Work or Want," or "Save more—Buy less" are warning signals indicating that the country's economic government is fundamentally wrong. The healthiest and most effective incentive for working as much as feasible is to give people a chance to buy good things or to go abroad on a holiday when they work hard. And it is only when people know that their money will buy something good, not only today but also later, that they will save.

THE LIMITS OF FORCED CAPITAL FORMATION

Among the war-devastated countries of Europe, Belgium stands out as a country that followed the line of sound common sense and, instead of indulging in fashionable "austerity" and pursuing the will-o'-the-wisp of forced capital formation on a gigantic scale, opened its frontiers to consumer goods and thus gave people the necessary incentive to work. It seems that the country did not have cause to regret its decision. Clearly, the Belgians recognized the great danger of forced investment's creating an inflationary pressure at a time when the warehouses were empty of consumer goods. This is, incidentally, a point most meritoriously underscored in the so-called Harriman Report of November 8, 1947, in which distinguished U. S. economists reported to President Truman on the economic problems of the Marshall Plan. It is stated in this report that many European countries had overextended themselves with their collectivist investment programs and, in spite of their dearth of consumer goods, were aiming at a rate of accumulation far higher even than in the United States. The fully justified advice to these countries is to cut back sharply on their construction and modernization programs until the European economic recovery has made more progress.

But other views still prevail; witness the minister of a Western European country who, last fall, wished to convince another visiting American commission of the soundness of his country's economy and as the most conclusive evidence conducted the visitors from one building site to the next. More than that, his tactics succeeded. All of us are inclined to think that where something is being built, something useful is being done. But there is no particular merit in building as such; everything depends on whether it fits harmoniously into the economy as a whole. And in this respect the determining factors are, first, whether the total volume of building at a given moment is correct, and, second, whether within this setting the right things are being built. The fact that a country is busy building proves neither the one nor the other, if the country concerned is a collectivist one, where decisions regarding both the total volume of investment and its nature are taken without reference to the consumers. The consumers, of course, are just the people who are not asked what they want, which is no doubt why some collectivists, who have now lost some of their fashionable appeal, with involuntary humor still call such an economic system a "want-satisfaction" economy. The distinguishing feature of such an economy is that consumption can be compressed very much by controls to the benefit of investment, and it is a further distinguishing feature of collectivist systems throughout history that they have always taken advantage of this possibility and always tend toward a combination of maximum investment with minimum consumption. Their rationale is "austerity," but just as in the past the *bon plaisir du prince* was eventually hedged in by limitation, so it is becoming obvious today that collectivist-forced capital formation is not all plain sailing. Its limitations are clearly visible today, and they mean that ambitious government programs, drawn up without consideration for natural human reactions, must be cut back.

"Austerity" is bad economics and a false calculation, because it works against people's willingness to work and to save, both so necessary today. But then, this glum philosophy is tailor-made for all planners, collectivists, and "commissars." It gives them an occupation, power, and importance. It lends their speeches the dignified accents of unworldly asceticism and patriotic concern and supplies them with an opportunity to make the consumer the scapegoat for their misconceived economic policies. We may say in all seriousness that they seem to have taken the habit of considering the consumer as someone who gets in the way and causes trouble, but whom, unfortunately, no one has yet managed to abolish. In their eyes it is sheer impudence for the consumer to wish to spend the money he has earned on buying something he wants, and it is improper of him to demand "luxury goods." He is curtly put in his place, and an attempt is made to intimidate him with economic sophisms. It is certainly not going too far to say that the mentality today prevalent throughout the world is well described in these terms, with the sarcasm it deserves.

When people can no longer buy the "luxury goods" they would like to have, they prefer to buy the luxury good called leisure and to work less. But this, of course, is the one luxury good which really does the most serious harm today to the countries of Europe.

X

The Formation and Use of Capital*

TRANSFORMATIONS IN THE ECONOMIC SYSTEM

On looking back over the course of the Western world's economy since the war, we find growing evidence of a change of outstanding importance. Nearly everywhere, not altogether excluding even Switzerland and the United States, profound transformations have taken place in the ways of capital formation and in the manner of its use, and this has led to one of the most serious upheavals in the economic system. We can hardly refuse to admit, at this stage, that what has come to pass in the sphere of capital formation and investment is one of the principal causes of today's grave economic disturbances. In these circumstances, it seems opportune to try to discuss the essentials of these processes and their consequences.

The crucial point is that in nearly all economies capital has increasingly come to be formed and used by methods very different from those that until ten years ago were regarded as normal for an essentially free economy. These new methods have imparted a more and more collectivist aspect to this part of the economic process, which we call the capital sector. To put it briefly: Everywhere, a diminishing proportion of investable funds, and in certain leading countries only a small fraction of them, has been drawn from the traditional source

* Neue Zürcher Zeitung, *October 17 and 18, 1952.*

of voluntary savings out of current income, and the decision regarding the total volume and the direction of investment has largely become a matter of government planning. The formation and use of capital have thus been increasingly withdrawn from the systematic context of the market economy even where the latter has in other respects been allowed to survive or, as in Germany, has been re-established by a radical reform. The consequences are plainly visible today in the capital sector's being out of tune with the economy and the economic order as a whole, to a degree that in some countries has led to the gravest disturbances. On close inspection, mismanagement in the capital sector will be seen to be the chief trouble with postwar economic developments. The problem it poses for economic policy in all countries must be counted among the most important and difficult of all. Its solution cannot be long delayed if governments are in earnest about re-establishing an efficient economic order and putting a stop to the present crisis, the most visible expressions of which are permanent inflation and balance-of-payments deficits, instead of muddling through with the help of one expedient after another. These may seem rather bold statements not comprehensible at first sight; they need to be justified and explained.

In speaking of mismanagement in the capital sector as a mark of postwar economy in many countries, I have in mind two things: an excess of investment in the national budget and an economically faulty choice of individual investment projects. Characteristically, both types of mismanagement tend to coincide, since excess investment presupposes the same collectivist and inflationary economic setting, that is, the same disturbance of the free forces of the market economy, which is responsible also for the faulty distribution of the excessive volume of capital.

Now, the statement that excess investment is one form of mismanagement in a nation's capital account may need some explanation. Not everyone may understand at first sight how anything done in this respect could possibly have been too much after the terrible destruction of the last war. What about the proud and impressive testimony of postwar reconstruction and the figures of investment statistics? Is this not an achievement hard to fault? These are natural enough questions. Clearly, we shall have to settle exactly what is to be understood by an "excess" of investment. The clearest way of putting it, perhaps, is to say that all this investment would indeed be an achievement deserving of unqualified praise if, apart from Marshall aid, it had been financed by genuine savings.

There are two reasons, on that assumption, that this investment would be above suspicion as a serious source of disturbance. First, it would have been compensated by a corresponding reduction of consumption, and second, this offsetting reduction of consumption would have been voluntary and hence not associated with any compulsion disturbing the economic process. The first circumstance would have ensured that investment, compensated by a corresponding reduction of consumption, would not have overstrained the economy and thus led to the well-known consequences of inflationary pressure and balance-of-payments difficulties. And the second advantage of this kind of coverage of investment expenditure would have been that a voluntary, as against a government-imposed, reduction of consumption would have found its own place in the system of the market economy's regulatory and functional forces, instead of leading to today's equally well-known fiscal burden of compulsory public saving, with all its implications.

That this is a completely unrealistic assumption is something I need not be lectured about. Of course, there was not the remotest chance, even in the best possible conditions, of covering the extraordinary amount of postwar investment in Europe by genuine savings. I am ready to concede even more. There are good arguments for supporting the view that part of this investment was so urgent that, given the insufficiency both of the nations' genuine capital formation and of American aid for covering it, it was probably inevitable that they would fall back on methods exempting investment from the usual requirement of genuine saving, in spite of the perils involved. Be that as it may, the point at issue here is that such exemption cannot be granted with impunity, that it has serious consequences not to be overlooked, that these consequences can be described as "excess" investment, and that they are such that, whatever may in the past have recommended these methods, they should now be abandoned. It is time now to remember the limit imposed upon investment in our continent in its present state by the extent of its own genuine saving, except insofar as foreign capital aid can be counted upon. My purpose is to affix a warning at this boundary that has been transgressed so recklessly and with so much disregard of the danger involved.

With the purpose thus clarified, let us proceed. In many European countries postwar investment, however urgent and desirable it may have been, can be described as "excessive" to the extent that it was made possible by methods of capital formation that transgressed the limits of genuine saving and therefore amounted to a violation of the economy, to a strain on its strength, and to a disturbance of its system of regulatory and functional forces. The statistics of major European countries do, in fact, show that, disregarding American capital aid, the share of individual savings in investment coverage has shrunk to very modest proportions in comparison with what it used to be and has, indeed, become almost insignificant. Today's three leading sources of capital formation are credit creation, fiscal-forced saving, and self-financing out of corporation profits. There will be more to say presently about the revolution this has meant for present-day capital formation. Leaving aside for the moment the question of self-financing and its special problems, and concentrating on the extraordinary part played by credit creation and taxation as a means of forced capital formation, it ought to be clear now what they mean as methods of boosting investment, and why the volume of investment resulting from them is to be regarded as dangerously "excessive."

Insofar as investment has been financed by credit creation, this is a process identical with the well-known expansionary "cheap money" and "full employment" policies that are now coming in for increasingly sharp and unanimous criticism. Still fatally obsessed with the ideas stubbornly surviving from the Great Depression, many of the Western countries treated their current troubles as though they were due, as they were then, to a deflationary interruption in the circular flow and thought that in leaving so much of the function of financing investment to the additional liquidity pumped into the banking system by the central bank, they were merely closing the gap in the circular flow, and thus serving full employment without fear of inflation. Nor is this all. Following the dogmatic rut of ideas begotten by the Great Depression and, at best, appropriate to it, large-scale investment without prior saving, that is, without a corresponding reduction of consumption, was not only considered worth risking, or, indeed, required for the sake of economic equilibrium, but, beyond that, governments took it upon themselves even to raise mass consumption to a further considerable extent by means of a suitable social and wages policy.

And thus the policy of overinvesting has become one of the principal causes of the process fittingly described as "permanent inflationary pressure," the consequences of which need not be discussed again here. The reason that the volume of investment originating in credit expansion is to be qualified as excessive is that the resulting sum of investment and consumption exceeds the economy's production capacity at current prices and hence finds expression, domestically, in an inflationary rise of prices and, externally, in a balance-of-payments deficit. What this excess signifies is that money is spent twice over, and that the country spends on mass consumption and on investment more than is covered by goods. The simple truth has had to be learned again—a country not only can live beyond its means but also build beyond its means, electrify railways, renew machinery, and modernize factories beyond its means. In more than a few European countries it became possible after the war to point to a newly built power plant, to a new model railway station, or to the new cable standards of a railway line about to be electrified and to say: Here is your balance-of-payments deficit and your dollar shortage.

THE SOCIALIZATION OF CAPITAL FORMATION

Today there must be few people to whom it is still necessary to explain that the policy of permanent inflationary pressure is dangerous and that, by virtue of simultaneous efforts to raise mass consumption, it has become a very serious mistake. It is this inflationary pressure that is the main source of all the postwar economic disturbances on the national and international scale. Even though it may be assumed that this is at long last generally understood and admitted, this knowledge has unfortunately come so late that it has become all the more difficult to go into reverse—witness Great Britain's agonizingly slow recovery.

The other of the two methods of artificial investment expansion, forced capital formation through taxation, seems to come off a good deal better in this respect. By taxing away purchasing power and using it for investment, the government achieves a simultaneous reduction of consumption. This method of capital formation, which in 1951 contributed only a little less than half the total in Great Britain but is now so important, therefore has the merit of avoiding inflationary pressure with all its consequences.

But the government is not thereby absolved from the reproach of abuse and over-straining the economy. On the contrary, it may be argued that the immoderate growth of the share of capital formation and investment resting on fiscal compulsion is one of the main causes of a revolutionary transformation no less dangerous and no less far-reaching than that due to permanent inflationary pressure and, for reasons that need no further explanation in this context, closely connected with it. The transformation I have in mind is that everywhere the proportion of national income claimed and administered by the state directly or indirectly (through the social services) has even after the war remained at a level that, quite apart from its revolutionary social effects, is in the long run incompatible with the system of regulatory and functional forces that is the condition of the Western countries' free economy and society. Fiscal socialism, as this erosion of the market economy by the budget may be called, and inflationary pressure for the sake of "full employment" (maximum investment and simultaneous maximum consumption by the masses) are the two contemporary developments that share the common effect of undermining our economic and social system in a manner as fatal as it is insidious, because it is creeping and not easy to diagnose. But they are seen to share also a common cause, which is an excess of investment dissociated from the solid foundation of normal capital formation.

There is only one fitting conclusion to be drawn from all these considerations. The true source of the trouble is the disproportion between the volumes of investment and saving in the economy. But, fatefully, deficient saving, in its turn, is, to no small extent, the very consequence of this whole system of forced capital formation resting on the devaluation of money, unduly heavy taxation, destruction of wealth, the impairment and blunting of the incentives to produce and save, the curtailment of capital returns, and an overall policy undermining long-run confidence. Once more, we are moving in a circle: the attempt to make good the shortfall of genuine savings by inflationary credit creation not only generates economic consequences so grave that this policy has to be abandoned but at the same time is one of the main causes for the insufficiency of saving. Does anyone still need to be told that this vicious circle has to be broken through at last?

What all this amounts to is that we have finally come to un-

derstand how dangerous are the ways taken by capital formation and how threatening to the foundations of our economy
and society. Genuine saving in all its forms, not least in that
of equity investment that is so stunted today in most countries,
must be restored to the preeminent position from which,
through misunderstanding its function, we have shortsightedly
allowed it to be displaced during the last twenty years. This
can only be done by a radical reform of the system as a whole
with all its now typical collectivist and inflationary aspects and
its overemphasis on fiscal methods. After the rush of socialization in capital formation, the time has come to acknowledge
that it has consequences that no reasonable person can gloss
over, and that are such as to make it imperative to retrans-
form socialization into individualization, thereby reinserting
this decisively important process into the overall system of an
efficient economic order. No one with even the slightest understanding will need more than a hint that what is at stake
is, in fact, more than the economic order as such; it is the whole
foundation of a free society.

In this light, the task is seen to be of such momentous importance that it must be considered as cardinal to the whole of
our economic and social policy. We are at one of the great
crossroads, where decisions of almost incalculable implications
have to be made. It is here that we must make our stand if we
are to succeed in stemming the sinister, trampling march of
a proletarianized mass society with its mechanized, compulsory
social welfare system and its ultimately inevitable goal of a
totalitarian mammoth state. This demands, above all else, that
the center of gravity in the responsibility for people's lives
should be shifted from the state back to where it belongs by
all standards of common sense and historical experience—
to the individual surrounded by his family, to free organi-
zations, to the broad masses of the people themselves.

However much corporative capital formation, which is
known as self-financing, may have gained in importance, it is
no satisfactory substitute for the shortfall in personal capital

formation from income. If a horrible neologism may be permitted, I would say that in the overall and long view the "corporatization" of capital formation in its present dimensions is only fractionally better and less dangerous than its socialization. To be sure, it was irreplaceable as a help to rapid postwar reconstruction in many countries, but here again it must be realized that this was only an expedient, whereas considerations of many kinds, which cannot be further discussed here, compel us to regard a lasting shift from personal to corporate capital formation as a degenerative process that can hardly be taken too seriously.

To return to our original theme, mismanagement in the capital sector, we recall that it takes two forms. Having discussed excess investment in the relative sense defined, it remains to add a few remarks on the second form of mismanagement, the economically faulty choice of investment projects. In addition to allowing a disproportion to arise after the war between the total volume of investment and the national budget, Europe committed a second sin; having violated the economy as described above, and thereby having additional investment opportunities alongside those opened up by Marshall aid, many countries used these opportunities in a manner that cannot be described otherwise than economically wrong. The economies were overstrained by excess investment, but, directed to wrong purposes as it was, this overexertion led neither to the hoped-for cure of the economy nor to its balanced progress, but left behind it tensions and distortions of all kinds.

Two problems were involved in restoring order to the economy, namely, the proper readjustment both of the total volume of investment and of its use in individual cases. Neither has been solved satisfactorily. There should be no disagreement nowadays with the view that what is responsible in both cases is the attempt to solve the problem of economic adjustment by methods that, being both collectivist and inflationary, invalidate the economy's own steering mechanism. It is not

hard to prove that in all cases of patent misinvestment interference by economic planning and an inflationary distortion
of value relations had prevented this steering mechanism from
functioning properly.

Every well-informed person knows the concrete cases to
which this applies. Strictly speaking, two separate things are
involved: misallocation as regards the share of individual
branches of industry, and misallocation as regards the amortization period of capital investment, or, so to speak, errors
"in breadth" and "in depth." A well-known example of the
first type of misallocation is the deficiency of investment in
German heavy industry as a result of its not having been
included until recently in the reforms re-establishing the
market economy in Germany and, in addition, of its legal
structure's and economic reputation's having been severely
undermined by all sorts of interference. Instead of taking
timely steps to remove the main cause of this maladjustment,
that is, the controls that distorted iron and coal prices, a device
was thought up that is truly worthy of our age, namely, to
raise capital for heavy industry by a compulsory loan exacted
from those sections of German industry to which the free
market had restored economic health, and then to pump in
that "investment help" under political pressure—via Parliament, government departments, and the official confedera-
tion—instead of through the market. This pumping method
took so long to prepare that in the meantime the original conditions had altered considerably.

What is meant by misallocation "in depth" is illustrated by
the example of all those countries that committed the error
of orienting their investment programs too much toward long-
term projects, that, while seductive to the constructive imagination of the planners, sacrificed the hard enough present to a
distant future and disregarded the principle that at a time of
extraordinary capital shortage, the right investment to choose
is one that yields quick returns and has a short amortization
period. Neglecting projects close to the consumption stage,

investment was directed to those remote from consumption. Now that Marshall aid, the main source of those investment funds, has dried up, the resulting disproportions are coming to light, most strikingly in France with its much praised but, in this sense, badly misplanned Monnet Plan, as well as in Austria.

Notwithstanding these experiences with planning methods in the allocation of investment capital, the view is still widely held that ours is a time when not only the volume but also the type and direction of investment should be determined no longer by the market and its regulators—namely, free prices, a rate of interest truly reflecting the market's supply, and demand schedules and capital returns conditioned by competition—but, instead, by government planning and the state's fiat. It is perhaps with reference to this particular problem of the economic order that faith in planning, which otherwise is now so badly shaken, has survived longest in many European countries. Unfortunately, it was not the least of the numerous and serious errors of the whole system of Marshall aid that it gave almost dogmatic force to the belief in the necessity of the planned guidance of capital use. The time is now ripe for an impartial reappraisal of that phase in European reconstruction, and in such a reappraisal this constructional defect of Marshall aid will come in for extensive criticism, all the more so as its aftereffects are still with us and cannot be masked even by uncritical production statistics.

If we look at the principle of the matter and ask what forces are to be entrusted with responsibility for the use of capital and the alignment of investment with the economic order as a whole, we find that, as in other spheres, we have a choice only between the market method and the collectivist one. Since the latter method has come to predominate in so many countries, and not only capital formation, but also the use of capital has been socialized to a large extent, it is time to point out the significance of the resulting transformation: without detriment to such concessions as are unavoidable, it is one that, in the long run, is not compatible either with an orderly economy or a free society. Experience should help us to see through all the assurances to the effect that only government planning and official orders can take care of the selection of national investment priorities and avoid wasting scarce capital on less urgent projects; experience should also help us to recognize that all these assurances can obscure neither the absence of objective standards of priority nor the danger of decisions that, in the last resort, are arbitrary and hence lead to misinvestment. Only a doctrinaire can still refuse to admit that socialization of capital use is one of the things to be viewed with increasingly grave concern and that investment guidance by the market, through free prices, unmanipulated rates of interest, competitive returns, and well-organized captial markets must be restored to its due position, a position that planning methods wrongfully contested with unfulfilled promises.

XI

Keynes and the Revolution in Economics: Economics Old, New, and True*

With the possible exception of Protestant theology, there is hardly a branch of learning today that, like economics, is split into two almost irreconcilable camps with almost no dialogue passing between them any more. This split has its origin in an exceedingly bold revolution in economic thought dating back fifteen years and, perhaps by an unjust simplification, associated with the name of the late Lord Keynes, who died in 1946.

THE REVOLUTION IN ECONOMICS

Radical rethinking is not alien to other disciplines. To take theoretical physics as an example, we all know how far quantum mechanics and the theory of relativity have deflected that science from Newton's classical tradition. But this revolution in the physical concept of the universe has not created a rift between the "old" and the "new" schools. As and when the new theories asserted themselves by irrefutable proof or empirical probability, they became the common property of science, and there was no sound of venomous dispute, all the less so as the practical applications of physics in everyday life were not affected by this palace revolution in theory. The revolution in economics, on the other hand, has so far essentially

---

* Universitas, *December, 1952, pp. 1285–1295.*

done nothing but shock and divide. It originated in a theory that combines provocative radicalism with far from fully convincing argumentation, with a precision that proves to be apparent rather than real and throws up problems of the most confusing kind. Furthermore, thanks to its influence on actual economic policy in our time, it has become a force that has a decisive bearing on the life and interests of every individual, indeed of whole nations and classes and, with the mere term "full employment," has furnished both one of the most seductive and one of the most dangerous slogans to the political life of the mid-twentieth century. As a result, economics is today split into two camps apparently without prospect of reconciliation, and it would be hard to find a parallel to this split in the whole history of the science.

HEALING THE RIFT

The adherents of the Keynesian School, or of the "new economics," as it is widely called, are, like all revolutionary leaders, inclined to regard the victory of their doctrine as complete. The idea of so serious and genuine a rift offends their sense of domination. But if the rift is to he healed—and to do so is a task that is gaining in urgency but perhaps steadily losing in difficulty—the first step must be to acknowledge its existence and full implications.

It is probably still not generally realized just how deep is the rift and how critical, therefore, the inner predicament of economics. One of the most distinguished of contemporary economists, whom I met again recently after many years, said to me that he was not prepared to enter into a discussion of the last ten years' literature, which, because it was essentially inspired by Keynes, he regarded as useless, not worth reading, and stultifying, and I frankly confess that while I would not make this temperamental judgment my own, I would far sooner see him in charge of a central bank or an economic government department than any of the authors of the literature he condemns. As eminent a mind as Professor F. H. Knight, of Chicago, not long ago described the "new economics" of Keynesian origin as the worst of the fashion crazes that from time to time afflict our science and as a return to the dark Middle Ages, and Schumpeter, to name another master, remained to his dying day in hardly less vehement opposition, no matter how politely elegant the style in which he couched it.

RIGID FRONTS

The revolutionaries' answer to these legitimists of economics is vehement self-assertion and barely veiled contempt, such as are habitual to the "enlightened" in dealing with those who remain in the dark. They seem to regard themselves as all the more superior in that they can point with obvious pride to the difficulty of their literature and to the use of mathematics, which lifts the "new economics" almost to the lofty heights of physics. A leading Keynesian in the United States, to give an example, recently dismissed one of Hayek's books with the contemptuous remark that there was no breath of the "new economics" in it and that the author had thus behaved like an astronomer who failed to take account of the Copernican revolution. The columns of this very publication were recently the scene of the tragi-comic spectacle of a reviewer's (V. Muthesius) thinking he was lavishing special praise upon an English book by stating with relief that the author had not fallen victim to the Keynesian School, which remark, in turn, called forth the protests of adherents of the "new economics," who clearly felt the object of the reviewer's praise needed to be defended against such an insult. They seemed anxious to counter any impression that there might be a dissenter among England's ranking economists by suggesting that, at any rate in that country, the "new economics" had permeated everywhere—not reflecting, perhaps, that if the theory's domination really were as absolute as all that, the chronic crisis of the British economy is not much of a recommendation for it. Conversely, if the Germans compare the economic developments of their beaten country with those of the victor's, they have reason to note with some satisfaction that at any rate they victoriously withstood the onslaught of the Keynesians.

But enough of this description of a conflict and opinions and theories that is so sharp that one cannot but agree with Professor J. M. Clark, of Columbia, when he declares that the Keynesian revolution has split economics into two spheres of logic, where the sense of one is nonsense in the other. It can easily be imagined what disastrous consequences this disintegration of traditional economic theory has had for economic policy in practice. The remarkable advances of economics, in research, organization, and external influence alike cannot obscure the cracks that have appeared in its foundations and that certainly signify an extremely serious retrogression in comparison with the "old economics." ...* There can surely be no doubt that the disintegrating and confusing influence of the "new economics" must be taken into account by anyone wishing to gain a serious and unbiased understanding of the agonizing economic history of the last ten years, with its "repressed inflation," its *ad hoc* experiments, and the Sisyphus labor of international reconstruction failing over and over again.

EXPEDIENT INTO DOGMA

This is a depressing state of affairs, a clear view of which is continually obstructed by the fact that it is not easy to say just what is the essence of Keynesian economics and what constitutes the revolution it brought about. What did Keynes want,

* *There follow a few lines of quotation from Professor Sir Roy Harrod, the source of which is not identified and the original text of which cannot now be traced, even by their author.—Ed.*

and what have his disciples—typically overzealous like all adepts—learned from him?

To put it in a nutshell and, hence, inevitably in simplified terms: Quite rightly, the Great Depression of the 1930's had appeared to Keynes as a gigantic circulatory disturbance marked by a series of deficiencies of income and demand, which, regardless of their original cause, kept entailing others; he considered it as basically due to a breakdown in the mechanism that should ensure that the decision of some individuals to save, and thereby forgo spending their income, finds its normal compensation in the decision of others to invest. Whereas the "old economics" had focused attention on the ordering and guiding mechanism of the system of individual prices and wages and had viewed the economic process mainly as one of continuous readjustment of production and of redistribution of factors of production in response to this guiding mechanism, the world was now faced with a situation that could not be interpreted in terms of that theory. It was a disturbance to be explained no longer as the result of wrong prices or wages, as an expression of a wrong distribution of factors of production; rather, it was to be explained only as a disproportion between the economic aggregates of the circular flow (saving and investment, income and expenditure, decline and renewed creation of purchasing power), and the cure lay in removing that disproportion. In other words, it was a case where a deficiency of "effective demand" was the true cause of mass unemployment and as such had to be removed by a policy that, in bold reversal of sound economic thought, put the main emphasis on "spending," on boosting "effective demand," and, in taking this course, on neither being frightened by the danger of inflation nor waiting for prior savings.

Had Keynes stopped there, he would have done no more than the rest of us, who at that time advised a policy beginning with the "spending" end. He would have secured for himself only a modest little nook in the Valhalla of economics, but, on the other hand, no one could have said of him that he did more harm than good. But the crucial point is that he did not stop at calling for extraordinary means in an extraordinary situation. He went much further. He declared the method of thinking in aggregates to be the only valid one, now and in the long run. And together with the method, he elaborated its results—his diagnosis of an extraordinary situation and the treatment accordingly prescribed—into a general theory in which "deficiency of demand" is always around the corner, and economic policy must always be poised to close this "gap" in order to ensure eternal "full employment." It is only with this that he really brought into economic thought a revolution that thrusts aside the previously ruling method and puts an opposite one in its place, literally standing on its head most of what theory and sound common sense have so far considered right and proven. That is the calamity, and that is the reason that the adherents of the "old economics" cannot be reconciled with those of the "new economics" so long as this torrent of exuberant destruction has not been forced back into its bed.

A BIASED APPROACH

This is not the place to demonstrate in detail why, for all its seductive brilliance and elegance, the chain of thought that led Keynes to these bold conclusions does not hold. Our main concern on this occasion is with the result of this revolution for economic theory and policy. A whole generation of economists (especially in the Anglo-Saxon countries, but likewise wherever else it is thought important to be in the swim) was so one-sidedly brought up to operate with economic aggregates that it forgot the things that until then were the real content of economic theory and that never should be forgotten: namely, that the economic order is a system of moving, and moved, prices, wages, interests, and other magnitudes. Keynes's aggregative functions made the plain mechanism of prices look outdated and uninteresting, and we witnessed the development of a sort of economic engineering with a proliferation of mathematical equations.

This new method was one part of the training of the new generation of economists and economic policy makers; another was the idea that saving is, at best, unnecessary (since investment takes care of saving afterward *via* the multiplier and the marginal propensity to save) and, at worst, harmful. It follows that a policy measure is good when it increases effective demand and bad when it threatens to diminish effective demand.

THE DANGER OF INFLATION UNDERESTIMATED

The danger of inflation was reduced to a remote theoretical possibility; the thing to be feared constantly was what was described as deflation. Budgetary deficits, leveling taxes that diminish both the ability and the willingness to save, "cheap money policy," a combination of growing popular consumption and investment stimulation, expenditure and credits on all sides, mercantilist foreign-trade policies with the twin purposes of mitigating the effects of those other policies on the balance of trade and of creating export surpluses as a further stimulant for the domestic money flow—all of these practices now received the blessing of economic science.

NOT WITH IMPUNITY . . .

Years ago, in an obituary of Keynes in the *Neue Zürcher Zeitung,* I wrote that while it is legitimate to think that there exist times when a resolute increase in the money supply averts trouble, it is not with impunity that a man of outstanding intelligence may give the blessing of his authority to the inflationary inclinations of government, which are strong

enough as it is. It is legitimate to think that in certain circumstances the growth of the public debt is the lesser evil, but not
with impunity may this be turned into a maxim. It may happen that mass unemployment cannot be quickly removed by
any means other than an increase in effective demand by means
of credit expansion, but not with impunity may the proven
rules and institutions be flouted with barely veiled contempt,
lest, without these long-run guardians of an orderly economic
process, the economy become subject to permanent inflationary pressure. There may be some previously overlooked problem to discover in the process of saving, but not with impunity
may people be deprived of the feeling that they are doing the
right thing by saving and setting aside from their income a
reserve for themselves and their children instead of spending
as long as the money lasts, and then, when there is none left,
relying on help from the state, which is accumulating debt
upon debt. Just as a ship in distress may have to cut away its
masts and jettison its cargo, so there may be hurricanes in
economic life that force us temporarily to neglect the principles of sound economic and monetary policy, but not with
impunity may these principles be declared as outdated just
because they are inconvenient for the full employment policy
rigidly pursued after the shock of the Great Depression.

"TO THE TROPICS WITH THE EQUIPMENT FOR A POLAR
EXPEDITION"

We ought not to forget that this is the seed that Keynes has
sown. No honest person can overlook how abundantly it is
bearing fruit. There is no other explanation for the utterly
wrong postwar orientation of the Western world, which,
taught only to fear and combat deflation, followed the banner
of "full employment" right into permanent inflation. In spite
of all the warnings of the old-style economists, the danger was
recognized too late, so that it has become exceedingly diffi-

cult to face about and abandon the wrong position. As I wrote some years ago, it was like a man going to the tropics with the equipment for a polar expedition, and I was pleased to see in a recent article by Professor Erich Schneider, of Kiel,[1] that he took up the simile with a slight variant.

It is time to admit honestly and openly that such is the nature and such are the effects of the Keynesian approach, the last manifestation of which was the United Nations Experts' Report of December, 1949, soon thereafter recognized as untimely and quietly shelved.

There is not much to be gained by pointing out that Keynes was a man of genius to whom we owe remarkable and fruitful stimulation. There are few who would deny it, and I myself in my above-mentioned obituary have compared him with Adam Smith, albeit with strong reservations. Nor is it much help that Keynes himself at the end of his life was troubled and tried to restrain the excessive zeal of his followers, and that, flexibly open-minded as he was, he himself, had he lived to do so, might well have written the most effective correction of Keynesian economics. What for him was intellectual working capital with a rapid turnover has been turned by the less agile into fixed investment capital, the productivity of which is defended by all means, including monopolistic protection. Keynes cannot be absolved from the reproach that in the exuberant vitality of his mind he did not make sufficient allowance for this.

KEYNES AND THE MARKET ECONOMY

Finally, it is cold comfort that Keynes himself always regarded himself as a liberal, professing his belief in the freedoms of the bourgeois world and meaning to serve them after his own—in our view, strange—fashion. The desire to recon-

[1] Frankfurter Allgemeine Zeitung, September 4.

cile his theory with the market economy is laudable, but practical experience has proved that this theory has instead become one of the supporting pillars of an opposite economic policy of the collectivist and inflationary kind. It can be shown that there are profound reasons why one could hardly expect it to be otherwise. And has not Keynes himself in his magnum opus outlined this development clearly enough, as proof of how little he was in earnest about the market economy? If the countries of Europe are today grouped according to the style of their economic policy, there are those with a market economy on one side, and those with a collectivist, inflationary, full-employment policy on the other. It is the latter that cause most concern, even to the more impartial representatives of the "new economics." It really seems grotesque that recently a French author, J. Cros, in a study entitled "Le Néo-Libéralisme," contrasted Keynes as "le véritable néo-libéral" with such muddle-headed writers as Lippmann and Röpke.

IDEOLOGY AND ANALYTICAL TECHNIQUE COMBINED

The developments of the last ten years have in fact so compromised the Keynesian approach, and compromised it so openly, that it is easy enough to understand the attempt to water it down and present it as a mere analytical technique, which can now, with disinterested impartiality, be switched from the struggle against deflation to that against inflation. When, however, this attempt is combined with the claim to illuminate us with the pure light of Keynesian theory, then the legitimists among the rest of us economists will be forgiven for displaying some surprise at such agility. After we have spent years warning the adherents of the "new economics" of precisely those dangers that have materialized, we have some difficulty in getting used to their now stealing our thunder in the name of the selfsame "new economics." At the very least we shall, no doubt, be permitted a few words on the subject.

First of all, we have to admit that the use of the Keynesian analytical technique in combating today's inflation in the full-employment countries is in a way quite legitimate. We do, after all, use it ourselves when we say that these countries "live beyond their means," in the sense that the sum of consumption and investment releases more purchasing power upon the economy's goods than can be satisfied at current prices, so that inflationary pressure develops and with it a deficit in the balance of payments. We could, of course, have learned that from the "old economics" as well, but we do not deny that the technique of thinking in flow aggregates has been refined by the "new economics."

But if we concede that much and thus make a step toward reconciliation, it would not be unfair to expect that the adherents of the "new economics" in their turn should frankly admit two things: first, that in fact a passionate ideology has been turned into a mere analytical technique, and second, that if this technique has now to be applied to a situation exactly opposite to Keynes's assumptions, this has not happened, to put it mildly, entirely without the help of the Keynesian ideology. They might even be expected to admit that the fact that it is so desperately hard to deflect the full-employment countries from their inflationary course is not least to be ascribed to the firm hold gained in the meantime upon public opinion in those countries by the Keynesian ideology, with its sole emphasis on the fear of deflation, full employment at any price, expansion and reckless spending—so much so that some pessimists doubt whether the task can be achieved without grave social and political upheavals.

A BRAKE AGAINST INFLATION, BUT . . .

This alone throws light on the great difficulty of applying the analytical technique of the "new economics" with fine impartiality to inflation or deflation in turn, according to the situation. A number of serious objections may be raised against the possibility of such symmetry. It is bound to be heavily lop-sided insofar as the Keynesian approach at best always remains latent inflationism. This inflationism at once becomes virulent in the presence of any disturbances, including those which, because they are accompanied by unemployment and a shrink-ing volume of business activity, look like "deflation," even though they are to be interpreted, not according to the "new economics" as a disproportion of the economic aggregates, but according to the "old economics" as a result of wrong values (prices or wages) and a wrong distribution of the factors of production. What happens then? What happens when exces-sive wage increases cause unemployment? And, above all, how about the difficulty that disinflation in a full-employment sit-uation tends to be associated with such pseudo-deflationary symptoms?

The point is that even though the "new economics" is re-duced to a mere analytical method of a neutral kind and in the present situation agrees in its conclusions with those of the "old economics," the desired synthesis will be a good deal more difficult than meets the eye. It will hardly be possible at all unless the exponents of the "new economics" make up their minds to surrender their method's and their theory's claim to domination and to evacuate a good many more positions than they have already given up.

The idea of continuous manipulation of aggregates with a view to counteracting now an inflationary, now a deflation-ary, tendency, as the case may be, is indeed most seductive. It is not, of course, the sole privilege of the "new economics" but has always been a guideline of sensible economic policy. But it remains a dangerous idea so long as it is not purged of all Keynesian vestiges far more radically than has been done so far. Keynesian analysis will always look at the danger of in-flation through a diminishing glass and at the danger of defla-tion through a magnifying glass, and in matters of economic policy, to change the metaphor, will always limp with the inflation leg. So long as the analysis remains spellbound by the "new economics" to the extent of working only with aggregates, its underlying models are bound to misrepresent the nature of inflation and even more so of "deflation." Nothing could be better proof of the inner bias of the whole approach than the fact that it took so much time and persuasion, and the present inflationary tendencies had to grow to such massive proportions, before at least the more circumspect among the champions of the "new economics" bowed to the evidence and changed over from an anti-deflationary to an anti-inflationary course. The analytical machine worked out with so much ingenuity by Keynes and his disciples does indeed possess a brake against inflation. But the machine is so constructed that this brake comes into play only at breakneck speed and, moreover, has the awkward habit of cutting out again immediately after the first effect.

A HIGHLY UNMATHEMATICAL CIRCUMSTANCE

This is one of the main reasons why the Keynes-inspired theory of continuous anti-deflationary and anti-inflationary compensation, brought about chiefly by means of what is known as compensatory fiscal policy, has not so far proved its worth in practice. Expansion causes no trouble, but when it comes to the contraction demanded in the boom, which, in compensatory fiscal policy, implies swinging the budget from deficit to surplus, it has never worked, not in the United States, nor in Switzerland, nor anywhere else. "Under the 'compensatory' theory," we read in the Guaranty Trust Company's *Guaranty Survey* of September, 1952, "the last twelve years should have witnessed an unbroken series of substantial budgetary surpluses. The contrast between this and the actual record would be amusing if it were not so tragic. Experience so far indicates that what is in theory a two-sided influence actually operates on one side only—the inflationary side—

and that the inflationary effects tend to be strongest at times when they are least desired." The reason lies not only in the lopsided character of the philosophy underlying this compensatory theory. It lies also in the damnably unmathematical circumstance that one cannot talk Parliament and public opinion into saving and economical management, by exceptionally praising them as virtues, if all the rest of the time they are reviled as folly and sin, not to speak of modern mass democracy's built-in obstacles. This is something that has not been accorded the attention it deserves, thus giving away the theory as a typically intellectual construction that forgets the social reality behind the integral calculus.

XII

The Fight Against Inflationism*

Was it Disraeli or Gladstone who once said that apart from love, nothing turned men's heads so much as thinking about money? Be that as it may, there is hardly another field in all the institutions of organized society that is, like this one, both extremely difficult and decisively important for the health or sickness not only of the economy but of society as a whole. It is well to remember to what extent our epoch is one of crises and revolutions because it is one of inflations (occasionally interrupted by a deflation), and it is equally well to reflect on the baneful part played therein by the fact that when men—and especially responsible men—think about any question relating to money, their thought has come adrift from the anchor of clear principles. Nor should it be forgotten that the gold standard had one merit that outshines its weaknesses, and that was to be just such an anchor that saved money from becoming the plaything of every conceivable theoretical speculation and, in practice, preserved it from the attentions of an aimless monetary policy that has done mischief after mischief to the economy and society of our time.

MISES'S MONETARY THEORY: 1911, 1924, and 1953

Anyone who, such as the author of this review, belongs to a generation of economists who lived through the shattering ex-

* Zeitschrift fur das gesamte Kreditwesen, *February 1, 1954.*

perience of witnessing the unexampled failure of monetary theory and the simultaneous collapse of monetary policy in the inflations after World War I, and especially the most pernicious of all, the German inflation, will always think back with undying gratitude to one book that at that time, thirty years ago, became a vertible beacon for us. However much we may have differed later from its author's views on other matters, or indeed from his whole social philosophy, we shall never forget that book of his, nor the services it rendered us and continues to render us, even though we may not always be aware of them. I mean Ludwig von Mises and his book *Theorie des Geldes und der Umlaufsmittel,* which was first published in 1911 and which I got to know in its second, 1924, edition. Nothing could be more welcome to me than to have a topical opportunity to talk about it again, not only in gratitude to its aged author, who today, in his apartment in New York, carries on his intellectual work with undiminished vigor, but also in loyal remembrance and with an emphatic reaffirmation of the significance that this book still possesses for us today—indeed, perhaps quite especially today, when the end is at hand for yet another epoch of confusion in monetary theory and error in monetary policy in the wake of, though not unquestionably caused by, Keynes and his doctrine, and when no further delay must be brooked in returning to theoretical clarity and practical reason in all matters concerning money and credit.

Such an opportunity presents itself today. It is afforded by the recent publication of a new English edition of our—now American—friend's standard work under the title *The Theory of Money and Credit.*[1] This new edition not only makes the book accessible once more, but it is also enriched by up-to-date additions. Once more we can enjoy the logical sequence of clear ideas limpidly stated, spiced in the author's characteristic fashion with the salt of irony and the pepper of indignation about the errors and aberrations that have worked such mischief. Once more we draw pleasure from the courage

---

[1] *Yale University Press, New Haven, Conn., 1953.*

and keenness with which he goes to war against these errors and aberrations with weapons drawn equally from the armory of the classical theory of money and the modern theory of value. Once more we follow him through these classical chapters, from the "functions of money" to the "problems of credit policy," and once more we wish that many others may confide themselves to his guidance. Once more we recall what it meant for ourselves at the time to read his pioneering analysis of credit creation, the functions of interest, forced saving, and the monetary causes of cyclical fluctuations, and once more we enjoin as many others as possible to do likewise. Even those who have absorbed all these things to such an extent that, as often happens, they forget the pioneer will suffer no harm if they take advantage of this very readable new English edition to refresh their notions at the source.

"MONETARY RECONSTRUCTION"

It is rare for a book of this kind still to be fresh enough almost half a century after its first publication to be so well worth a new edition. This is a great distinction. But inevitably the book has, in the interval, acquired the patina of a work written at a time in which the problems, experiences, and issues, while still interesting, are largely not ours and have been replaced by others. It is one of the species of books whose honorable but slightly melancholy destiny it is to diminish their own topical interest by helping to create a new *communis opinio*. Their glory is to eclipse themselves rather than to endure the much less glorious fate of being overtaken and eclipsed by others; for us, on the other hand, it is a duty not to forget this.

The author of this book possesses enough worldly wisdom not to mind about this, and it is to be hoped that he will not despise the implied compliment just because of its honesty. In our turn, we have to thank him all the more warmly for the freshness, free from any sign of patina, with which he has built

a bridge from the classical parts of his book to the present; I
mean his addition of a long, final part under the title "Monetary Reconstruction," in which he tells us what conclusions
he draws from his theory in regard to the major problems of
contemporary monetary and credit policy. All those who know
him—and who doesn't among economists and economic policy
makers?—will have a pretty shrewd idea of what these conclusions are likely to be. Anyone who agrees with them will be
gratified at the force and decisiveness with which they are
expressed. And anyone who rejects them will, it is to be hoped,
not read them without pausing a little to reflect on the words
of a man whose hair has turned to silver in a lifelong, honorable fight for freedom and reason, who has more experience
than most and an unusually keen intelligence, nor without
asking himself seriously whether Mises is all that wrong when
he exposes the inflation of our time as "the true opium of the
people administered to them by anti-capitalist governments
and parties" and closes the volume with these sentences, which
may here be quoted as characteristic of the book and its spirit:
"The present unsatisfactory state of monetary affairs is an
outcome of the social ideology to which our contemporaries
are committed and of the economic policies which this ideology begets. People lament over inflation, but they enthusiasti-
cally support policies that could not go on without inflation.
While they grumble about the inevitable consequences of
inflation, they stubbornly oppose any attempt to stop or to
restrict deficit spending. . . . There cannot be any question
of the gold standard as long as waste, capital decumulation,
and corruption are the foremost characteristics of the conduct
of public affairs. Cynics dispose of the advocacy of a restitution
of the gold standard by calling it utopian. Yet we have only
the choice between two utopias: the utopia of a market economy, not paralysed by government sabotage, on the one hand,
and the utopia of totalitarian all-around planning on the other
hand. The choice of the first alternative implies the decision in
favor of the gold standard."

NOT "DEFLATION-BLIND"

These passages are characteristic of the thrust of the whole book. It seeks out inflationism in all its intellectual and political hideouts and challenges it to combat. It is not that the author is blind to the possibility of deflation and its economic ravages. On the contrary, one of the most interesting and topical passages of the book is the part where he recalls the destructive consequences of the deflation that occurred both after the Napoleonic Wars and after World War I because the gold price was not adjusted to the price level lifted by inflation— a mistake that is being repeated today as long as the American buying price for gold is not appropriately raised from its present thirty-five dollars per ounce. But since the worst after-effect of such illusionist policies invariably is that the consequences of deflation brought about in this way merely furnish inflationism with new arguments, the only result is a reinforcement of the secular trend toward inflation—a distressing trend that beyond doubt is with us for good, that draws sustenance from everything, including the mechanism of modern democracy, the prevailing ideologies, mass psychology, the tissue of interests, and the structure of modern society, and that is the creeping poison of our civilization.

The resistance of economics against this secular inflationary trend has become dangerously weak. The oversubtle theories of our time—and here again Keynes has to be named as the starting point—have eroded this resistance by arguments that have proved too much for the mental constitution of many and that, therefore, make one wish the author had taken issue with them in detail. But this is not to belittle the merit of a book in which resistance against inflationism has gained the strength to be derived only from a clear mind and incorruptible judgment.

XIII

The Dilemma of Imported Inflation*

I

Among the difficult and increasingly pressing problems of any policy to counteract the inflationary tendencies of an overheated boom, the question of international complications deserves particular attention at this moment. This question can perhaps best be studied in the case of Germany, where a dramatic worsening of the situation is giving rise to a lively discussion. The essential points involved are of such outstanding general interest that it is worth extending the German discussion to the international scale.

Germany is an especially striking example of a country whose countercyclical economic policy has landed it in an apparently paradoxical situation, precisely because of the international complications involved. While in Germany an altogether exemplary attempt is being made to dampen the boom by a restrictive credit policy, unusually high surpluses keep recurring month after month in the German balance of payments and are a dangerous source of expansion counteracting the restrictive credit policy and, to a large extent, offsetting its anti-inflationary effects. A country that, quite rightly, tightens credit domestically, because it is afraid that overexpansion of the economy may lead to a progressive de-

* Neue Zürcher Zeitung, *July 28, 1956, and October 7, 1956.*

terioration of the currency, finds that this selfsame currency is much in demand on the international market as a "hard" currency, of which there is a "shortage"—all characteristics that are not at all those of inflation. And the more that country does to resist internal inflation of its currency, the more stubbornly the balance of payments keeps registering a surplus, with all its expansionary effects.

The case is not peculiar to Germany alone; there are other countries in a similar position, including Switzerland. The point is that alongside domestic credit expansion, external economic relations have proved to be another dangerous source of inflation, because of the monetization of the balance-of-payments surplus. How to plug this source is a question much debated in Germany at present. Should imports be encouraged, and by what means? Should exports be curtailed, and by what means? Could tariff reductions of a politically feasible magnitude be expected to give any appreciable relief? If not, would it help to export capital, especially in the form of the advance redemption of Germany's foreign debts? Is the surplus in the German balance of payments going to last, or is it merely the result of forces whose effect is temporary, so that it is safe to just sit back and wait? Or, on the contrary, is the external equilibrium of the country so fundamentally disturbed that one has to think seriously of revaluing the mark unless certain other countries, especially France and England, devalue their currencies? And if this idea is to be seriously entertained, what would be the best technique of revaluation? Instead of taking the risky step of fixing a new par value for the D-mark, would it not be better to let the exchange rates float within a wider margin? And to this end, would it not be enough to relieve the central bank of its obligation to purchase foreign exchange and to limit its functions to mere intervention?

These are some of the most important questions on which the discussion in Germany turns. It is tempting to comment upon them, and maybe one might even hope in this way to make a clarifying contribution here or there. On this occasion, however, I prefer to refrain and instead to do my best to be of service by trying to define in precise terms the general nature of the problem now under discussion in Germany. I shall also try to demonstrate that no reasonable decision can be taken otherwise than in the light of a grave dilemma that countries like Germany, Switzerland, and Belgium have to face at present. I anticipate. A way out has to be found from an extremely grave dilemma, and unless this is clearly grasped there is little point in waxing indignant at the idea of revaluing the currency—in the lenient form, say, of broadening the margin within which exchange rates are allowed to fluctuate —and to do so in the name of the unexceptionable ideal of stable exchange rates, or in marshaling a lot of plausible enough reasons for rejecting as dangerous the sort of counter-cyclical tariff policy that Germany is timidly trying today. I have in mind the dilemma of imported inflation.

For a long time now, most of the countries of the free world have been pursuing budgetary, wage, and credit policies that must inevitably result in creeping inflation with all the con-sequences that we know only too well. It is, incidentally, a kind of inflation that, because of its now chronic nature, its extent, its causes, and its motives, is not comparable with the mild inflations of previous boom periods. Whether we can get the better of this chronic inflation of our time depends, in the sphere of ideas, on monetary cynicism's being defeated by the unshakable conviction that honest money is a paramount necessity and, in the sphere of interests, on the victory of the anti-inflationists over the inflationists. The prospects of such a double victory are extremely uncertain because of the erosion of monetary standards and of the growth of inflation-ary interests, in which trade unions and employers largely present a common front. The main factor of uncertainty is perhaps the extent to which we must, in any case, expect the sort of "democratic" or "social" inflation that has its roots in the great catchphrases of our time—such as "full employment," to name only one.

Effective resistance against this wave of inflation is not equally strong in different countries. We know well enough how things are going in such important countries as England and France. But even as regards the leading country of the Western world, the United States, we are more and more forced to recognize that, no doubt against the better judgment of the authorities responsible, the Federal Reserve System is proving to lack the strength for a credit policy strict enough to compensate the inflationary pressure of an expansionist wage policy now culminating in the steel strike. This means that we must expect the increasingly inflationary credit expansion of the United States to continue (perhaps even cumulatively), without being able to say with precision when and how it will come to an end. What dangers this spells for the future of the dollar has been shown by such experts as Melchior Palyi, of Chicago, or Philip Cortney, of New York. Their warnings cannot fail to impress, even though one essential reservation needs to be made, which is that, even allowing for an estimated total of close to fourteen billion dollars of the United States' short-term foreign indebtedness, six billion dollars of foreign investments in U.S. securities, and an indeterminable amount of dollar notes in foreign hands, the strain on the American balance of payments will be offset to the extent that the rest of the world keeps step with the American inflation or, on the average, even outpaces it. It need hardly be mentioned that this is in fact the case, and thus we have a repetition of the situation that developed immediately after the last war—in flat contradiction, it will be remembered, with the forecasts ventured by Keynes.

There are, on the other hand, just a few countries where the government or the central bank, or both, are not only wise enough but also independent and politically strong enough to put up an effective resistance against domestic inflationary pressures by means of an adequate discipline in monetary, credit and financial policy. But even if these countries, the most striking example of which is Germany, do manage to keep their domestic cost and price increases below the average of other countries, they find themselves with balance-of-payments surpluses that, as a symptom of the currency's "hardness," seem to contradict the warnings against the internal dangers of an inflationary overheating of the boom. In actual fact, of course, there is no contradiction, because what matters for the rate of exchange between currencies is not the absolute but the relative degree of inflation in any country. It's the old story of the one-eyed man's being king among the blind. However great the danger of domestic inflation in any country may be, if other countries on the average keep the reins even slacker, the first country's balance of payments will, at rigid rates of exchange, get into surplus, and its currency will be in short supply on the international market, just as though that country were deflating, while in effect it is still doing the contrary and struggling with inflation like Laocoon with the serpents.

What is so insidious about this situation, as we know, is that it is precisely that balance-of-payments surplus that opens up a new source of inflation, and one, to boot, that flows all the more copiously the more the domestic source of inflation is stopped up—or does so, at any rate, so long as other countries on the average let their domestic inflation gush along merrily. Given that it is uncontrolled inflation abroad that creates a balance-of-payments surplus for the country concerned, and given that this balance-of-payments surplus finds expression in an increase of the domestic money supply, it is correct to say that this is a case of imported inflation.

Now, the dilemma of such an imported inflation arises when we ask ourselves whether a country determined to defend the purchasing power of its currency should not have the right and the possibility of defending its currency from imported inflation as well. If the answer is to be affirmative, then one must accept also the means required for effective defense —and there can be no doubt that these means include an alteration of the exchange rate as a last resort, when all other methods fail and in particular in the absence of devaluation on the part of the countries that export inflation. If, on the other hand, we give a negative answer to the question, the strict implication is that countries such as Germany, Switzerland, or Belgium are condemned to leave the fate of their currency at the mercy of the American steelworkers, the election tactics of the Republican party, the trade unions of England, and the confusion of political factions in France. For if nothing is done to make the balance-of-payments surpluses disappear, and if the circumstances that generate them continue, then one would have to expect the restrictive policy at home eventually to be worn down by the contradiction of the persistent external surplus. Most probably the external hole opened up by imported inflation would gape all the wider, the more effectively the internal hole is plugged.

However, there are two circumstances that are likely to put an early end to this bizarre game. First of all, it is hard to imagine that balance-of-payments surpluses such as have recently occurred in Germany (especially vis-à-vis the European Payments Union) can go on for any length of time without disrupting the mechanism of international payments and without forcing the countries that export inflation to protect their curency reserves, either by putting up obstacles against German exports and subsidizing their own or by devaluation. Secondly, in the absence of drastic measures to re-establish the external equilibrium of a country like Germany, strong forces will be at work tending to bring about the same result *via* a rise in the internal level of costs and prices. Somewhere or other the fox must come out of the hole. The only question is whether this will fit our ideas of what is desirable.

The dilemma with which we are concerned can be described also in another way. The case of Germany—and it bears repetition that much the same applies to Switzerland and Belgium

—has revealed a situation in which any serious determination to defend the currency and thus to meet the paramount requirement of sound monetary policy implies contemplating so unorthodox a measure as softening up the stability of the rate of exchange. Even those who, such as the author, find such a prospect profoundly distasteful must admit that any softening up of the domestic purchasing power of money would be far worse.

It is a particularly unpleasant dilemma to face a country precisely when it is determined to keep its money sound. All the more severe judgment will have to be passed on the circumstances creating such a dilemma. It should be unnecessary even to mention that it would be a complete perversion of the facts to put the blame on a country like Germany and to reproach it for not emulating the pace of inflation elsewhere, but instead to feel that at this juncture the right policy is one of credit restriction. It is beyond comprehension that certain voices abroad—regrettably including, it would seem, the Organization for European Economic Co-operation—seriously advocate vigorous domestic expansion as one of the measures to be taken by Germany in order to re-equilibrate its balance of payments. Of course, the countries that are right are those that hold back and put the brake on, because they are alarmed at the dizzy pace of the drive, and not those that are reckless or weak enough to permit this pace, which is bound to end in catastrophe.

It is true that a country of Germany's type, which restricts credit in a situation of persistent balance-of-payments surplus, is doing exactly the opposite of what the gold standard would have prescribed. But it hardly needs stressing that this is not a serious argument against such a policy, though it is a very weighty one speaking in favor of the much maligned gold standard. If we still had the gold standard, there simply would not be, as indeed there never was in the history of the gold standard, an international inflation of today's dimensions, which is creating the dilemma of imported inflation for any country that is reasonable. It is a strange logic, indeed, to blame a country such as Germany for not behaving as would have been natural under the gold standard, when it is precisely the nonexistence of the gold standard, and indeed the absence of any genuine international monetary system, which has created this distasteful dilemma. For there is another thing that we are forced to admit, and that is that such international differences in the degree of inflation as now exist, together with the extreme developments in external payments, prove that we were under an illusion when we believed that after smashing the gold standard we had constructed a new, valid, and resilient international monetary system.

And here we have also the answer to another objection, to wit, that adjustment to international cyclical changes is the price to be paid by every single country if it desires genuine integration into the world economy. While this argument is justified as such, it does presuppose that the cyclical fluctuations, and thus the extent of deflation or inflation to be accepted by individual countries, remain within tolerable limits, and that the country principally responsible for world economic conditions, the United States, lives up to its international responsibilities in this respect and does not, instead, pursue some ideal such as a chronic "controlled inflation." But since we are getting rather far from this condition, the admonition of internationally responsible behavior is certainly to be addressed to countries other than those that are defending the last vestiges of reason in monetary and counter-cyclical policy, even at the cost of thereby being saddled with the dilemma of imported inflation.

But here I cannot forgo a remark directed more especially to Germany. Before such countries try to escape the dilemma by raising the value of their currency, they should first exhaust all other possibilities. Above all, they will have to remember that this ultimate step would be illogical so long as they have not removed the last remnants of exchange control, which is the mark of a soft and not of a hard currency. Present-day events in Europe surely drive home the lesson that those who, two years ago, considered that it was premature to want to re-establish currency convertibility were wrong. No one can fail to realize that what is happening now could not have happened if we had at that time succeeded in bringing off the bold venture we had in mind. In the meantime, the situation has become so serious that we must ask even more pressingly whether the time has not come for Europe's hard-currency countries, which are determined to fight inflation on all fronts, to proceed to joint action and, among other things, jointly to seize the initiative in at long last re-establishing convertibility. The urgency and the gravity of this question, however, will be grasped only by those who have some inkling of what is at stake for the free world.

II

A few weeks ago I discussed in this newspaper the grave consequences that follow from the extremely unequal inflationary pressure in individual countries, especially for those where that pressure is weak. That article was criticized by some, approved by others, but at any rate seems to have aroused so much interest that I am led to believe it would not be unwelcome if I were to take up the subject once more, to add a few more considerations in an attempt to clarify some controversial points, and to examine in depth the phenomenon we call imported inflation, which is as interesting as it is troublesome in practice.

Nobody will contest that the dilemma of imported inflation has lost nothing of its importance in the meantime. If anything, the tension between the few countries with low inflationary pressure, and consequently a balance-of-payments surplus, and the numerous countries with high inflationary pressure, and consequently a balance-of-payments deficit, has increased rather than diminished, and so the oneway flow of gold and foreign exchange from the latter to the former countries has, on the whole, continued unabated. In the case of Germany this flow has indeed reached an unprecedented maximum. While the surplus countries seem to be relying on an attitude that the physicians maliciously call "expectative therapy" and, by and large, to be behaving like so many Micawbers perpetually hoping that "something will turn up," the deficit countries are feeling the pinch more and more from one month to the next, from one week to the next. Unless there is some decisive change, we can see the moment coming when measures to end this extreme tension in international payments will brook no further delays, from whatever side they are introduced. Since the situation of a balance-of-payments surplus, together with its inflationary tendencies—which can be offset by domestic credit restrictions, even if these entail the maintenance and possible exacerbation of the tension—is indubitably far less immediately alarming and menacing than the opposite situation of a balance-of-payments deficit, it is the deficit countries that are more likely to introduce drastic measures, insofar as we must expect any initiative in this direction to come from the force of circumstances rather than from farsighted wisdom.

A continuing surplus in the balance of payments (that is, an external account that has to be balanced by an inflow of gold and foreign exchange) tends to expand the money supply in the country concerned and thus may become an autonomous source of inflation. This much is an elementary proposition that is surely generally undestood. This relative inflationary effect of a balance-of-payments surplus is matched in other countries by the relative deflationary effect of a balance-of-payments deficit. Since the balance-of-payments surplus is a result of high inflationary pressure in these other countries, inflation is in this way "imported" from countries with a higher inflationary pressure to countries with a lower one. It must be added, though, that this effect takes place only on two conditions.

First, it must be assumed that the rates of exchange do not adjust to changes in the ratio of the different countries' monetry pressure and purchasing power, but remain fixed. This is the point to keep in mind as an explanation of why there was no such thing as an "imported inflation" during the period of the great postwar inflation after World War I. The reason is simply that at that time the rates of exchange between the countries suffering inflation and the others were movable. "Imported inflation" had to wait for our own age, which harbors the strange belief that gaping divergences in the monetary policy of individual countries can be reconciled with fixed rates of exchange. This is a pious fiction of monumental dimensions, which was only possible in the first place because our newly constructed international monetary system, whose architects pride themselves so much on their achievement, skill lacks one essential element, namely, free and genuine currency convertibility. Without this fatal defect the present situation of tension could never have arisen, let alone continued for so long.

This is one of the conditions of "imported inflation." The other is failure to offset this "import" by restrictive credit policy in the surplus country. If anyone would argue that the whole theory of "imported inflation" was unconvincing because, after all, in Germany the surpluses had by no means regularly generated the increase in money supply and rise of prices predicted by the theory, then this argument simply would prove how successful domestic credit restrictions were in compensating for external expansion. Unfortunately, the dilemma of imported inflation is precisely that successful dis-inflationary policies at home constantly reproduce or even reinforce the cause of the balance-of-payments surplus, that is, relatively lower inflationary pressure at home than abroad. If things were left to themselves both in the surplus and in the deficit countries, without counteracting, respectively, the inflationary effects of the surplus by restrictions, or the deflationary effects of the deficit by further expansion, the tension would eventually solve itself. But it would be a solution to be paid for by the surplus country with inflation of the "imported" kind.

Naturally enough, the surplus countries defend themselves and thereby attract further flows of gold and foreign exchange. The deficit countries resent this. Instead of blaming themselves and their undisciplined monetary policy, they turn on the surplus countries—and especially on Germany, which is their most important and most striking representative, and in any event a country at which everyone is quite used to throwing stones—and reproach them with violating all the rules of propriety by failing to turn the tap of credit full on, in spite of the balance-of-payments surplus. This argument is supported by certain circles that sympathize with the deficit countries and their lax monetary policy (among others, the Economic Commission for Europe).

It should at long last have become clear that such reproaches are as foolish as they are unjust. Their ultimate implication is that any country should allow its own strength in fighting inflation, this scourge of our age, to be paralyzed by other countries' failure to muster the same strength. What these reproaches seem to say is this: if we are politically and socially too weak to cope with this "black spider," then you should not be better off either. Just how biased this attitude is will be clear if we reflect that none of those who are so ready with such reproaches would dream of contesting any country's right to defend itself against "imported deflation," the exact opposite of imported inflation, of which there was so much talk in the early postwar years. Does all this by any chance conceal the belief that we should apply unequal yardsticks in the two cases, and that the fight against inflation is no longer to be counted among the foremost aims of monetary policy? If that is so, it should be stated frankly. The surplus countries would know what to answer: we do not happen to hold such perverse views, and we have no intention of letting yours be imposed upon us.

One of the first points to be quite clear about is the monetary origin of the balance-of-payments surpluses that bring inflation into the country. These still seem to be not generally understood. The present situation is the clearest possible evidence of something we should have learned by experience, namely, that whenever there is any appreciable differential between the strength of inflationary pressure in different countries, the country with weaker inflationary pressure will have a balance-of-payments surplus and a "hard" currency and the country with stronger inflationary pressure a balance-of-payments deficit and a "soft" currency. That was the reason that, in spite of considerable inflation in the United States, there was a dollar shortage after the war (because inflation was a good deal stronger in the European countries than in the United States), and that the position previously occupied by the United States in relation to the rest of the world is now occupied by the group of hard-currency countries (Germany, Switzerland, Belgium) in relation to the rest of Europe. We have gotten to know a D-mark shortage and have watched with our own eyes how such a thing comes about.

It should help to clarify matters if we reflect that the calamity of the balance-of-payments surplus is merely the mirror image of the opposite misfortune of the balance-of-payments deficit. This latter is one with which we are familiar, and we have finally learned that it is not an act of God and has nothing to do, directly, with the laziness or poverty of the country's inhabitants but is the resultant of all the forces that, at a given rate of exchange, cause demand on the foreign exchange market to exceed supply. There are few who would deny that among these forces crucial importance attaches to "relative" inflation, or the "monetary ratio," as one might call it for short, with a view to characterizing the well-known divergence between monetary and credit policy at home and abroad.

We merely need to look at this the other way around to understand the case of the balance-of-payments surplus. Just as Sweden has a "soft" currency, not because it is poor or unproductive, but only because it indulges in a stronger dose of inflation than is the rule in the leading industrial countries, so Germany has today a "hard" currency, not because it is in any way particularly industrious, efficient, or rich, but because it rations itself to a much lower dose of inflation than is the rule elsewhere. The "monetary ratio" is favorable to Germany, as it is favorable to Switzerland and Belgium, not because these countries are particularly virtuous, but because others sin much more—which doesn't prevent the sinners, as we have seen, from denouncing the lesser sinners as "cynical" (to repeat a term actually used in England!).

Since, at unchanged rates of exchange, the "monetary ratio" is at the core of the tension, these considerations unfortunately also suggest that measures that do not touch this core cannot bring any genuine solution, even though they certainly are not totally ineffective. This applies more particularly to the reduction of import restrictions in the surplus country. So long as the above-mentioned basic cause of the tension remains, this cannot be expected to do more to remove the German external surplus than a solution of the dollar shortage could be expected from the reduction of American import tariffs alone. However, if the reduction of import restrictions is going to do less for the re-establishment of international equilibrium than many people expect, this is, of course, no reason against any such reduction, but, on the contrary, a reason for pushing it as far as is politically possible and defensible.

In this connection it is well, too, to pour plenty of cold water on the hopes which many Micawbers—to call once more on the immortal character from *David Copperfield*—in Germany pin on the moment when the growing impetus of rearmament will call forth large imports of military supplies. No doubt this will have some effect, but it is hard to see how much increases in imports can, in themselves, bring about a turning point. Either these rearmament imports will, as is desirable and to be expected, be financed in such a way as to cause no inflationary effects, in which case the purchasing power skimmed off for rearmament purposes by taxation or government loans will not be available for a corresponding amount of civilian imports or for sales of domestic civilian products, which thereby will be freed for additional exports. Taking an over-all view, nothing would then have changed in the mechanism of the balance-of-payments surplus. Or else we assume that rearmament will be accompanied by a certain amount of additional inflation, in which case the tension will be relaxed not by arms imports, but by inflation. But this solution can be had at any time, even without rearmament—except, of course, that there are strong reasons for resisting it.

Capital exports, on the other hand, are incontestably a powerful means of counteracting balance-of-payments surpluses and their inflationary effects. But in this respect there is a radical difference between Germany and Switzerland. Switzerland is structurally a capital-exporting country with a relative abundance of capital and, accordingly, low rates of interest, and hence this method of relieving the balance of payments is a natural one. For Germany it would not make sense, because Germany is a country with a relative shortage of capital and, accordingly, high rates of interest, both un-equaled among other industrial countries, and hence it is natural for Germany to have an inflow and not an outflow of capital. But if, in the present situation of persistent balance-of-payments surpluses, Germany gave free rein to these tendencies, the situation would only get worse. The external surplus would become even larger and the inflationary pressure generated by it even stronger, and to counteract this latter development Germany paradoxically would have to respond to capital imports with further domestic credit restrictions.

Thus, it is only logical that the authorities in Germany resist capital imports, however natural and economically reasonable these may be as such. What is left of German exchange control serves essentially no other end than to fight this capital flight in reverse. But it is logical only in the context of a wider paradox that, in the case of Germany, exacerbates the ordeal of the dilemma of imported inflation—the paradox, that is, that a country with a relative capital shortage finds that its successful fight against domestic inflation forces it to behave as though it had an abundance of capital, merely because of the tensions generated by fixed exchange rates and widely divergent purchasing power parities. The dilemma of imported inflation is bad enough. But if the "dilemma of capital imports" is superimposed upon it, then it is hard to think how the situation could be more contradictory.

XIV

Robbing Peter to Pay Paul:
On the Nature of the Welfare State*

There are certain things that no one in his right mind regards
as anything other than bad. Their virtually unanimous condemnation provides economic policy with a few elementary
guidelines that are beyond dispute today. No one wants poverty, sickness, or prolonged unemployment, and there is no
one who would seriously contest the necessity to combat them.
Much the same really applies to inflation, and even though
there are a few groundlings among professional economists
who would have us believe that a long-run, simmering inflation, at any rate, is not altogether a bad thing, the only interesting point in this argument is what it tries to obscure, to
wit, the bankruptcy of a certain brand of economic theory and
policy.

The position is entirely different as regards the welfare state.
Even among its critics—and there are now very many of them
—there is hardly one who would reject all the ideas and
arrangements associated with this concept. But this circumstance constitutes both a serious danger and a difficult problem; for once we accept the principle of compulsion, which is
inseparable from the welfare state even in the case of social
security, as a means of assisting the individual in his struggle
against the vicissitudes of life—where, then, is the limit? Might
we not find that things get out of hand, as happened with

* Frankfurter Allgemeine Zeitung, *January 22, 1958.*

progressive taxation, where, too, there was no stopping it once the principle had been adopted, rather rashly as we now realize? We are in the predicament of the sorcerer's apprentice; almost anywhere we turn our horrified eyes, we see that the welfare state has a built-in, irresistible tendency to further growth. More and more areas of compulsory aid keep being discovered; more and more population groups are drawn in; the assistance rendered grows more comprehensive and the projects adopted more elaborate:

> *Water on water rushes—*
> *It brings still more inside:*
> *Oh, and a hundred gushes*
> *Engulf me like a tide.*

It would be hard to deny that the modern welfare state progresses by its own momentum and, in striking analogy with the principle of progressive taxation, that there is nothing in its conception to set a limit to it. To expand the welfare state is not only easy, but it is also one of the surest means for the demagogue to win votes and political influence, and it is for all of us the most ordinary temptation to gain, at no cost to ourselves, a reputation for generosity and kindness. The welfare state is the favorite playground of a cheap sort of moralism that only thoughtlessness shields from exposure. But what is equally bad is that to turn back on this path is as difficult as to turn a car on a narrow, steep Alpine road. This is what we realize to our consternation once it is beyond doubt that the road leads to the abyss. We have a warning example in Lord Beveridge, who rightly sounds the alarm today when faced with the consequences of the British welfare state, but who, we can only hope, must have enough self-criticism to remember the outstanding part he himself played in the creation of that welfare state as an advocate of inflationary "overfull employment."

Now we can see the problem quite clearly. If the welfare

state can be compared to a powerful machine that has neither brakes nor reverse gear, but a vigorous forward movement, and if, at the same time, there can be no question of destroying that machine, the problem arises of how to control its power. If the welfare state has no built-in self-limiting capacity, then the necessary limits must be drawn from outside, lest it outgrow us and ultimately become the ruin of a free and prosperous society, not to speak of depriving man of the dignity of being responsible for himself. To be sure, most of us do not deny that state help is indispensable and that many of the welfare state's new institutions are a bitter necessity. There is no need to lecture us on this point, and indeed it would probably be easy to persuade us that, notwithstanding the overall verdict of "too much," there are cases here and there where not enough is being done. That is not the point, therefore. The point is how we can make sure that if we give them an inch they don't take a mile, or more. To this end we need some sort of rules, principles, criteria, and distinctions that enable us to resist a current that threatens to carry us away. There is hardly a more important task than this. All the more regrettable is it that it has barely been begun or perhaps is still not clearly understood.

According to the sound principle that it is best to proceed *a minore ad maius,* from the less to the more important, we may begin with a rule that might be called one of tactics, or emphasis. Given that the road of the welfare state carries one-way traffic only and that we are traveling along it fast without any reasonable hope of reversal, the first thing to make sure of is that from now on no further step is taken without being considered with the utmost care and extreme reluctance, without the economy wresting it from its conscience, as it were, like everything else in life that is difficult to undo. If in doubt, leave out—that should be the rule, the minimum of wisdom, to insist upon. Not only should the burden of proof as a matter of course rest upon those who advocate any further step along this road, but that proof should also be required to meet the severest possible tests. Over and over again the arguments should be scrutinized and the evidence sifted, the pros and cons carefully weighed, before any decision is approached, and even then it is best to sleep on it. Let all those who are responsible for Germany's "dynamic old-age pensions" examine their conscience; are they sure they have met these requirements? Or are they not, rather, in the position of Lord Beveridge? And in Switzerland and Great Britain, do those who now yield to the temptation to follow the German example really take the burden of proof more seriously?

There is a special implication in all this for those of us who are responsible for our advance on this road not as practical politicians, but merely intellectually, and thus bear what is perhaps the heaviest responsibility. It is, to say the least, a moot question whether the broad masses themselves are always and everywhere keen on the modern welfare state. What we hear from Sweden and other welfare-state paradises may well give us pause. There can be no doubt at all, on the other hand, that there exists a broad and extremely influential group of people who are out for prestige and power, and who not only have the greatest interest in the progressive expansion of the welfare state but are determined to make the utmost of the opportunities it offers for social demagogy. I have in mind the group of people made up of so-called progressive leaders of public opinion, of officials of the public and private social security bureaucracy, of politicians adept in trimming their sails to the prevailing wind of mass sentiments and mass opinions, and finally of all those marching under the ideological banner of what I would call "progressism." Regrettably, there is every reason to believe that in modern mass democracy the joint pressure of this group is so strong that we are infinitely more likely to get too much welfare state than too little, and there is far more danger of excess than of harmful abstinence. That is the direction in which the tide is flowing; that is the line of least political and social resistance, which the Western peoples are tending to follow in any case, whatever we may do for or against it.

Since in practice all the danger lies in the direction of an abuse of the welfare state principle, those vested with intellectual responsibility can be in no doubt about their correct attitude. The further expansion of the welfare state does not need their vote, for that is taken care of—and to a larger extent than suits us—by the political and social forces of the age. They can, therefore, safely adopt the rule of shifting the weight of their vote to the other side and of placing the stress on the dangers and limits of the welfare state. Cheap moralism is anything but moral for anybody, but for the responsible intellectuals it is nothing short of immoral. Their duty is to make themselves unpopular, just like the author of this article, and to say what, as it is, hardly anyone says.

In other words, it is safer in this case, as in so many others, to err on the side of exaggerating criticism rather than encouragement. The responsibility we shoulder in the first case is incomparably lighter than what falls to us in the second. The welfare state does not need our kindly help, since it can get along very well without it. But the dignity of the free individual and the good health of society do need our help, because they are jeopardized by the mushrooming welfare state. The time has come when the responsible statesman, the social scientist, and the leader of public opinion must form an alliance in order to strengthen the forces of moderation, caution, hesitation, and preservation, which are threatened with defeat, however much we may do. If this attitude requires courage, that is all the more reason for adopting it.

So much for the tactics, for the correct distribution of emphasis. One step further and we are in the wide field of another set of questions, namely, that mere common sense suggests that the aims of the welfare state can more expediently be achieved by doing one thing rather than another, without thereby making the welfare state more "unsocial." In such cases one would really have to be quite hopelessly dogmatic to fail to realize that lack of intelligence does no good even to the welfare state. To take an example from the important area of social medicine, there are surely few people who would deny the necessity of giving financial aid in certain cases to certain groups, in order to help them regain their health. But there are intelligent and less intelligent ways of achieving this aim. It would be plain foolishness and failure to appreciate the elementary laws of psychology and economics, for instance, to seek to deny the necessity of the sound old principle of letting the patient normally meet some part of the cost of re-establishing his own health, thus giving him an interest in claiming assistance only after serious consideration and within reasonable limits of expense. Since exceptions have to be made anyway for emergency cases, there is no excuse for not applying this principle of automatic control through cost-sharing in health insurance, and it would be hard to find an answer to the question of why anyone who pays out of his own pocket for his clothes, his radio set, and, above all, for the innumerable ways of ruining his health should not also pay a modest part of the cost of restoring it.

It cannot be gainsaid, of course, that behind such questions of administrative technique and organizational expediency there are ultimately some problems of a fundamental kind. And this brings us to the heart of the matter. We are bound to look differently even upon questions of this kind if we hold different views on the true meaning of public social assistance. The basic distinction lies in which of two things we want: a helping hand for those who really need it, or who may be presumed to need it, or public social assistance as an instrument of a welfare state that deserves the attribute "socialist" because it aims at the progressive socialization of the satisfaction of wants and at economic and social equalization, without regard to the income and wealth of the individuals encompassed by the welfare state. The gulf that divides these two views could not be deeper and more unbridgeable; for the first of them is conservative (or, if another term is preferred, "evolutionary"), whereas the other is revolutionary, and the first is in conformity with the principles of the market economy and is indispensable if the market economy is rightly to be called "social," whereas the other is hostile to it and erodes it.

However much it may be a matter of pressing concern to work out this distinction in precise terms and to make a clear choice, we are still very far from such clarification. Yet it is one of bitter necessity, so that we may stand firm against all attempts to obscure the decision and to pervert the idea that no one should fall below a certain minimum into the contrary idea that no one should rise above a maximum as near as may be the same for all. Nor, indeed, have we as yet gone the whole way in following through the practical consequences of those two social philosophies. Again it is social medicine that can provide us with plenty of instances for practical application in specific cases.

If we look at the difference in another light, we shall see quite clearly that it is really a difference in people's social approach, in the aims by which they set their course. On the one side are all those who put the whole stress upon the individual's responsibility for himself and his family, who regard this responsibility not solely as a burden but as the essence of his human dignity, and who wish to develop and strengthen this sense of individual responsibility as well as both the willingness and the ability to assume it. In this view state aid is a subsidiary means, a rear position in case the front line of self-help and voluntary mutual aid collapses. On the other side are those who reverse this system of defenses, and who labor to prove that our basic idea, which is rooted in the individual, is ridiculously old-fashioned, unworthy of anyone progressive, utopian, reactionary, philistine, or even economic nonsense. Their basic idea is the conception of society as a colossal machine with its tubes, valves, and thermostats pumping

incomes this way and that, or else as an enormous pot to which
people contribute unequally but from which all draw equal
rations.

Any discussion between these two camps is difficult, but not
hopeless. It is not in all circumstances useless to show the representatives of that second group their own social philosophy
more clearly than they often see it themselves, and thus to try
to chasten or even to shock them. The best result, however,
may be expected from demonstrating that the further the
modern welfare state progresses, the closer it comes to a critical
point beyond which consequences are inevitable such as even
the warmest well-wisher of this development cannot reasonably want without risking exposure as a diehard. This critical
point—or, we might say, the point at which the soup boils
over—can be determined in three ways.

The critical point is reached, first, when it costs so much to
run the welfare state that even its beneficiaries, the masses,
begin to be clearly aware of the financial burden involved,
and when it becomes a matter of practical importance for
everyone to work out whether, when all the pumping is done
in all directions, he is better or worse off. It is almost impossible to answer this question today, a circumstance that adds
to the unease and the misgivings that seem increasingly to
characterize the spiritual climate in the typical welfare-state
countries. At that point there looms yet another question,
namely, whether the beneficiaries of public social security
would not be better served if the welfare state left them more
money to make provision for themselves.

Secondly, the critical point may be defined as the point
where a vicious chain reaction sets in—where, on the one hand,
the welfare state's compulsory aid paralyzes people's willingness to take care of their own needs and its financial burden
considerably weakens people's ability to do so, while, on the
other hand, this limitation of self-provision makes people more
and more dependent upon compulsory public aid and increases their claim on it. Just when this point will be reached

not only depends on the proportions that the welfare state assumes in any country but also on the degree to which the people's inclination to save and their sense of responsibility for their own affairs resist the pressure of the welfare state; it also depends on the tax system and on other circumstances. The Scandinavian countries provide the most striking illustration of this boiling point, but it would be rash to assume that Germany or Switzerland could not likewise be raised to this temperature, if only the fires of the welfare state continue to be kept good and hot.

The Scandinavian countries are also, together with such others as France, a good example of how the boiling point can be reached in yet a third way. This is perhaps the most critical point of all, because it makes it so crystal clear that the welfare state eventually nullifies itself. It is the point where the welfare state becomes one of the principal causes of chronic inflation, which, in its turn, is one of the many blots on the scutcheon of our time. How this mechanism works cannot be explained here in detail, but I may perhaps be allowed to plead that I have not shirked the issue—a discussion of it will be found in my book *A Humane Economy*.[1] I would, however, stress one aspect that is often overlooked. Such a welfare state not only exports inflation to other countries that, like Germany, were more successful in containing chronic inflation, but it also sponges on them to the extent that month after month it builds up a debit position in the European Payments Union. The welfare state lives beyond its means, but that can be done only if others foot the bill.

To let someone else foot the bill is, in fact, a general characteristic of the welfare state and, on closer inspection, its very essence. There may be more charitable ways of saying this, but that does not alter the fact. But the point is not only that someone else pays, but that he is forced to do so by order of the state. That the welfare state necessarily implies compulsion is de-

[1] *Henry Regnery Company, Chicago, 1960.*

fensible, for how else could its aims be achieved? What is wholly indefensible is any attempt to suppress, obscure, or simply deny this inconvenient and ugly fact. Compulsion is so much of the essence of the welfare state that we should really call it the compulsory welfare state, if we want to call a spade a spade and forestall any attempt at camouflage. There is a good case for such plain speaking, the more so as strangely little is ever said, and *sotto voce* at that, about the nature of the welfare state as a compulsory institution.

In spite of its alluring name, the welfare state stands or falls by compulsion. It is compulsion imposed upon us with the state's power to punish noncompliance. Once this is clear, it is equally clear that the welfare state is an evil the same as each and every restriction of freedom. The only question on which opinions may still differ is whether and to what extent it is a necessary evil. It seems obvious that a convincing case for this can be made out only within very narrow limits.

Not long ago the French historian P. Gaxotte characterized our age by saying that never before had there existed in the world so many jails filled with so many harmless and even perfectly honest people. If this is so, the welfare state as one of the main areas of state compulsion must bear its share of the responsibility.

XV

The U. S. Balance-of-Payments Crisis: Diagnosis and Treatment*

When a country such as the United States seems to suffer from a stubborn balance-of-payments deficit, an ailment whose symptom is loss of gold reserves, it is tempting to react in the same way as the economic layman almost invariably does react to such a process. One looks at the balance of payments as though it were a pair of scales; one notes that one pan, with payments to foreign countries, is going down, and the other, with payments from abroad, is rising; one concludes, therefore, that the trouble is that obviously there is too much in one pan and too little in the other. It follows, so the argument goes, that it is high time the government saw to it that something should be taken away from the heavier pan and added to the lighter one. From there just one more step leads to the notion that the disequilibrated scales can be set right by any measure that increases receipts and diminishes disbursements. And so there is serious talk about import restrictions and export subsidies, exchange control, incentives to capital imports, and obstacles to capital exports.

In point of fact, an alarmingly large section of opinion regarding the present balance-of-payments crisis of the United States is just at that level of lay economics, and the measures apparently under contemplation are of the same ilk. Since the U. S. trade balance continues to be in surplus, as before, the

* Neue Zürcher Zeitung, *November 25, 1960.*

213

cause of the trouble is supposed to be the deficit on capital account—in other words, an excess of unilateral capital transfers from the United States to abroad. From this the conclusion is drawn that this excess must be diminished and aligned to the other side of the balance of payments. Given that a large part of the U. S. unilateral capital transfers is of a political nature, the U. S. government feels constrained to turn this tap down a little, without regard to the consequences this might have on the world political situation. At the same time, other governments are to be induced to take over some part of these political expenditures, and more especially the German government, which is regarded as eminently capable of doing so in the light of the same sort of considerations, namely, the persistent surplus in the German balance of payments. This assessment of German solvency is supported in Germany itself by those who explain the German external surplus as being in large part due to insufficient exports of German capital and to the receipt of unilateral dollar payments (maintenance costs of American troops in Germany) and who thus play into the hands of the American wishes.

All these arguments and measures are clearly flawed by an elementary error in economics, as no one who has been trained in economics can fail to see. What sort of error it is becomes quite clear once we appreciate that the whole problem is one that should be familiar to at least the older generation of economists. It is all over again the problem of the transfer of German reparations after World War I and of Germany's capacity to pay.[1] At that time, the predominating view was, at first, quite simply that Germany's capacity to make unilateral payments to abroad depended upon its ability to achieve a corresponding balance-of-payments surplus. This thesis led to a prolonged and interesting—but now, alas, forgotten—discussion, which eventually made it clear that the balance-of-payments surplus was not the condition but the

---

[1] See *the article on the Transfer Problem in this volume.*

result of the German reparations, and was the measure of how much Germany was actually paying by its own efforts.

If a country—thus ran the lesson we then learned anew—makes more capital payments abroad than it receives and, therefore, runs a deficit on the external capital account, as was the case of Germany's paying reparations and is now the case of the United States' paying out development aid, grants, and the costs of U. S. troops stationed abroad, then this country must necessarily register a surplus on goods and services account matching the amount actually disbursed to balance the capital account. These are the key words: the amount actually disbursed to balance the capital account. Everything depends upon an appropriate volume of purchasing power having first been withdrawn from the total volume of domestic income and expenditure and upon the country's being rich enough to take this domestic withdrawal in its stride. The problem, therefore, lies primarily not in the balance of payments but in the country's ability to raise the required resources domestically.

Now, it is beyond doubt that nothing has happened in the United States during the last few years that might suddenly and seriously have weakened the country's ability to make domestic resources available for foreign payments. Whether and to what extent these payments are to be made remains a political question, which it is not our business to pronounce upon. If anything, the economic margin for such payments has widened rather than narrowed, given the recent years' continued growth in the prosperity and economic strength of the United States. If, today, the U. S. government means to ease the pressure on the balance of payments by cuts in its unilateral expenditure abroad, this would alter the structure of the U. S. balance of payments in such a way that one would expect a corresponding decrease on the credit side of the goods and services account. If, conversely, the German government meant to diminish the balance-of-payments surplus by deliberately stepping up unilateral foreign payments, this would alter the structure of the German balance of payments in such a way that one would expect a corresponding increase on the credit side of the goods and services account.

This will sound less paradoxical if we understand where the problem really lies. The problem lies in the *adjustment* that is necessary if sudden and major changes in the balance on capital account are to be so offset in the goods and services account that a new equilibrium comes about. Such an adjustment needs time and may entail difficulties and frictions. That these latter should not be overestimated and that in fact there are strong forces tending to re-equilibrate the balance of payments in the case of unilateral capital transfers in the content of the transfer theory on which economists eventually agreed more than a third of a century ago now.

Here we come to the heart of the matter. What is at the bottom of the U. S. balance-of-payments difficulties is a problem of equilibrium, not one of ability to pay, and it is a problem pertaining to the whole of the economy, not to the balance of payments alone. The United States is not one cent the poorer or the less able to pay because of its balance-of-payments deficit, nor is Germany one cent the richer or the more able to pay because of its persistent balance-of-payments surplus, just as France was by no means poor and insolvent so long as it ran an external deficit and suddenly became rich and solvent when it adjusted the exchange rate of the franc, stopped any further inflation and thereby turned its balance-of-payments deficit into a surplus. If the United States is today suffering from a balance-of-payments crisis, the reason is that the U. S. economy as a whole is no longer in equilibrium with the economies of other countries. This equilibrium depends upon two factors, which are, on the one hand, the American price and cost structure in comparison with that of other countries, and on the other, the exchange rates, that is, the hinge on which the price and cost structures turn.

It is wrong, therefore, to say that the United States has a payments gap because it imports too much or exports too little, or exports too much capital or imports too little of it.

The correct answer is that the American balance of payments has ceased to be in equilibrium because the American economy has gotten out of equilibrium with the major countries abroad. And this has happened because in view of all the circumstances, which include more particularly the economic recovery of the European countries and their increased competitive strength, the United States has become too expensive, or less competitive, or has failed to reconcile the total volume of its domestic income and expenditure with its external payments, or whatever other form of words one might choose to indicate a state of affairs that basically turns on one fact only. That fact is that even the affluent society, to use Galbraith's well-known description of the American economy, can eventually live beyond its means. All this is, of course, subject to the reservation that nothing is changed in the conversion factor between the United States and the rest of the world, that is, in the dollar rate.

As regards the question of the main cause of the disturbance in the equilibrium of the American economy, this is a matter on which far-reaching agreement had eventually been reached. Some of the economists who now rest content with the theory that the gap in the U. S. balance of payments is due to American foreign aid and military expenditure abroad were until a short while ago among the leading critics who warned against the effects of the wage inflation. And in fact the American payments crisis is one of these rightly feared effects, and it would seem that last year's steel strike was the last big drop that caused the bucket to overflow. The true situation becomes quite clear if we consider the possibilities of effective treatment. In this respect there are two things that surely can hardly be doubted. One of them is that there certainly exists a dollar rate, that is, a conversion factor, that would give rise to a new equilibrium, and secondly, it is obvious that if, for thoroughly commendable reasons, the dollar is not to be devalued, equilibrium can be re-established by weakening the upward push of American costs and prices.

Given that in fact a devaluation of the dollar would, for political reasons alone, be a great misfortune for the whole of the free world, everything depends upon such a weakening of the upward push of American costs and prices. To avoid devaluing the dollar—not to speak of such an unspeakable thing as American exchange control—therefore implies a restrictive credit and financial policy in the United States. The present administration is open to the reproach that it has not done enough in this respect and has not been consistent enough. If the new Kennedy administration is to do better, it will have to be a good deal more energetic than its predecessor in turning off the taps in Washington, instead of turning them on still further, as Kennedy and his advisers have announced so far. The hopes of the United States and of the whole free world, in this as in other respects, therefore lie in the new president's being converted from Saul into Paul—and may he soon see the light on the road to Damascus. To put it in terms of a symbol: we could all relax if the president were to replace his purely inflation-minded adviser Galbraith with a man such as Professor Haberler.

The difficulties and hardships of such a policy of adjustment by internal monetary discipline will be the less, the more co-operation the United States gets from the European countries with balance-of-payments surpluses. The country that could render the United States the greatest service is the one whose balance-of-payments surpluses are an extreme case, and that country would thereby render itself an even greater service. That country is Germany, which is being exhorted at present to relieve the United States by taking over some of the political foreign expenditure. It has been argued here that, quite apart from political misgivings, the idea of such relief rests on a mistaken diagnosis of the ailment. On the other hand, the United States could expect truly effective help from Germany if Bonn and Frankfurt were at long last to decide which of two courses to take: either to give a free rein to the inflationary effects deriving from the balance-of-payments surpluses, thus diminishing the domestic purchasing power of the currency, or else to raise the external purchasing power of the D-mark. The case of Germany is the exact opposite of the American one. Across the Atlantic an anti-inflationary damper is definitely preferable to devaluation, and equally definitely it would be better on this side to revalue rather than to let inflation rip, that is, to let the purchasing power rise externally rather than to diminish it at home.

XVI

World Without a World Monetary System*

Were it not for the pitch-black storm clouds of world politics gathering about Berlin at the moment and overshadowing all else, it would be much more evident that the aspirations, cares, and dangers centered on the problem of international monetary relations have assumed a degree of importance almost without parallel. The debate sweeps along this way and that, one project after another keeps cropping up, and it almost looks as though the economists and financial experts of our time were all possessed by the novel ambition of having their name associated with some "plan" of international monetary reform. It would be astonishing if a clear view of essentials had prevailed in all this, although it may be hoped that the mists will eventually disperse. But the landscape we shall then see does not promise to be bright and sunny. As things are at the moment, the author's modest intention is not to propose a new "plan," but to mark out a few points of orientation in this confusing debate.

On more than one ground it seems reasonable to begin with the revaluation of the German currency, which was rightly hailed as a dramatic event a few months ago not so much because of its extent, which was modest enough, as because of the principle involved. To be sure, there were critics at home and abroad who opposed this measure and who, once it had been

* 1961.

carried out against their opposition, condemned it; but even among them there must be few today who would refuse to admit that it sprang from a compelling and irresistible logic, such as is seldom found in economic policy. Even the bad losers among these critics, who, with a somewhat defective logic involving them in contradictions with their former rejection of revaluation, reproached it for not being sufficiently effective, must in all honesty ask themselves what would have happened without revaluation in a situation of continuing balance-of-payments surpluses, virtually no diminution in the overheated temperature of the boom, and strongly rising wages.

But by and large nobody seems much inclined to indulge in such skirmishes after the event. The subject of revaluation has passed into history with a speed that is all the more astonishing in view of the urgency with which the measure was needed and the relief it brought. Of course, it would be wrong to say that it is already forgotten, though even that would be no surprise in the giddy pace of our time. The almost complete calm on this battlefield so hotly contested not long ago reflects, among other things, the attitude of the erstwhile opponents; the champions of revaluation are not in a mood of noisy exultation, given that the one and only fireworks display turned out to be rather meager, and on the other side there is even less inclination to court ridicule by denying the salutary effects of revaluation. Another point that certainly counts is that just because revaluation was opposed so vociferously, aggressively, and stubbornly and therefore was carried out only so late and in such a small dose, it was welcomed by the people with all the more gratitude and made an impression that promises to be lasting. That is of the greatest importance at the level of politics and morals. But it does nothing to alter the fact that no more shots are fired on this front.

For this there is a special and profound reason, and it brings us to the heart of the matter. Even the advocates of revaluation always knew that it could not be a once-and-for-all gesture by which to throw open the door to a paradise of lasting equilibrium and secure protection against imported inflation. Nobody could nurture illusions that it would be more than a provisional answer to a much more far-reaching and serious problem. That problem, which was behind Germany's imported inflation and after revaluation still awaits a solution, has come to the forefront in all its clarity and gravity now that the provisional answer has been given and recognized as provisional. It is the problem of the, in the long run, intolerable inadequacy of the international payments system. To say it even more plainly, the problem consists of the fact that a number of essential tasks to be fulfilled by an international monetary system either are not fulfilled or are done inadequately. The world possesses no world monetary system, not even in its noncommunist better half, or none worth the name. This, of course, has been the case ever since the previous world monetary system, the only one that ever existed in our historical era, that is, the gold standard, was swept away by the whirlpool of the Great Depression thirty years ago, having already undergone dangerous denaturation after World War I by being reissued, as it were, in the cheap, popular edition of the Gold Exchange Standard. But all this has become clear only now.

We had, after all, to consider one thing after another and to cross each bridge as we got to it. It is not so long ago that we had to count ourselves fortunate if only we managed to remove some of the very worst obstructions in international payments, above all, exchange control, and thus to reintroduce the conditions of a reasonably free and multilateral international economy. Hard battles had to be fought sometimes until, through a series of stages, among which the European Payments Union was outstanding for all its interim nature and defects, convertibility was finally achieved for most of the major currencies, albeit in different degrees of perfection. This was inestimable progress, but as and when it came to pass, it inevitably threw into relief the fundamental defects of the international monetary system. These defects were never in doubt from the outset, of course, and now, when the re-establishment of convertibility or the degree of its perfection puts them plainly in evidence, it would be foolish to indulge in a more or less shamefaced nostalgia for the good old days of inconvertibility and exchange control, and to blame these defects on the convertibility at long last achieved once more in at least acceptable, average degree. If I break my leg and eventually am well enough to walk again, it would be silly if, in view of the dangers to which I am now exposed in street traffic, I pined for the idyllic days when I had to keep to my bed. If I am run over now, it is not my successful recovery that is to blame, but the lack of traffic discipline.

But what is it all about? Where are the problems? These are the questions that should be put first, and it is the frequent failure to do so sufficiently firmly that is one of the main reasons that the current debate is so confused, as I indicated earlier. It does indeed suffer to an unusual degree from one person talking of one thing and another of some other thing, with no agreement as to what particular problem is to be discussed at any given moment. It is true that there is probably a broad consensus of opinion nowadays about what the basic trouble is, to wit, the plain fact that we have no international monetary system, in the sense that we had one in the days of the gold standard, and that since the latter's demise we never managed to replace it by anything that could take over its functions. This is an uncontestable fact, however much we may reject any return to this model as foolishly utopian, and however superior a smile we may affect when we meet one of the rare, benighted personalities who thinks that the door to this paradise is not hopelessly bolted and barred. It still remains a fact, and it would be a good thing if everybody at last admitted it openly.

But what do we mean by saying that there exists no international monetary system? What are the problems that have to be solved if we are to have such a system again? This is where the semantic confusion begins. To begin with one of the "plans" most often mentioned today, the Triffin Plan, it is clear that its originator primarily has in mind a problem of a particular kind, the problem of what we call international liquidity. He regards it as the most serious and the most urgent, because in his view the leading reserve currency, the dollar, needs to be relieved of a burden that threatens to impair either the American payments position or international liquidity. If the U. S. runs a deficit in the balance of payments, as it has been doing in recent years, the rest of the world, to the extent that it registers corresponding balance-of-payments surpluses, receives an injection of additional liquidity. In parentheses, it should be stated that the American deficit is not, as many seem to think, due to the dollar's being the leading reserve currency, but to the external equilibrium of the American economy's having been upset for various reasons, which include, above all, inflation in the United States too strong in relation to the shift in international competitive strength and to inflation in Europe. But let's return to the main argument. Conversely, if the U. S. external deficit is eliminated by a change in its causal factors, Washington can indeed heave a sigh of relief, but international liquidity is squeezed. To put it in a nutshell, the blanket is too short and has to be lengthened. This could be done by raising the price of gold, and up to this point the idea of the Triffin Plan does in fact hardly differ from certain notions of the champions of a higher gold price. The special feature of the Triffin Plan is that it proposes to replenish international liquidity not by the simple method of raising the gold price, but by international book assets.

International liquidity certainly is a genuine problem. That much should be generally admitted. Central banks need a mass of maneuver to act as a buffer against the continuous shocks emanating from the balance of payments. One can even go further and grant it as probable that the liquidity base of today's world economy has, in view of the extraordinary growth of its payments flows, become so narrow that, following the absolutely desirable normalization of the American balance of payments, it may indeed give rise to that serious problem that the author of the Triffin Plan assumes in common with the advocates of an increase in the gold price and with the authors of several other plans. But it needs to be added at once that, while the problem of international liquidity as such must be taken seriously, it is by no means a simple problem.

It is not easy to define the idea in such terms as to forestall its abuse. There is, for instance, the question of how to decide whether the balance-of-payments difficulties of any particular country involve a genuine liquidity problem, as seems to be assumed in the case of the stand-by credits in support of sterling, or are simply a reflection of that country's continuously "living beyond its means" and in the name of liquidity asking that the payments gap for which it is itself responsible be plugged up by the solvent countries, which indeed is what the mechanism of the European Payments Union amounted to for years. Every banker knows the type of client who asks for a short-term credit to tide him over a momentary "illiquidity," whereas in fact he is heavily in debt. One would hardly expect it to be otherwise in international affairs, especially in our age when the experts themselves are dominated by an ideology taken as scientific truth ever since Keynes, the ideology, that is, of a more or less veiled inflationism or, at the very least, of open anti-anti-inflationism fighting tooth and nail against admitting that the true cause of balance-of-payments difficulties lies in the financial extravagances of modern mass democracy.

In effect, the doors are wide open to an abuse of this postulate of "international liquidity." Even now it is misused to an alarming extent, and we have reached the point where anyone who talks of "liquidity" as a rule means something very different, to wit, a sort of immunity from the consequences of an economic, social, and fiscal policy that undermines the balance-of-payments equilibrium as well as confidence in the country's currency and international credit-worthiness. This abuse of a word that, correctly understood, refers to a legitimate and very serious problem, is, to repeat, even now most alarming. But this is nothing against what we would have to expect if, as the Triffin Plan proposes, an international super-bank were to be set up, so constructed that the book assets it administers —and creates!—would replace gold as the "definitive money" of the world economy, and the decision regarding the allocation of the "liquidity" would be left to that bank's managing directors. The countries that accept monetary discipline and that need no such allocations but are called upon to finance them will assuredly be those whose central bank governors would regard it as irresponsible to join an institution that offers them "international" book assets in place of gold and gold-guaranteed national currency reserves and thus becomes a mousetrap for their good money. This suggests that such a "politicalization" and "institutionalization" of the international monetary system, as intended by the Triffin Plan, would not only fail to guarantee any such system but would, just like the Keynes Plan of the now remote past, most probably founder on an insufficient willingness on the part of national governments and central banks to castrate themselves by their own hand.

But the same danger signals retain their validity even within the narrower setting of a Triffin Plan restricted to Europe, as has been talked of recently. Even supposing, however, that the Triffin Plan is politically feasible and solves the problem of international liquidity better than has been done so far, it can still only do so to the detriment of another problem, which is the real problem of the international monetary system. The Triffin Bank would be free from the "golden brake" (Schumpeter) and endowed with the money-creating possibilities of a bank that itself, within certain limits, has no liquidity problem of its own, but would have to serve the liquidity demands of its more unsound clients and would certainly be under the influence of the prevailing anti-anti-inflationist ideology; it would be hard indeed for such a bank to resist the temptation of inflationary policy or at least of lending its support to existing inflationary tendencies. The reproach that Jacques Rueff, nowadays the butt of so many attacks, rightly makes to the present monetary arrangements in the world, namely, that they inflate international credit in the same way as a genuine gold exchange standard, would apply even more forcefully to the Triffin Plan. It does, in fact, amount to a sort of super-gold exchange standard on the international scale, with its only difference from a national one being that there would be not even any possibility of the inflationary kite-flying's correcting itself by the sort of run on the currency that Rueff is afraid of.

If we are now to state the real and central problem of an international monetary system, we might formulate it as follows. The world suffers from the elementary incompatibility of three things, namely, convertibility of such a passable, average degree as has now been re-established, stability of exchange rates, and the freedom of each country to choose whatever degree of monetary discipline at any given moment seems to lie on the national line of least political and social resistance. Since this line happens to vary a great deal from one country to the next (by way of illustration: on the average of the years 1953-1956, the working days lost annually per 1,000 workers numbered 575 in the United States, 205 in France, 135 in Great Britain, 70 in Germany, and 9 in Switzerland), and since, furthermore, some countries are more and others less prepared to follow that line according to the greatly varying anti-inflationistic allergy of the population (it is very high in Germany, to the despair of inflation-minded experts in Anglo-Saxon countries) and to the equally varying degree of monetary cynicism in high places, convertibility at fixed rates cannot possibly be reconciled with the autonomy of national monetary policies. Where the clash can lead has been made plain by the example of the German currency.

Thus, the heart of the problem is the elementary incompatibility of the two postulates of an international monetary system, namely, free convertibility and stability of exchange rates, and the considerable differences in the degree of monetary discipline. This conflict must be removed, and that is the alpha and omega of the international monetary system to be striven for. But the conflict can be removed only by sacrificing one of the three incompatible elements.

Which is it to be? Not free convertibility, in any circumstances—that much is surely common ground, although some of the reform proposals do, on closer inspection, imply a curtailment of convertibility.

What about sacrificing the stability of exchange rates? This may in certain circumstances save the situation, or at least be regarded as the lesser evil, as the devaluation of the French franc at the end of 1958 as well as the recent revaluation of the D-mark have proved convincingly and, it is to be hoped, finally. But it has become equally clear that we cannot get by with such once-only corrections so long as we have to live with considerable differences in national monetary discipline and hence with the permanent danger of serious balance-of-payments disturbances and imported inflation. In that event, the countries with relatively strict monetary discipline would be faced with the choice either to strike sail and submit to inflation's being foisted upon them from outside in whatever degree is deemed fit by the ideological inflation-mongers and the trade union bosses of the United States and Great Britain, or else to cut the rope that forces them into the wake of inflation elsewhere and to try their luck with the famous floating rates of exchange.

This leads us into a subject that cannot possibly be fully discussed on this occasion. But through all the controversies it should be clear that this is an experiment lacking the background of practical experience, and a hazardous experiment at that, to be considered only as a counsel of despair. We may wish that it were agreed also that the postulate of stable exchange rates, while not ranking nearly as high as that of free convertibility, nevertheless does come immediately after the latter. Without stability of exchange rates any international monetary system would be flawed at an important point, because it would lack a major condition of international economic integration. Just how important this condition is will be seen if we reflect that national economic integration (among the separate regions of one country) is unimaginable with fluctuating rates of exchange between, say, regional currencies. In view of all this, the utmost reserve is indicated in regard to this expedient, not to mention the ultimately decisive fact that in any case it is hardly feasible in practical politics.

When all else fails, of course, a determined resistance to inflation may, as a last resort, require that serious consideration be given to the solution of cutting exchange rates loose from the anchor of parity. But it would be an act of defeatism with respect to the true task, which is to create a world monetary system at last. If we do genuinely want such a system, then —and this brings us to the third point—every effort must be brought to bear on removing today's considerable differences in monetary discipline, at least among the leading industrial nations, and on achieving a uniform international pace. Naturally, this would make sense only if that pace were set by the countries with most monetary discipline. The thriftless should be induced to fall into line with the prudent, rather than forcing the prudent into the laxity of the thriftless, as is the aim or effect of so many of the current "plans."

These are the clear marching orders to be acknowledged by all who desire both an international monetary system and a successful defense against world inflation, and who are not prepared to achieve either an international monetary system at the cost of national monetary stability, or national monetary stability at the cost of an international monetary system. It would be unreasonable to expect this attempt at definite orientation to be combined at once with a hard proposal for giving effect to the aim so defined. Only two things may be stated.

The first of them is that if even the classical gold standard was unable to assert itself otherwise than step by step, the new international monetary system will be even more dependent on a nucleus of countries that make a start with it. This idea seems to be in the air today, witness especially an article by a man of no less authority and distinction than the former president of the German central bank, Dr. Wilhelm Vocke,[1] and it does indeed make sound common sense. Its implication is that, within the area of this club of countries committed to equal maximum monetary discipline, the two postulates of the international monetary system, namely, freedom and stability in the foreign exchange market, can be met without inflationary consequences. Conversely, however, this means that the club members cannot in future guarantee stability of exchange rates in relation to other countries unable or unwilling to fulfill the membership conditions of the club. It should be a point of honor for every country to belong to this club of the prudent and trustworthy, for not to do so would be tantamount to an admission of not being credit-worthy.

The second remark is this: The authors of most of the reform proposals current today seem to think that the problems of an international monetary system can be solved without gold as the basis of the monetary system, at least internationally, and without respecting gold as "definitive money." This is an illusion of which we must rid ourselves. What this means in practice cannot be discussed in detail here, but there is just one point that should not be passed over in silence. It is that this high esteem for gold rests upon the rather unfashionable conviction that the basic idea of the gold standard has been the victim of a character assassination during the last twenty or thirty years. We have witnessed the emergence of a sort of

[1] Neue Zürcher Zeitung, *July 19, 1961.*

fable convenue in this respect, a myth of very special kind, a tissue of unfounded and unproven assertions and accusations that have long wanted scientific revision. Another point should be made clear beyond doubt. Any plan that does assign to gold the function of "definitive money" in an international monetary system simply cannot take for granted that today's completely archaic gold price will adjust itself of its own accord to the international system of values. But this means also that any deliberate adjustment of the gold price as a cardinal value of the world economy is justifiable only to the extent that this condition of a new monetary system is strictly safeguarded against inflationary abuse.

When all is said and done, the conditions of an international monetary system firmly based on gold are identical with those of victory over today's world inflation. Anyone inclined to smile at even a so modestly conceived return to gold as a foolish utopia should, therefore, in all honesty admit that world inflation cannot be defeated. If anything is foolish in all this, it is surely that smile.

All the experts, or would-be experts, in currency matters can be divided into two main groups, those to whom gold is a thorn in their flesh and who therefore might be named chrysophobes, and those who have a predilection for gold and who shall be baptized chrysophiles. The intellectual genealogy of modern chrysophobia as a new trend remains to be written. It can be traced from John Law, where all the arguments can already be found, to Keynes and his adepts; and the agreement of Hitler and Khrushchev on this and on other matters is a fact that does no credit to chrysophobia but, instead, to gold, which is hated by all Jacobins and collectivists. Chrysophobia does, in effect, have a penetrating odor of ideology and of a sort of world do-goodery, and few things are as characteristic of our age as the complete ascendancy of chrysophobia over chrysophily. It is a form of indignation about something allegedly antiquated, primitive, anti-progressive, reactionary, profit-minded, a form of social rationalism extolling something as progressive, enlightened, and superior, a sort of doctrinairism in the sense of an attitude's riding roughshod over the facts.

This is where chrysophily is quite different. To be sure, it is also founded on certain value judgments, of a liberal, anti-collectivist, anti-étatist, and anti-nationalist kind, but in addition it rests on one of the most durable and uncontestable facts, namely, on the anthropological circumstance that everywhere and all times, and notwithstanding all chrysophobic ideologies, people have regarded and still regard gold as the ultimate store of value, as the most liquid good, as a refuge when all else fails. Funnily enough, this applies to the chrysophobes themselves, when they don't talk but act. When John Law, we are told by Michelet, decamped after his chrysophobic bubble burst, his bag was found at the frontier to contain large quantities of gold and precious stones; Hitler, however much he was given to ranting against gold, shamelessly caused it to be wrenched from the dentures of his victims, and Khrushchev is not deterred by his obscene cracks about gold from taking good care of it as the indispensable key to the most coveted goods of the free world.

Just why people have this attitude to gold is an interesting question in its own right. The answer to it will have to take account of many things, but, above all, of the following. The anthropological fact of *auri sacra fames* is an expression of the almost instinctive preference for an ultimate store of value that, determined as it is by a *consensus saeculorum*, is truly international and independent of governments and their folly. Chrysophiles consciously avow this preference. They see in gold the inestimable merit of anthropologically conditioned, para-governmental anchorage of the national and international monetary and payments system.

The earth is far from being the best of all possible worlds. And yet there are things in it of wonderful wisdom; for instance, the circumstance that the economic order associated with the ideal of freedom is infinitely more productive than that resting on unfreedom. But, strangely, men are inclined to disregard just such lucky accidents of creation, especially if they happen to be intellectuals, clever but unwise. This applies also to gold. It is a miraculous circumstance that there should exist a rare product of nature on which civilized mankind has been able to agree as an ultimate store of value. The chrysophile considers it foolish to disregard this unusual lucky accident, and he feels that if gold did not exist, it would have to be invented, were it not that it is the essence of gold to be one of those natural things that, like language, cannot be invented. But he is convinced that the wisdom of gold will eventually always triumph over the folly of its detractors.[2]

[2] *Cf. Charles Rist,* The Triumph of Gold *(New York, 1961), an English-language edition by Philip Cortney of collected essays by the great French economist who died in 1955.*

XVII

D–Mark and Dollar*

We seem to be inured nowadays to the unusual and the un-precedented. Yet even for us it should make sensational read-ing that the United States government is trying to lay its hands on part of the German foreign exchange reserves in order to speed up and facilitate the re-equilibration of the American balance of payments. To begin with, it is striking enough that this is not even couched in the form of a request but put for-ward as a demand, which, together with indignation about the Germans' unwillingness, thus is in all the more blatant con-tradiction with the principle generally accepted so far, at least among the economically highly developed countries, that it is the economic and monetary policy of each nation's govern-ment and central bank that are primarily responsible for its own balance of payments.

The demand has other unusual features. One's memory would have to be very short indeed if one remained insensitive to the charm of such a demand, addressed by the leading and the richest economic power in the world to a country that only ten years or so ago was regarded as a cripple barely able to stay alive, and that the very economists who are now close to the American government branded as the prototype of a coun-try bent on a catastrophic economic policy. To choose such a country for such a remarkable demand, with the explanation

* *1961.*

that it is the richest, is perhaps not a very polite form of belated tribute to the economic policy that brought that country to its present state, but it is all the more sincere for that.

It is, then, significant that Germany is the only country to which such an American demand has so far been addressed, and it will repay thinking over why this should be so. It needs no explanation that the government that puts forward this claim is, apart from any other motives, following the line of least political resistance, which means, among other things, that it feels especially sure of the political and ideological loyalty of the country chosen for this demand. If it is held to be good politics to aid those countries whose loyalty is in doubt, it needs only a step to reverse the flow of funds when a country not only appears to be financially strong but also seems to give no cause for concern as regards its loyalty. This can be considered a sort of distinction.

But leaving this circumstance aside, and assuming that the only determining factor is the financial strength of the countries that could possibly be approached for help in equilibrating the American balance of payments, the case still is not fully explained. The gold and foreign exchange reserves of Italy and Switzerland, too, have been rising steadily in the last few years and at a rate quite comparable to Germany's. If that were enough to motivate the American demand, one may well ask why Washington did not approach Rome and Berne as well. This would, of course, not be a clever thing to do, but apart from this purely tactical consideration, there must surely be some other reason that has to do with the economic peculiarity of the German case.

This is the crux of the matter. More will have to be said presently on whether the American approach to Bonn is justified by convincing economic logic. But even though, as will probably have to be concluded, it is nothing but the translation of bad economics into world politics, it does give expression to a few undoubted facts. The American demand on Germany is not the product of arbitrariness and chance. On the contrary, it dramatically underscores two circumstances. The first is that, similar developments in Italy and Switzerland notwithstanding, Germany does occupy a special position in this respect, insofar as year after year it chalks up balance-of-payments surpluses, which for various reasons have caused the problem of imported inflation to be more pressing, more stubborn, and more intractable in Germany than in any other comparable country. The second meaning of the American demand is that it establishes a link between the balance-of-payments difficulties of the United States and the opposite ones of Germany. The deficits on one side and the surpluses on the other are, in fact, inseparable parts of one and the same worldwide economic process that seriously upsets the balance of international payments, a sort of earthquake in the world economy with the United States and Germany as the two epicenters, not for the first time in modern economic history.

It is no exaggeration to describe the gravity of the problem in these terms, as witnessed by, *inter alia*, the clash of opinions in Germany regarding the nature of the problem and its best solution. This clash is not incomprehensible if thought is given to what is at stake and what the opposing groups are after.

One of these groups stresses the danger of external surpluses for the domestic purchasing power of money and maintains that the only way of averting this danger is to up-value the external purchasing power of the D-mark. That this group is in a strong position is apparently not denied even by its opponents. There is no easy answer to its argument that the danger, of which it has been warning for years with logic hard to refute, has for some time now begun to materialize, and that all the measures taken against it—barring the one of raising the external purchasing power of the currency—have proved ineffective, both against the source of the domestic diminution of purchasing power, that is, the inflationary effects of the balance-of-payments surplus, and against this diminution of purchasing power itself.

To be sure, economics is notoriously a field of conflicting opinions, but, so the representatives of this group maintain, there has seldom been a case so clear-cut and so compellingly logical as the one here under discussion, and in economic policy hardly another case where all considerations speak so overwhelmingly in favor of one single measure, namely, to raise the external value of the German currency in order to save its internal value. But this is the one measure that is unacceptable to those who officially or unofficially determine the course of German economic policy. They have marshaled continuously changing reasons, one less convincing than the other, in an attempt to explain their refusal to the public, which, of course, is easily confused in money matters, and in so doing have displayed unusual intolerance for the counterarguments originating largely from professional economists. For the representatives of the first group this is a most discouraging experience, which serves better than most to illustrate the almost insuperable difficulties of conducting a sensible economic policy in our day.

The first group feels that its patience is being tried almost beyond endurance, for the price that has to be paid for the rejection of their recommendation seems to be rising all the time, while the chance of deriving some benefit from following it is diminishing to the extent that the danger to be averted, imported inflation, is becoming a reality. While it is getting increasingly harder to deny the upward push of costs and prices inflated by the overheated boom and overfull employment, and while obviously nothing can be done about it by persuasion, and while the monetary restrictions applied from time to time are bound to make the external source of inflation gush all the more strongly, the temptation grows to ease the pressure of external surpluses by artificially expanded capital exports. Whether this expedient would be effective is highly doubtful, but it would most certainly denude Germany of resources and make a country still relatively poor in capital even poorer. Now that the Americans are making ready to take part in this preposterous game of pumping, they are told that German balance-of-payments surpluses must not be confused with German wealth of capital. Such a confusion does, in fact, rest on a mental short circuit unforgivable in a professional economist. But it is often overlooked that the same confusion underlies the plan to combat balance-of-payments surpluses by government-promoted capital exports. The mistaken assessment of Germany's capacity to pay, as expressed in the American demand, has previously been fully shared by responsible Germans, and it is encouraged by all those in the second group who explain the German external surplus as being in large part due to the dollar expenditure of the American army stationed in Germany, thus unwittingly giving the Americans their cue.

There was never any reason to doubt that a country such as Germany—and Germany less than any other country, for the topsoil of international goodwill is there still extremely thin —could not go on year after year sucking up gold and foreign exchange like an ominously thumping, giant suction pump, without becoming subject to increasing pressure to do something to ease the situation of those pumped empty. Germany will have to pay ransom, and this now has to be added to the high price to be paid for a policy that fails to find an effective solution to the problem of imported inflation. The ransom has to be added to the rise in costs and prices, to the boiling temperature of overfull employment, and to the strains and stresses caused by the ineffective measures against the import of inflation. This is all the more provoking as the moment approaches when the domestic diminution of purchasing power will eventually prove inescapable, the bitterest entry of all to close this bitter-enough, giant reckoning.

So much for the first group. In contrast with it, the second group, the opponents of revaluation, have long been in the weaker position, on the defensive. Their embittered resistance is not quite inexplicable; there are a number of reasons for it. First of all, there is the conflict of interests. While the first group cannot seriously be reproached with selfish motivations, since defense against inflation has always—at least so far—been acknowledged as being eminently in the public interest, it is obvious that in asking for measures against this special form of inflation they are affecting important, sensitive, and very well-organized group interests, that is, the interest of export industries and all the other beneficiaries of an inflationary super-boom. It is true that the advocates of revaluation are not, after all, suggesting that those so affected should sacrifice their special interests to the common interest. It had been thought that it was enough to appeal to an enlightened and farseeing egoism as against an unenlightened, shortsighted one, since the export lead deriving from the undervaluation of the D-mark was bound to be eroded by the rise of domestic costs and prices, so that the only question was whether the special position of German exports was to be brought to an end by external increase or by an internal decrease of purchasing power, with or without hardship to the savers and owners of life assurance policies. But it seems that such an appeal demands more than it was thought reasonable to expect.

There are yet other considerations which must be given their due if justice is to be done to the second group, the opponents of revaluation. It has to be conceded that inflation of such dimensions fed by balance-of-payments surpluses is a novelty rather taxing for people's capacity to reason and make decisions. It is true that Switzerland, rightly regarded as the paragon of conservative monetary policy, gave the example of how to stop the import of inflation by revaluing the currency, when for years after the last war it deliberately allowed the dollar rate for other than export proceeds (finance dollar) to decline. But this example has generally fallen into oblivion and, in any case, it needs an expert to understand it. Furthermore, to alter the exchange rate is in fact something unusual and contradicts the ideal of a stable external value of money, an ideal that certainly has a lower priority than that of a stable internal value of money but still should be infringed upon only in emergencies. To alter the exchange rate even in the direction of revaluation, otherwise always regarded as something most desirable, cannot, therefore, be an easy decision for a government and a central bank that, for reasons deserving respect, regard stable exchange rates as a lofty aim. And thus they have clung to every conceivable argument that might absolve them from the choice between the once only sacrifice of this aim and the irrevocable sacrifice of the even higher aim of defense against inflation. It is a tragedy that in so doing they only got caught more deeply in the dilemma and had to pay for their hesitation a price that kept rising and is only now apparent in its full measure.

To do justice to the second group, finally, the subject of the controversy must be seen in the international setting to which it belongs. The particular form of inflation under discussion has not primarily come about through monetary laxity in Germany (or Switzerland), but in other countries. What gives it effect is that Germany has been so successful in combating the other forms of inflation that it now finds itself saddled unexpectedly with the new form of imported inflation, but when trying to combat it with the weapons that proved effective in the defense against other forms of inflation, discovers them to be blunt against this insidious form and now lacks the political strength to apply the only remaining effective weapon—that of adjusting the exchange rate, unusual though it is and repugnant to every honest central bank governor. Germany, like Switzerland, has gotten into such difficulties only because the world is still without an international monetary system that enforces an alignment of monetary discipline as the old gold standard did. Imported inflation, therefore, is an expression of a serious defect of today's world economy. It is a shock imparted to the balance of payments of these countries by other countries that are suffering from the opposite trouble of massive external deficits and thereby are exporting their own domestic inflation, which is fed by well-known internal sources. The leading position among these other countries has for some years been occupied by the United States.

This, roughly, is how the two fronts face each other in this embittered battle of opinions. With the best will in the world for doing justice to the second group and understanding its position, the inescapable conclusion is that the factual arguments of the first group are in large part irrefutable and for the rest are more convincing. Although everything essential has by now been said by both sides, the discussion keeps throwing up new points of interests. This applies especially to Professor Rudolf Meimberg's soberly factual and therefore engaging study *Zum Streit über den Wechselkurs der D-Mark*[1] but also to the contributions to the debate recently published by the *Frankfurter Allgemeine Zeitung* of January 28, 1961.

Most interesting of all was the method with which the American economist Professor M. Palyi, who rightly enjoys a high reputation in Germany as well, intervened in the debate to lend a hand to the opponents of revaluation. They celebrated this intervention as a triumph of their cause but realized perhaps too late that it really means a *reductio ad absurdum,* if so intelligent a man feels compelled to sacrifice all other positions and limits himself to an all but authoritarian condemnation of any alteration of exchange rates as *dirigiste*—as though a stable exchange rate were not in any case a "political" price requiring to be "directed" by the central bank, and as though in many cases, such as that of the French franc or of the peseta, there had eventually been any other way except to alter the exchange rate. For the rest, there is nothing for it in his eyes, and inflation simply has to be imported. Here, at last, is the admission that in fact the choice does lie between imported inflation and revaluation; while this has the merit of honesty, it is purchased at the price of cynicism. Whoever now cold-bloodedly opens the floodgates to imported inflation

---

[1] *Frankfurt am Main, Fritz Knapp Verlag, 1960.*

is indeed safe from the reproach of double-dealing but has to accept blame for having shamefacedly or shamelessly capitulated to inflation, which so far had rightly been generally termed a crime. He forfeits any credibility as an opponent of inflation, in any shape or form.

After these critical remarks, I am all the more pleased to find myself in full agreement with Professor Palyi on the point that the opposite balance-of-payments trouble of the United States, which directly or indirectly is the main source of Germany's imported inflation, is essentially the consequence of internal inflationary pressure. To put it more precisely: the American balance of payments has ceased to be in equilibrium because in view of all the circumstances, including especially the economic recovery of Europe and Japan and their increased competitiveness, the United States has become too expensive and less competitive under the impact of domestic inflation, mainly of the wage-push type, and has failed to reconcile the total volume of domestic income and expenditure with its external payments. The *Wall Street Journal* of January 26 puts it neatly by saying that it is as clear as anything could be that the United States got into their present difficulties by paying out too much abroad and, at the same time, by giving free play at home to deficit spending and inflation. Contrary to some other strange theories given currency, even by people who have to be taken seriously, this is the only diagnosis of the American balance-of-payments crisis that fits the facts and answers economic logic. It is gratifying to note that this opinion is shared by some of the most distinguished American economists, as witnessed, above all, in the article by Professor Gottfried Haberler, of Harvard University, in the January issue of *Lloyds Bank Review*. But, of course, this was to be expected.

Since the war the United States has chronically suffered from domestic inflation, now wage inflation, now budget inflation, now investment inflation. But as long as the European countries and Japan were economically weak and for the rest

outdid the United States in inflationary policy, the strange result was that American inflation was associated with a dollar
shortage. But once these countries had powerfully improved
their capacity to produce and compete—and in addition had
learned monetary discipline, while in the United States wage
inflation, especially, continued, and American competitiveness was impaired by trade union and fiscal policy—the dollar
shortage turned into today's "dollar flood," even though at
long last visible progress was made under President Eisenhower in the battle against inflation.

This diagnosis is at the same time the explanation for a very
strange phenomenon. I have in mind that fact that, contrary to
all experience and expectations, cyclical stagnation in some
parts of the world economy, notably in the United States, is
associated with high balance-of-payments deficits and an unprecedented boom elsewhere, especially in European countries
such as Germany, Switzerland, and Italy, which have high
external surpluses. One would have expected the exact opposite, and the normal course would have been for the stagnation
tendencies of the United States to spread to the industrial
countries of Europe via a flow of payments and a borrowing in
the opposite direction, from Europe to America. Thus, the
American sneeze would have given Europe the flu, or worse.
Nothing of the kind happened. Europe skips about all the
more merrily, the more America keeps coughing. The profound reason is that the causal chain in the United States begins not with stagnation, but with a swing of the balance of
payments into deficit as a result of the circumstances described,
and it is this deficit that generated stagnation at home and inflationary surpluses in Europe and, via the latter, an overheated boom and overfull employment.

But this diagnosis also provides the key to the cure of the
dollar weakness. American credit and monetary policy must
set their course toward restriction until domestic inflation disappears and with it the external deficits. That is the crucial
point, and no deflection from it is permissible by references to

the high foreign payments commitments of the United States. What is to be thought of such popular references I had occasion to discuss a few months ago in my article "The U. S. Balance-of-Payments Crisis: Diagnosis and Treatment."* The Eisenhower Administration was, therefore, on the correct course in keeping the country short. If it is blamed for not being consistent enough, it is only fair to make allowance for the predicament in which the U. S. executive and central banks find themselves in view of a wage inflation so strong and so stubborn that they would have to turn off the money and credit tap more sharply than they dare, in view of the slowdown caused thereby. The result might easily be a combination of stagnation, further price and wage pressure, and an external loss of blood continuing unarrested.

By contrast, President Kennedy, to judge by his program as announced, is hardly on the correct course so far. This is the distressing but inescapable conclusion. Homoeopathy is being undeservedly discredited by an attempt to cure an external deficit, such as the United States suffers from today, by an increased dose of its cause, namely, monetary expansion. This is all the more regrettable, as the new President should not find it too difficult to solve the dollar problem with the correct means without inflicting paralyzing stagnation on the country. The answer is to combine a policy of continued monetary and fiscal discipline with tax reliefs for undistributed profits and with an effort to persuade the trade unions, surely a promising approach in the case of a Democratic president notably sympathetic to the labor movement.

Such a program holds out the prospect of all the quicker success and all the fewer sacrifices for the United States, and the more it can count on help from the European end. It is quite natural that Washington should look first to Bonn in this connection, for the D-mark does in fact exercise a suction effect that can no longer be denied. It is not good politics and

* See *Chapter* xv *of this volume.*—Ed.

is even less good economics to take the money back from the Germans in more or less elegant fashion and via more or less plausible detours. But the Americans are not in the wrong in expecting something of Germany. There are only two things Germany can do. Either Germany does what recently a group of Kennedy's advisers in an excess of cynicism suggested the Bonn government should be forced to do, namely, to administer a hefty dose of inflation to the German economy, or else, if this is repudiated with overwhelming justification and understandable indignation, Germany must at long last offer Washington the revaluation of the D-mark. If it does neither the one nor the other, it will have an extraordinarily difficult task in protecting its till. Thus, the right treatment for the dollar has its counterpart in the right treatment for the D-mark.

XVIII

F. A. Kramer: *In Memoriam**

If one individual among the many who mourn the untimely death of this unique man may be permitted a personal testimony, I would condense everything into this one sentence: I have lost a friend to whom I was tied by years of common work in hard times, by an intimate mutual understanding in everything we had at heart, and by the deepest affection, and whose life and work I respectfully acknowledge as those of a truly wise and God-fearing man. Would that thousands knew what example he set by his firm and unswerving faith in the highest, by his steadfast courage in defending what he had recognized as right, by the judicious application of his exceptional mental faculties, and by a spirit of sacrifice that gave him, long marked out for an early death as he was, the strength to make his life's work, the *Rheinischer Merkur,* the rallying point of the Christian and humanist freedom forces in Germany. Thousands should know that here was a man of unusual gifts of mind and character, who sacrified his health, comfort, peace, and finally his life to his work and, with it, to a cause that numberless Germans knew as their own. In thanking him for it here, I wish that we may be joined in this expression of gratitude by all those who, even though only from afar, can appreciate what it meant in the despondency of our time to see this man's fight against the deadly forces of disintegration, of world ruin,

* *Undated manuscript, first published in* **Gegen die Brandung,** *1959, believed to have been written at the time of Kramer's death in 1950.*

the simultaneous destruction of the divine and the human, excess, perversity and unfreedom. They cannot express their gratitude better than by associating with their memory of our dead friend respect for his example and loyalty to his aims and standards.

It was during the war that we met on Swiss soil, brought together by a common concern for the fate of our Western culture and for a European solution to the German question. At our very first meeting I was impressed with the political acumen of my friend, with the clarity and precision of his thinking, with his unusual power of expression and his intellectual integrity. Immediately there was created between us the sort of concord that roots in the deepest layers of the soul and hardly needs to be stated and confirmed in detail. And so it came that despite the distance between Geneva and Berne, where he lived, we developed an increasingly close collaboration, of which the direct results unfortunately were scant, although the indirect effects have proved all the more significant and lasting.

One of our main tasks, as we saw it, was to avail ourselves of all the ways and means offered by the diplomatic life of a neutral capital in order to counteract the pernicious tendencies that threatened early to push the Allies' policy onto the track that ultimately led to Teheran, Yalta, and Potsdam. It was a desperate struggle against an extent of delusion and misjudgment that even then filled us with ominous forebodings for the future. It was my friend who, because he lived in Berne and devoted himself wholeheartedly to this struggle, had to shoulder the main burden of this wearing and discouraging activity. An account of our experiences, which naturally would have to include the intrigues of the German socialists and communists, then still linked by a common "left" ideology, would mean taking a living example to describe the historical and psychological background of an Allied policy that was not only bound to fail in solving the German question but ended up by surrendering the bulk of Europe and Asia to Russian com-

munist imperialism. Not all Germans were Nazis; it was needful to look out at once for the forces on which to rely for the
sound reconstruction of Germany—these forces were not only
on the Left, for communism was nothing but a variant of
totalitarianism—and it was only at one's peril that one could
try to drive out Satan by Beelzebub. We would say all this only
to realize in the end that we were talking into the blue and, to
boot, were becoming suspect as "reactionaries." It was my
friend who suffered most from this psychologically, and I am
sure that it was then that the ground was prepared for his illness. The logical outcome of all this was that discussions with
the American representative were broken off when we talked
of the incurable naiveness of a policy that placed blind faith in
the communists and of the necessity of combating the red
totalitarianism just like the brown.

The highest marks must be given, in this context, to the
intelligence and loyalty of Allan W. Dulles, the author of a
just book on the German opposition, whom President Roosevelt had sent to Berne on a special mission during the war.
But it was through his mediation that one of our greatest
disillusionments was to come to us.

It was on the day when the foundation of the "Free Moscow
Committee" was announced, in 1943, that I made Dulles's
acquaintance. When he asked what this meant, I replied: "It
means that Moscow has a German program, but the West has
none." He went on to ask what I advised should be done, and
I said the West should make haste to catch up with the East's
political and propaganda lead by making up its mind about a
Western solution to the German question in opposition to
the Moscow-inspired one, and by promoting the creation of an
appropriate Western committee of Germans. I was asked what
sort of thing I had in mind and explained that I thought the
purpose would be best served by a committee made up of
representatives of the Christian churches. Such a committee
should be formed without further delay, and its first duty
should be to issue a carefully prepared manifesto by which to

lead the Germans back to the firm ground of Western values and traditions. But something else needed doing as well. The Allies should imagine in what an appalling state of spiritual bewilderment the Germans would be. At their entry, the Allies would find a nation of human beings upon whose heads the world was collapsing after terrible suffering. Only a few would understand why this had to come, what Hitler and national socialism signified, why there had been a war, what inhuman and hateful things had come to pass, and why it all ended as it did; and greater still than their physical hunger would be the spiritual hunger of these people, who in their stupor would want to know what had really happened to them and why, and once they had grasped that, would come to see a new goal of life and community. The Allies should engage the good services of an honest German at one with his people, an intelligent man with powers of expression, to write a pamphlet in this sense, and this should right away be printed in millions of copies to be distributed at the Allies' arrival, together with the soup kitchen rations, in the name of our Christian, German committee. I knew of only one man who would fill the bill, my friend Dr. F. A. Kramer.

All these ideas and proposals were accepted with the utmost readiness, and all the rest again fell to the lot of my friend, who set about carrying out the project untiringly and with admirable skill. The committee was founded after we had succeeded in interesting excellent representatives both on the Catholic and the Protestant side, including a well-known socialist. We agreed upon an action program, and, most important of all, my late friend, who, upon my proposal, was also entrusted with this literary task, delivered his manuscript for the pamphlet. It had cost him weeks of the most painstaking work and, as was to be expected, was eminently suitable for the purpose. The rest was now up to the Americans. And then the crushing blow fell. Obviously in response to a hint from Washington, Mr. Dulles, who so far had impatiently urged us on, called the whole thing off. The work of months was merely destined to disappear in the files of the State Department, and instead of the millions of copies that Mr. Dulles had led us to believe would be printed, we got the kind offer that if Dr. Kramer cared to have the pamphlet printed, the Americans would take the beggarly total of five hundred copies. The pamphlet was later published under the title "Vor den Ruinen Deutschlands" in Germany (Historisch-Politischer Verlag, Koblenz) and in Switzerland (Europa-Verlag, Zürich).

We had had our lesson. If it was in any case undesirable for the Western powers to have a German policy, because and insofar as this was against communist plans, it was altogether out of the question to encourage any sort of political and spiritual activity by Germans who had gained a reputation for being reactionaries on account of their appeal to tradition, Western civilization, homeland, family, property, and Christianity, and of their warning against any and every form of totalitarianism. In the name of the policy of "unconditional surrender," such hopelessly "unprogressive" Germans had to be cast off at once.

This is the story, told here for the first time, of what was probably the only attempt, and one that failed miserably, to oppose Moscow's declared German and European policy during the war by a joint German-American initiative based on those ideals by which the West stands or falls. I break my silence not in order to open old wounds, but in order to honor the memory of my friend, who played the main part in this attempt and, with the support throughout of his courageous wife, sacrificed his strength and his last financial reserves.

When history took the course that we had tried to stem with our weak forces, he regarded it as his natural duty to be among the first to return to his country and to devote himself to his last breath to the same task, even amid the ruins. He was irreplaceable, and the more grievously we shall miss him.